# OPEN HOUSES IN NEW ENGLAND

A *YANKEE BOOKS* TRAVEL GUIDE

# OPEN HOUSES
# IN
# NEW ENGLAND

by Mary Maynard

*YANKEE BOOKS*

**We would like to thank the following for the use of their photographs:**

Deep River Historical Society, Inc., G. Allen Brown, Henry Whitfield State Historical Museum, Connecticut Historical Commission, The Antiquarian & Landmarks Society, Inc., Keeler Tavern Preservation Society, Inc., Torrington Historical Society, Inc., American Clock and Watch Museum, Inc., The Preservation Society of Newport County, Simsbury Historical Society, Norwood Historical Society, Paul Revere Memorial Association, Edith Wharton Restoration, Inc., Victoria Beller Smith, Vermont Division for Historic Preservation, Eric Gilbertson, Richard S. Kanaski, Saint-Gaudens National Historic Site, Jeffrey Nintzel, Norman McGrath, The Musical Wonder House.

Printed in the United States of America.

**Distributed in the book trade by St. Martin's Press.**

If you have any questions or comments concerning this book, please write:
Rodale Press
Book Reader Service
33 E. Minor Street
Emmaus, PA 18098

Cover Design • Dale Swensson, Bar Harbor, Maine
Cover Photograph • Courtesy of Longfellow National Historic Site,
                 Cambridge, Massachusetts
Composition • High Resolution, Inc., Camden, Maine

Library of Congress Cataloging-in-Publication Data

Maynard, Mary
       Open houses in New England/by Mary Maynard.
             p.    cm. — (A Yankee Books travel guide series)
       Includes index.
       ISBN 0-89909-347-7
       1. Dwellings — New England — Guide-books.    2. Architecture.
Domestic — New England — Guide-books.    3. New England —
Description and travel — 1981- — Guide-books.    I. Title.    II. Series
F5.M39    1991
917.404'43-dc20                                    91-26018
                                                      CIP

1 3 5 7 9 10 8 6 4 2

# CONTENTS

## MASSACHUSETTS

## VERMONT

## NEW HAMPSHIRE

## MAINE

# INTRODUCTION

*O*pen Houses in New England is a comprehensive guide to more than 600 houses throughout this six-state region that are open to the public. In almost every corner of New England, from the Canadian border to the shores of Connecticut, you are invited to step inside an open door for an intimate glimpse into the lives of the people who have lived here for the past three centuries.

For the most part, the houses described within these pages are historical ones, landmarks of our heritage that have been carefully and lovingly preserved by local citizens. Some are former homes of notable people— presidents, heroes, politicians, inventors, artists, and writers. Many are architectural gems, both humble and magnificent. All together, they represent the rich and varied culture of what constitutes New England.

Preservation has always been important to New Englanders. The largest number of restored houses open to the public in the country are concentrated here. These houses date from the earliest seventeenth century wood frame dwellings, such as the Fairbanks House, in Dedham, Massachusetts (1636), to the modern technology exemplified in the Zimmerman House, in Manchester, New Hampshire (1952), designed by twentieth-century architect Frank Lloyd Wright.

The furnishings and collections within the houses cover an even broader span of time. They range from the meager possessions the Pilgrims brought to this country or the crude implements they fashioned for survival, to the lavish European and China-trade treasures imported by the new settlers as they grew in wealth and stature. Some of the finest collections of early Americana can be found here in New England, and knowledgeable guides are eager to show them off.

While the millionaires' mansions of Newport, the stately homes of wealthy sea captains and merchants of Portsmouth, Salem, or Nantucket, and the historic villages of Deerfield and Plymouth have long been among the major New England attractions to visitors, not to be overlooked are the myriad less well-known houses scattered throughout this area that have their own special stories to tell. This book attempts to highlight as many as possible, for each one contains a unique legacy of some person, place, or event that gives personal insight into this place we call New England.

All of the house listed here are open to the public on a regular basis or by appointment. Some are closed during the winter months because they are not heated. It has become increasingly popular, however, for many of the houses to stay open through the Thanksgiving and Christmas holidays, when they are festively decorated and special events are held (and warmed by roaring fireplaces!). During the spring and summer months many historical societies, with the help of local garden clubs, feature "house and garden" tours. During these tours other interesting and historical houses that are privately owned are also open to the public.

Several inns, taverns, and bed and breakfasts have been included in the book because of their particular historical significance, but they are only a few of the countless number of such properties in New England that welcome guests. Inns and taverns, sometimes called "ordinaries," were an important and necessary part of daily life in early times. In most cases they began as private homes whose owners extended their hospitality to wayfarers. The selectmen in each town were mandated by law to provide for accommodation of travelers as well as their livestock. Local taverns, such as the Golden Ball, in Weston, Massachusetts, or the Keeler Tavern, in Ridgefield, CT, not only provided food and shelter, but generally became social centers for the community as well.

Every attempt has been made to make the information in this book as accurate and up-to-date as possible. Visiting hours and days are apt to change from year to year, so it is always best to telephone before you go. (When a phone number is not listed, you can often get imformation from the local library or town clerk's office.) Admission prices are subject to change as well, so they are not listed. For the most part, such fees are nominal (except for the historic villages such as Deerfield, Mystic Seaport, and Old Sturbridge), and in many other houses, a small donation is acceptable.

The houses are listed alphabetically, first by state and then by town. The year the house was built immediately follows its name and is in parentheses, followed by the address and telephone number. A brief description is then given, followed by an anecdote or bit of history pertaining to the property. Each descriptive paragraph concludes with the name of the organization that maintains it, the dates and hours it is open, and whether or not there is admission.

At the conclusion of each chapter you will find a list of additional houses in each state that are also open to the public. Space prohibited us from describing every house in detail, and some of these houses are either in the process of restoration or do not have regular visiting hours at this time.

Some abbreviations have been given:

SPNEA: The Society for the Preservation of New England Antiquities

DAR: The Daughters of the American Revolution

I am indebted to the above organizations as well as to the countless state and local historical commissions and historical societies that have so graciously and willingly supplied me with information and photographs for this book. I am awed by the virtual army of volunteers who not only give so freely of their time and energy to help preserve each local landmark but are equally proficient and dedicated to their task.

# CONNECTICUT

GENERAL DAVID HUMPHREYS
HOUSE (1698)

## Ansonia

*General David Humphreys House (1698)*

37 Elm Street
203-735-1908

Originally built as the "mansion house" for the town clergy, this large, red Georgian-style house, with Federal windows and doors, later became the home of General David Humphreys (1752–1818), statesman, poet, aide-de-camp to General George Washington, and considered the "Father of Industry of the Naugatuck Valley." It has been carefully restored to its original state and contains eighteenth-century furnishings. An unusual feature is the double feather-edge paneling throughout the building. The house is operated by the Derby Historical Society and has excellent programs on "living history" for school children, lectures for adults, assistance with genealogical research, and a nice gift shop. Open year-round, Monday–Friday 9:00–4:30. Free.

# Branford

*Harrison House (c. 1724)*

124 Main Street
203-488-4828/488-8835

Built by Nathanial Harrison in 1724 as a "two-over-two" house and occupied by his descendants until 1800, this is now a carefully restored classic colonial saltbox with a center chimney, hand-hewn oak corner posts, huge chamfered summer beams, and exposed joists. Period furnishings, such as four-poster and rope beds, seventeenth-century chests of Branford origin, old china, and early paintings can be seen throughout the house. One room is set aside for Brandford archives, memorabilia, and photographs. There is also a large herb garden and a barn displaying farm implements. Owned by SPNEA and operated by the Branford Historical Society, it is open June 1–September 30, Wednesday–Saturday 2:00–5:00 and by appointment. Christmas Open House. Free, donations accepted.

# Bridgewater

*The Captain's House (c. 1850)*

*The Elijah Peck House (1820)*

Main Street
203-354-4394

The Captain's House, a small plain frame dwelling, is the birthplace of Captain William Dickson Burnham, who ran away from home when he was 14 and went to sea on a clipper ship. He was to make a fortune at his trade as master of various ships and was among the first to establish a steamship line to the Hawaiian Islands. Upon his death in 1919, he bequeathed the bulk of his estate to his home town of Bridgewater for educational purposes. Completely restored and relocated, the house contains a collection of local history and furnishings, particularly articles from various old general stores and the old post office in Bridgewater. Both the Captain's House and the adjoining dwelling—the Elijah Peck House, a furnished, two-storied, clapboard dwelling—are maintained by the Bridgewater Historical Society, Inc., and are open May–September on Saturday afternoons. Free.

MILES LEWIS HOUSE (1801)

# Bristol

*Miles Lewis House (1801)*

100 Maple Street
203-583-6070

Here is an excellent example of a post-revolutionary mansion, standing as erected with the exception of a new staircase and minor repairs. It is a large, elegant, white clapboard structure with twin chimneys and a wide central hallway. Operated by the American Clock and Watch Museum, it now houses one of the most extensive collections of American horology in the country. Clocks and memorabilia of clockmakers are attractively displayed in period rooms. It is open March 1–November 30, daily 11:00–5:00. Admission.

# Canterbury

*Prudence Crandall House (c. 1805)*

Canterbury Green
203-546-9916

This handsome, large, white, Georgian-style house was the site of New England's first black female academy, opened by Prudence Crandall in 1833. Three period rooms contain permanent and changing exhibits on Prudence Crandall and her school, the

PRUDENCE CRANDALL HOUSE
(C. 1805)

lives of black persons in pre–Civil War Connecticut, and local history. The museum offers year-round special events, a research library, and a small gift shop. Operated by the Connecticut Historical Commission, it is open January 15–December 15, Wednesday–Sunday 10:00–4:30. Admission.

# Clinton

## Stanton House (1789–1791)

63 East Main Street
203-669-2132

The site on which this house stands is considered the birthplace of Yale University. Adam Stanton bought this property from the Reverend Abraham Pierson, the first rector of Yale College, who taught his first students on this site. The house has 13 rooms and eight fireplaces and a large wing that houses a general store, first operated by Stanton and later by his son, from 1804 to 1864. Three generations of Stantons lived here, and the house is filled with their eighteenth- and early nineteenth-century possessions. It is operated by the Hartford National Bank and Trust Company and is open June 1–September 30, Tuesday–Sunday 2:00–5:00 and by appointment. Free.

# Cos Cob

*Bush-Holley House (c. 1685)*

39 Strickland Road
203-869-6899

Originally a small saltbox, this interesting house grew with successive owners, acquiring several wings, a two-story front porch, and added chimneys. In the late 1900s it operated as The Holley Inn, attracting many of the leading American Impressionists of the day. Such writers and artists as Childe Hassam, Lincoln Steffens, Louis Comfort Tiffany, and Willa Cather spent their vacations here. Furnished with eighteenth- and nineteenth-century antiques, reflecting the lifestyles of its former occupants, the museum features works by many turn-of-the-century artists. The house is headquarters for the Historical Society of the Town of Greenwich, Inc., and is open year-round, Tuesday–Friday 12:00–4:00, Sunday 1:00–4:00. Tours by special appointment only. Gardens. Admission.

# Coventry

*Nathan Hale Homestead (1776)*

South Street
203-742-6917/247-8996

THE STRONG HOUSE (EARLY 1700S)

### *The Strong House (early 1700s)*

South Street
203-742-7207

This is the family home of Connecticut's state hero, Nathan Hale. ("I only regret that I have but one life to lose for my country.") The rural setting, much as it was when the Hales lived here, and the 10-room Georgian-style homestead, with many of the original furnishings and memorabilia (including Nathan's Bible, silver shoe buckles, and trunk), reflect the lifestyle of a prosperous farming family of the period. Just down the road is **The Strong House**, a fine old nicely furnished saltbox, which is the ancestral home of Nathan Hale's maternal family. The Hale Homestead is owned and maintained by the Antiquarian & Landmarks Society, Inc., and the Strong House (with picnic grove) is owned by the Coventry Historical Society. Both are open May 15–October 15, daily 1:00–5:00. Admission.

# Danbury
### *John and Mary Rider Homestead (1785)*

Scott-Fanton Museum
43 Main Street
203-743-5200

Built by John Rider, a carpenter and cabinetmaker, this is a very good example of a successful middle class craftsman's home of the late eighteenth century. Many of the furnishings were made by John Rider and his son. There are also a revolutionary war display, old carpenter's tools, exhibits on local history, and a Charles Ives Parlor. (Charles Ives, American composer and organist and Pulitzer Prize recipient, was born in Danbury.) The Dodd Hat Shop segment of the museum shows how hats were made in colonial times—pointing up Danbury's prominence in the nineteenth century as the hat capital of the world. The house is owned by the Danbury Scott-Fanton Museum and Historical Society, Inc., and tours are conducted year-round, Wednesday–Sunday 2:00–5:00. Library hours are Tuesday–Friday 10:00–5:00, and Saturday and Sunday 2:00–5:00. Gift shop. Donation.

# Darien
*Bates-Scofield Homestead (c. 1737)*

45 Old King's Highway
203-655-9233

This homestead is a classic Connecticut saltbox with a massive center chimney. It features a kitchen with a seven-foot-wide fieldstone fireplace and a buttery, a weaving room with early equipment, crewel embroidered curtains, and period furnishings throughout. There is a research library and a Colonial herb garden on the property. It is operated by the Darien Historical Society and is open year-round, Tuesday–Friday 9:00–1:00, and Thursday and Sunday 2:00–4:00. Donation.

STONE HOUSE (1840)

# Deep River

*Stone House (1840)*

South Main Street
203-526-2609

This unusual stone house was built by Deacon Ezra Southworth with stones from his own quarries. It is now a museum house with nineteenth-century furnishings. On display is a piano made from the famous Charter Oak Tree (where the original state charter was hidden in 1687), locally made cut glass, Indian artifacts, old costumes, and a marine room with many items relating to local Connecticut River history. It is operated by the Deep River Historical Society and is open July and August, Sunday, Tuesday, and Thursday 2:00–4:00. Donation.

# Derby

*Osborne Homestead Museum (1850)*

500 Hawthorne Avenue
203-734-2513

Adjacent to Osbornedale State Park stands this attractive Federal-style house, which was the former estate of Frances Osborne-Kellogg, a successful businesswoman of her day. Originally built as a farmhouse, the house has undergone periodic modifications and additions, evolving into the impressive structure it is today. Its restored interior displays the original contents of the estate, which include a significant collection of antiques and fine arts. The grounds are beautifully landscaped with formal flower gardens, ornamental shrubs, and flowering trees. It is open April–December, Friday 10:00–3:00, and Saturday and Sunday 1:00–4:00; grounds open daily, 8:30–3:30. Donation.

# Essex

*Pratt House (1732)*

19 West Avenue
203-388-5816/767-0681

The earliest part of this house was built in 1645 by Lieutenant William Pratt, one of the first settlers of Essex. The gambrel-roofed central section was added by his grandson in the mid-eighteenth century, and the large central chimney section was built by his great-grandson in 1732. This well-preserved museum house illustrates the evolution of one family's adaptive use of land and property. The furnishings, dating from the seventeenth to the early nineteenth centuries, include Queen Anne side chairs, Connecticut redware china, copper and silver lusterware, and an outstanding collection of Chinese courting mirrors. An authentically restored herb garden is at the rear of the museum. It is owned and operated by the Essex Historical Society and is open June–September, Friday–Sunday 1:00–4:00. Special Christmas exhibit. Admission.

# Fairfield
*Ogden House (1750)*

636 Old Post Road
203-259-1598

This eighteenth-century saltbox farmhouse is furnished to portray the lives of its original owners, Jane and David Ogden, and their seven children, who left a complete inventory of the house. Trained docents give visitors a unique glimpse into the lives of its late-colonial-Revolution era inhabitants. Highlights of this simple, modest early home are the well-equipped

OGDEN HOUSE (1750)

lean-to kitchen and authentically laid-out vegetable and herb gardens behind the house. It is owned and operated by the Fairfield Historical Society and is open mid-May–mid-October, Thursday and Sunday 1:00–4:00. Donation.

# Farmington
## *Hill-Stead Museum (1898–1901)*

35 Mountain Road
203-677-4787, for information, 203-677-9064

Conceived in the style of an American colonial farmstead, this handsome house on a 200-acre estate was designed by Theodate Pope, one of the first woman architects invited into the American Institute of Architects. It was built as a retirement home for her parents, industrialist Alfred A. Pope and his wife, to house their distinguished collection of French Impressionist paintings and decorative arts. Hourlong tours on the quarter-hour are given Wednesday–Friday 2:00–5:00, and Saturday and Sunday 1:00–5:00. The grounds and gardens are open until dusk. Closed mid–January to mid–February and major holidays. Admission.

HILL-STEAD MUSEUM
(1898–1901)

### *Stanley-Whitman House (c. 1720)*

37 High Street
203-677-9222

This is one of the best preserved examples of the framed overhang style of architecture of early eighteenth-century New England. It is an unusual saltbox with a great central chimney, and its wide framed overhang is embellished with four hand-hewn "drops." It has been beautifully restored with many rare period furnishings and decorative objects. There are herb and flower gardens in the spring and summer, special fall activities, and a Christmas program in December. It is owned and operated by the Farmington Museum and is open May 1–October 31, Wednesday–Sunday 12:00–4:00; March, April, November, and December, Sunday 12:00–4:00. Closed January and February. Gift shop. Admission.

# Glastonbury
### *Welles-Shipman-Ward House (1755)*

972 Main Street
203-633-6890

Built by a wealthy Glastonbury shipbuilder, Captain Thomas Welles, as a wedding present for his son, this two-story frame house has been completely restored to its original appearance. It is noted for its enormous kitchen fireplace and elaborate paneling and woodwork in the parlor. It is furnished with period antiques, and the barn out back displays antique farm and shipbuilding tools. Special exhibits and events are held throughout the season. Operated by the Historical Society of Glastonbury, it is open May and June, (closed July), mid-August–October, Sundays 2:00–4:00 and by appointment. Herb garden. Admission.

# Granby
### *Abijah Rowe House (c. 1753)*
### *Weed-Enders House (1790)*

208 Salmon Brook Road
203-653-3965

These two houses are part of the original Salmon Brook Settlement in Granby and, along with the

Cooley School (c. 1870), have been restored and furnished by the Salmon Brook Historical Society. The colonial-style Rowe House was built by Abijah Rowe, a blacksmith and farmer, who made most of the hardware in the house. The Weed-Enders House, a small saltbox restored to its original condition, features changing exhibits of local history. Both houses are filled with interesting collections of both colonial and Victorian furnishings rooted in Granby's past. Owned and operated by the Salmon Brook Historical Society, they are both open every Sunday, May–October, 2:00–4:00. Free.

# Greenwich
## Putnam Cottage (c. 1690)

243 East Putnam Avenue
203-869-9697

This was originally the homestead of the Knapp family, who were among the first settlers of Greenwich. Timothy Knapp had a tavern here during the revolutionary war where General Isreal Putnam was forced to make a daring escape from the British in 1779. Rare "fishscale" shingles adorn this small red saltbox, where two huge fieldstone fireplaces dominate the first floor. Beautifully restored and furnished with period antiques, it is owned and maintained by the DAR and is open year-round Monday, Wednesday, and Friday, 10:00–12:00 and 2:00–4:00, and by appointment. Admission.

# Groton
## Ebenezer Avery House (c. 1750)

Fort Griswold
203-446-9257

Fort Griswold is the site of the 1781 massacre of American defenders by British troops under Benedict Arnold. This 10-room house, a conventional center-chimney colonial, was built here about 1750 by an ensign wounded in the battle of Fort Griswold. In 1971 the house was dismantled, numbered piece by piece, and re-erected on the present site, about a quarter-mile from its original location. The massive chimney is divided to serve five fireplaces—three on the first floor and two on the second. The second floor features a weaving room with spinning wheels and an old loom. It is furnished throughout with many period pieces belonging to the Avery family. It is open from Memorial Day to Labor Day, weekends 1:00–5:00. Free.

# Guilford

## Henry Whitfield House (1639)

Old Whitfield Street and Stone House Lane
203-453-2457

Built for the Reverend Henry Whitfield, clergyman and founder of the town, this is the oldest stone house in New England and the oldest building in Connecticut. It is a unique example of English domestic architecture and is furnished with an excellent collection of seventeenth- and eighteenth-century antiques. When first built it also served as a fortress and meetinghouse for early settlers. Exhibits include weaving equipment, the first tower clock in the colonies, and an herb garden. It is maintained by the Connecticut Historical Commission and is open April 1–October 31, Wednesday–Sunday 10:00–5:00; November 1–March 31, Wednesday–Sunday 10:00–4:00 (closed Thanksgiving and December 15–January 15). Admission.

HENRY WHITFIELD HOUSE (1639)

## Hyland House (1660)

84 Boston Street
203-453-9477

This classic colonial saltbox was built in the seventeenth century by George Hyland and added to in 1720 by Ebenezer Parmelee. (Parmelee made the first town clock in America for the church steeple—see Whitfield House.) It contains unusual interior woodwork, three walk-in fireplaces with seventeenth-century cooking tools, and is furnished with early, rare antiques. Hung in the lean-to attic is an original casement window from the 1600s which is one of three documented windows in the United States. There is also an herb garden on the grounds. It is owned and operated by the Dorothy Whitfield Society and is open June–Sepember, Tuesday–Sunday 10:00–4:30. Admission.

## Thomas Griswold House (1774)

171 Boston Street
203-453-3176/453-5452

Here is a classic Connecticut saltbox built by Thomas Griswold in the eighteenth century and lived in by his descendants until 1956. It is now a museum of local history, containing locally made furniture, books, photographs, memorabilia, farm tools, and a costume display. There is a restored blacksmith shop and a colonial garden on the property. It is operated by the Guilford Keeping Society and is open mid-June–mid-September, Tuesday–Sunday 11:00–4:00. Admission.

# Haddam

## Thankful Arnold House (1795–1810)

Haddam Green
203-345-2400

This is a most unusual house, built in three stages between 1795 and 1810 by Joseph Arnold. It is named in honor of his wife, Thankful, who bore him 13 children, and who was a direct descendant of John and Priscilla Alden. An interesting feature of this three-story gambrel roof house is a large stairway leading up to the side entrance. It is furnished throughout with period pieces. Operated by the

Haddam Historical Society, it is open June–September, Saturday and Sunday 2:30–5:00.

# Hadlyme
*Gillette Castle (1919)*

67 River Road (Gillette Castle State Park)
203-526-2336

This hilltop fieldstone mansion overlooking the Connecticut River was built by actor William Gillette, famous for his portrayal of Sherlock Holmes. It has 24 rooms, including a 1500-square-foot living room. The 42 doors in the castle each have a different carved wooden lock and bolt, all designed by Gillette. There are many eccentric and unusual features to this battlemented fortress, which would look more at home on the Rhine River. The property includes walking paths and picnic grounds. Operated by the Connecticut State Park and Forest Commission, it is open daily from Memorial Day to Columbus Day, 11:00–5:00, and on weekends from Columbus Day until the last weekend before Christmas, 10:00–4:00. Gift shop. Admission.

GILLETTE CASTLE (1919)

# Hamden
## *Jonathan Dickerman House (1792)*

105 Mount Carmel Avenue
No telephone

With the exception of its distinctive front roof overhang, this small house is typical of an eighteenth-century Connecticut farmhouse. The near-original condition of the house, devoid of plumbing or central
heating, reflects the conservative tastes and plain
lifestyle of a moderately prosperous farm family of
that era. The rooms are simply designed, with few
adornments other than a paneled fireplace, and are
furnished with some early period pieces. Exhibits and
lectures on local history are held here. It is owned
and operated by the Hamden Historical Society and is
open mid-June–early September, Saturday and
Sunday 12:00–3:00. Donation. Write P.O. Box 5512,
Hamden, CT 06518.

# Hampton
## *The Burnham-Hibbard House (c. 1834)*

Hampton Hill Historic District
No telephone

Of simple architectural style, this early nineteenth-
century, two-story, gable-roofed frame house (with
an ell added in 1897) reflects the life of this community in earlier days. Carefully researched and restored
as a living museum, it has on display four period
rooms on the first floor and four exhibition areas on
the second floor. Furniture, ceramics, textiles, and
memorabilia were all donated by Hampton families
and represent the diversity of the town's social history. It is owned and operated by the Hampton
Antiquarian and Historical Society and is open for
special affairs during the year and by appointment.
Write to the Antiquarian and Historical Society,
Hampton, CT 06247. Free.

# Hartford
## *Butler-McCook Homestead (1782)*

396 Main Street
203-522-1806/247-8996

A lone survivor on Main Street in downtown Hart-

ford, this large, white clapboard, multichimneyed house reflects the varied lifestyles of four generations of the family that lived there. All of the furnishings are original, and there are many interesting collections, including Victorian toys, Japanese armor, early American antiques, silver, and paintings. It is nicely landscaped with Victorian formal gardens that are open year-round. Owned and operated by the Antiquarian & Landmarks Society, Inc., it is open mid-May–mid-October, Sunday 12:00–4:00, and for a special Christmas display in December. Admission.

BUTLER-McCOOK HOMESTEAD (1782)

## *Isham-Terry House (1854)*

211 High Street
203-522-1984/247-8996

This imposing Hartford landmark is an elegant example of the Italianate style of architecture so popular before the Civil War. The brick exterior, painted cream color with dark green trim, is accentuated with long porches and cast-iron balconies, wide bracketed overhangs, and elaborate cornices. Lived in by the same family for 80 years, its interior of decorative wall and ceiling treatments, rich wood paneling and original gas lighting, remains intact. It is furnished with an eclectic array of Victorian antiques and paintings and special collections of glass, clocks, and porcelains. It is owned and operated by the Antiquarian & Landmarks Society, Inc., and is open mid-May–mid-October, Sunday 12:00–4:00. Admission.

## Nook Farm

351 Farmington Avenue and 77 Forest Street
203-525-9317

Located in the heart of Hartford's bustling insurance industry is an oasis of beautifully landscaped grounds and historic houses known locally as Nook Farm. During the mid-1800s Nook Farm incorporated more than 140 acres of scenic farmland, where a close-knit community of prominent writers and intellectuals of the day built their homes. Many of the houses were torn down during urban renewal and expansion of the city of Hartford but the following two homes remain much as they were when their illustrious owners lived there.

## The Harriet Beecher Stowe House (1871)

THE HARRIET BEECHER STOWE HOUSE (1871)

This nineteenth-century, buff-colored brick cottage with brown wood trim and a gabled roof was the

home of Harriet Beecher Stowe, author of more than 30 books, most notably, *Uncle Tom's Cabin*. The house is decorated throughout with many personal belongings of Mrs. Stowe, including the mahogany table on which she wrote her most famous novel, and some of her own original art work. The kitchen has been restored to illustrate many of her trend-setting ideas on "efficient" housekeeping presented in a popular book, *The American Woman's Home*, which she and her sister wrote in 1869.

## The Mark Twain House (1874)

This elaborate black-and-vermilion-painted brick Victorian, with its multiturreted roofline, balconies, and yards of "stick-style" railings, was the home of author Samuel Clemens, better known as Mark Twain. He himself described it best in his poem "This is the House that Mark Built"—"These are the bricks of various hue/And shape and position, straight and askew/With the nooks and angles presented to view . . . . " The interior of this 19-room house is as whimsical and interesting as the outside, with an eclectic arrangement of high-Victorian furnishings. Twain wrote some of his major works here, including *Tom*

THE MARK TWAIN HOUSE (1874)

*Sawyer* and *Huckleberry Finn.* The basement of the house contains a museum of Twain memorabilia, including his antique typewriter. (Twain was the first author to submit a typewritten manuscript to a publisher.) Nook Farm is operated by the Mark Twain Memorial and the Stowe-Day Foundation and is open year-round, Tuesday–Saturday 9:30–4:00, Sunday 12:00–4:00, and on Mondays June 1–Columbus Day. (Closed holidays.) An excellent museum shop is open until 5:00. Admission.

# Lakeville
## *Holley-Williams House (1808)*

Upper Main Street (Route 44)
203-435-2878

In this Classic Greek Revival house, with eighteenth- and nineteenth-century furnishings and portraits, lived five generations of Holleys. It overlooks the site of Furnace Village Forge, the first operational blast furnace in the state. Part of the iron empire of John M. Holley, the blast furnace produced cannons and cannon balls for the revolutionary war as early as 1762. The grounds feature a complex of original buildings and a lovely garden. The carriage house contains an exhibit on the Salisbury Iron Industry and a collection of locally made tools. The house is maintained by the Salisbury Association, and guided tours are given from July–mid-October, Thursdays and Saturdays 2:00–4:00. Admission.

# Lebanon
## *Governor Jonathan Trumbull House (1735)*

West Town Street
203-642-7558

Built by Joseph Trumbull for his son Jonathan and his wife and five children, this Georgian-style, two-story frame building is a modified rectangular house with a central chimney. Jonathan was the last governor of the colony and the first governor of the state. He was the only governor who actively supported the Revolution, and many leaders of the Revolution held councils here. The house is furnished with period pieces and a number of original Trumbull possessions, including a Queen Anne chair used by the governor in his pew in church. The War Office, where Governor Trumbull conducted his business,

and the Wadsworth Stable, where George Washington's horse slept, are also on the grounds. Owned and maintained by the DAR, the homestead is open May 15–October 15, Tuesday–Saturday 1:00–5:00 and Sunday by appointment. Donation.

GOVERNOR JONATHAN TRUMBULL HOUSE (1735)

# Ledyard

## *Nathan Lester House (1793)*

Vinegar Hill Road
203-464-0266

This is a typical farmhouse of the period and region, located on its original 100-acre site, which is now part of the town's historic district. Included on the grounds are many original buildings, as well as a farm museum containing early farm implements and machinery. The farmhouse, outbuildings, and land stayed in the Lester family until the early twentieth century, which accounts for their fine condition. Also on the property is the legendary Ledyard Oak. Operated by the town of Ledyard, the house is open from Memorial Day to Labor Day, Tuesday–Thursday 2:00–4:00, and weekends 1:00–4:00, and by appointment. Donation.

# Litchfield

## Litchfield Historic District

The Green, South and North streets

This small eighteenth-century settlement, founded in 1720 as a trading center and outpost in northwestern Connecticut, still has many of its original old houses clustered along "The Green." It is considered one of the best preserved New England towns in the state. While most of the houses are privately owned, many are open for special seasonal tours.

## Tapping Reeve House (1773) and Law School (1784)

South Street
203-567-4501

Judge Reeve built this house in 1773 for his young wife, Sally, the sister of Aaron Burr. He began his famous law lectures here, drawing students from all the states in the Union. As his scholars increased, he erected the small frame building next door, now known as the first law school in the country. Among its eighteenth- and nineteenth-century graduates were two vice-presidents, three Supreme Court justices, six cabinet members, 14 governors, and 130 members of Congress. The two-story frame house with central and end chimneys is furnished throughout with fine antiques of the period and exhibits of memorabilia of the many prominent graduates. Both buildings and the gardens are administered by the Litchfield Historical Society and are open mid-April–mid-November, Thursday–Monday 12:00–4:00. Admission.

# Madison

## The Allis-Bushnell House (c. 1785)

853 Boston Post Road
203-245-4567

This handsome, two-story colonial house was enlarged in 1860 with a Victorian wing. The colonial post and beam construction remains, however, as do other early architectural features such as corner fireplaces, corner cupboards, and paneling. The house is named after two families that lived here, the most famous being Cornelius Scranton Bushnell, the chief sponsor of the building of the ironclad ship S.S. *Monitor* and one of the organizers of the Union

Pacific Railway. The rooms contain period pieces and decorative arts, and there is a fine collection of toys and costumes on display. The house is maintained by the Madison Historical Society (gardens by the Madison Garden Club), and it is open from June until Labor Day, Wednesday, Friday, and Saturday 1:00–4:00. Donation.

# Manchester
## The Cheney Homestead (c. 1780)

106 Hartford Road
203-643-5588

Timothy Cheney, farmer, miller, and one of America's eminent clockmakers, built this home about 1780. His son George inherited it in 1875 and brought his bride, Electa, here to "keep house." They had nine children—eight boys and one girl—and the sons were eventually to form the famous Cheney Brothers Silk Mills (giving Manchester the nickname, "The Silk City"). Set on a hillside, the house is an early example of a split-level style, with a keeping room on the lower level, the "best parlor" on the second level, and bedrooms on the third floor. Many of the eighteenth-century furnishings were purchased in Philadelphia by one of the brothers, and one room is set aside as a studio, displaying works of art by Seth Cheney, another brother. The homestead is owned and operated by the Manchester Historical Society and is open year-round, Thursday and Sunday 1:00–5:00. Admission.

# Meriden
## Andrews Homestead (c. 1760)

424 West Main Street
203-237-5079/235-9790

Built by Samuel Andrews III, and later inherited by his son, Moses, this traditional New England saltbox has gone through many changes. But visitors to the house will still see many early construction details here, such as the original wide floorboards, the great fireplace with its deep dutch ovens, a huge exposed fieldstone chimney, a "hiding closet," and antique hardware. The furnishings are all donations from local families. There are also exhibits of toys and dolls and many display cases featuring products (now "collectibles") that were manufactured in Meriden.

The house is under the custodianship of the Meriden Historical Society and is open October–December and March–May, Wednesday and Saturday 2:00–4:00. Donation.

# Middletown

## *General Mansfield House (c. 1810)*
151 Main Street
203-346-0746

This Federal-style brick town house was built by Samuel and Catherine Mather, whose daughter married a Civil War hero, General Joseph Fenno Mansfield. The couple lived out their lives in this house, which has now become a repository for Civil War memorabilia and firearms. It is also filled with eighteenth- and nineteenth-century furniture, artwork, decorative arts, mostly from the Middletown area, and a genealogy library for researchers (by appointment). Owned and operated by the Middlesex County Historical Society, it is presently undergoing changes in visiting hours.

# Milford

THE BRYAN-DOWNS HOUSE
(C. 1785)

## *Wharf Lane Complex*
203-874-2664

Three houses, **The Bryan-Downs House** (c. 1785), **The Eells-Stow House** (c. 1700), and the **Stockade House** (c. 1780), form the Wharf Lane Historic District of Milford. The district is named for the old street, which ran from the town dock to the Milford Green and was the scene of the town's busy commerce by water in the eighteenth century. Some restoration work is still going on here, but the houses are furnished with a variety of interesting collections, including the Claude C. Coffin Indian Collection, containing over 4,000 prehistoric Indian artifacts. The complex, on the site of the old town wharf facing Milford Harbor, is maintained by the Milford Historical Society and is open from Memorial Day to Columbus Day, Sundays 2:00–4:30.

# Moodus

*Amasa Day House (1816)*

33 Plain Road
203-873-8144/247-8996
This simple, twin-chimney, center-entrance country house is located on the town green and is considered to be one of the earliest buildings in town. It was lived in by three generations of the Day family and is furnished in part with many of their belongings. Of

AMASA DAY HOUSE (1816)

particular interest is a magnificent shell-front chest of drawers made in the area. An unusual feature of the house is the original stenciled designs still found in two first floor rooms and the main stairway. The house is owned and operated by the Antiquarian & Landmarks Society, Inc., and is open May 15–October 15, Tuesday-Sunday 1:00–5:00. Admission.

# Mystic
*Mystic Seaport*

Route 27
203-572-0711

Founded in 1929, Mystic Seaport is a 17-acre waterfront site incorporating America's largest maritime museum, a collection of famous nineteenth-century ships, and a village of historic homes and workplaces gathered from around the New England area. Throughout the year there are daily demonstrations of working craftspeople, special events, seasonal cruises, lectures, art galleries, and restaurants, but the overall aim of this historic site is to preserve the authentic flavor of Connecticut's seafaring past. Three particularly interesting old houses to see here are the

THOMAS S. GREENMAN HOUSE
(1842)

**Samuel Buckingham House** (c. 1768 with an ell dated c. 1695), **The Burrows House** (c. 1812), and the **Thomas S. Greenman House** (1842). The latter house was built by Thomas Greenman, who with his two brothers, George and Clark, owned and operated a successful shipyard on the present site of Mystic Seaport. Both of the brothers' houses are located nearby. The Seaport is open every day year-round, 9:00–4:00. Admission.

## Denison Homestead (1717)

Pequot-Sepos Road
203-536-9248

Eleven generations of Denisons lived in this wonderful old house (also called Pequotsepos Manor), which is filled with their family heirlooms. Built as a typical foursquare plan, it is now the only New England home restored in the style of five eras (1717–1941). It has many fascinating architectural details, such as a rare trimmer arch over the kitchen fireplace that supports a hearthstone above, and summer beams, unconventionally running north and south. Besides the old colonial kitchen, each room has its own distinctive furnishings, including a Revolution-era bedroom, a Federal parlor, a Civil War bedroom, and an early 1900s living room. It is owned and operated by the Denison Society, Inc., and is open May 20–October 15 daily 1:00–4:00 (except for guided tours on Tuesdays). Admission.

# New Canaan

## Hanford-Silliman House (1764)

33 Oenoke Ridge
203-966-3333

This house was built by Sanford Hanford, a weaver and one of the early tavern keepers in the community, and his trades are emphasized throughout. There is a spinning and weaving room with early and modern equipment, and an eighteenth-century tavern room with an excellent collection of early pewter. Originally built as a center-chimney Connecticut saltbox, it evolved into a handsome Georgian-style home under the ownership of the Silliman family, who occupied it for more than two centuries. The house is furnished with many early pieces and a special doll exhibit. It is owned and operated by the New Canaan

Historical Society, which also maintains a complex of four other buildings, including the **John Rogers Studio and Museum**, housing a famous group of Roger's statuary. The house and museums are usually open year-round, Wednesday, Thursday, and Sunday 2:00–4:00 (check for seasonal changes). Donation.

# New Haven
*Pardee-Morris House (rebuilt c. 1780)*

325 Lighthouse Road
203-562-4183

The original house on this site was built around 1680, but was burned by the British in 1779 when they invaded New Haven. The following year, Amos Morris not only rebuilt the house, but added a ballroom. Georgian in character, the house has stone ends made entirely of granite. Shiny flakes of oyster shells used in the building of the house can be seen in the stone walls. It is furnished with some rare seventeenth-century pieces in the front room and some unusual eighteenth- and nineteenth-century "folk" painted furniture in other rooms. There are formal and herb gardens on the property. Owned and maintained by the New Haven Historical Society, it is open June–August, weekends 11:00–4:00 and by appointment. Admission.

# New London
*Joshua Hempsted House (1678)*
*Nathaniel Hempsted House (1759)*

11 Hempstead Street
203-443-7949

Constructed of unpainted oak, the large frame Joshua Hempsted House is one of the oldest houses in Connecticut, and one of the few New London houses that escaped the burning of that city by Benedict Arnold in 1781. The old house, with its ell added in 1728, was home to 10 generations of the same family. The diary meticulously kept by Joshua from 1711–1758 enabled the Antiquarian & Landmarks Society, Inc., to do an excellent restoration of the house. It is furnished with many of its original pieces and family possessions. The Nathaniel Hempsted House, also known as the Huguenot House, was the home of ropemaker Nathaniel Hempsted, grandson

of Joshua. This house also survived the burning of New London by the British in 1781. Built of granite on a granite ledge, it has been furnished to re-create the color and atmosphere of the mid-eighteenth century. An unusual feature of the house is its projecting beehive oven, which is used for occasional open hearth cooking demonstrations. Both houses are owned and maintained by the Antiquarian & Landmarks Society, Inc., and are open mid-May–mid-October, Tuesday–Sunday 1:00–5:00. Admission.

JOSHUA HEMPSTED HOUSE (1678)

## Monte Cristo Cottage (1888)

325 Pequot Avenue
203-443-0051

This was the boyhood home of a Nobel Prize–winning playwright Eugene O'Neill, and was used as the setting for two of his most famous plays, *Ah, Wilderness* and *Long Day's Journey into Night*. The simple, two-story, Victorian frame house with a wraparound porch and a side tower room, was named for the Count of Monte Cristo, Eugene's actor-father's most famous part. It is filled with memorabilia of the O'Neill family and is visited frequently by performers in O'Neill's plays. It is owned by the Eugene O'Neill Theatre Center and is open April 1–December 21 Monday–Friday 10:00–5:00, Admission.

## Shaw Mansion (1756)

11 Blinman Street
203-442-0391

This is another of the few New London houses to survive the burning of that town by the British in 1781, and although several small fires were set in the house by departing soldiers, neighbors rushed in to put them out. Made entirely of granite quarried on the site, it has several unique fireplaces made of paneled cement. During the revolutionary war the house served as Connecticut's naval office and was visited by Washington, Lafayette, Hale, and others. It is furnished with eighteenth- and nineteenth-century furniture, most of it belonging to the Shaw family and their descendants. Owned and operated by the New London Historical Society (which makes its home here), it is open year-round daily Tuesday–Saturday, 1:00–4:00. Admission.

SHAW MANSION (1756)

# New Milford

*Knapp House (c. 1808)*
6 Aspetuck Avenue
203-354-3069

This old frame house, built sometime between 1808 and 1817, is now part of the New Milford Historical Society Museum. (The entrance to the house is through the museum.) It is furnished with some of the original eighteenth- and nineteenth-century pieces left to the society in 1956 by the Knapp family, and with furnishings left to the society by another prominent New Milford family, the Boardmans (The Reverend Daniel Boardman was the town's first minister). The museum galleries display a collection of early portraits, miniatures, china, costumes, dolls, toys, and New Milford pottery. It is open May–October, Friday–Sunday 1:00–4:00, and by appointment. Donation.

# Newington

*Enoch-Kelsey House (1799)*
1702 Main Street
203-666-4995/666-4785

ENOCH-KELSEY HOUSE (1799)

Built in 1799 by farmer and tinsmith Enoch Kelsey, this center-chimney frame house was saved from destruction by the town of Newton when valuable wall paintings by a skilled artist were uncovered on its walls. The trompe l'oeil and freehand floral paintings are not only beautiful, but quite rare. The fireplaces, beehive oven, and paneling are all original, and the house is furnished with period pieces. As befitting its original owner, there is a good-size collection of tinware on display. Maintained by the Newington Historical Society and Trust, Inc., the house is open July–October, Thursdays 2:00–4:00. Admission.

## Kellogg-Eddy Museum (1808)

679 Willard Avenue
203-666-7118

This handsome, postrevolutionary era house, with Palladian windows and classical freestanding porch columns, was built by a prosperous farmer and businessman, Martin Kellogg, for his bride. Purchased by the town for its bicentennial celebration in 1987, it was restored at that time. It is noted for its finely handcrafted interior woodwork, particularly the intricate details in the fireplace mantels and ceiling frieze. The house is furnished with eighteenth- and nineteenth-century pieces collected from prominent local families, and features changing exhibits of antique items such as quilts, toys, and costumes. It is maintained by the Newington Historical Society and Trust, Inc., and is open year-round Thursday and Sunday 2:00–4:00. (Closed holidays and Thursdays in January and February.) Donation.

# Niantic

## Smith-Harris House (1845)

33 Society Road
203-739-0761

This house, an imposing, two-and-a-half-story frame Greek Revival dwelling, was originally called Brookside Farm. Owned by William H. Smith, who farmed the 103 acres in the summer, it was managed by his younger brother Herman and his nephew, Frank Harris. The house was purchased in 1955 by the town of East Lyme and restored. The furnishings were carefully selected to represent the mid-1800 period, when it was built. It is open July and August daily (except Tuesday), 1:00–5:00; September–December and April–June, Saturday and Sunday 1:00–5:00, or by appointment. Picnic facilities. Free.

## The Thomas Lee House (c. 1660)

Main Street
203-739-6070

This is the oldest wood-frame house in Connecticut, and it is still in its original state. Built by Thomas Lee in the early 1660s, the house began as a single room with a small chamber above. The room was called Judgement Hall and was said to be the one-time courtroom of Judge Thomas Lee. As Lee's family grew—to 15 children in all—the house was continually added to. It remained in the family for 250 years and was restored several times. The furnishings reflect the various lifestyles of the family as they lived here through the years. It is operated by the East Lyme Historical Society and is open June–September, Tuesday–Sunday 12:00–5:00. Donation.

# Norwalk

## Lockwood-Mathews Mansion (1864)

295 West Avenue
203-838-1434

Built by LeGrand Lockwood, a financier of the Civil War era, this magnificent mansion has been called "America's first château." Four stories high, it features a spacious octagonal rotunda surrounded by a series of decorative rooms (many in the process of restoration) and alcoves. Artists and artisans were brought from Europe to create the lavishly designed interiors of gilt, fresco, marble and wood inlay, etched glass, stenciled walls, and delicate murals. Saved from the wrecker's ball in the early 1960s, it has been under continuous restoration ever since. Recent efforts to acquire some of the mansion's original furnishings have been successful. One wing of the house is devoted to the Musical Box Society and has a large collection of music boxes on display. Hour-long guided tours are given from March to mid-December, Tuesday–Friday 11:00–3:00, and Sunday 1:00–4:00. Victorian gift shop. Admission.

# Norwich

## *John Baldwin House (1660)*

210 West Town Street
203-889-5990

Built by one of the founders of Norwich, this colonial home is very much a working household today. Visitors may chance to see impromptu demonstrations of spinning, weaving, natural dyeing, bread-baking, soap-making, and drying of herbs for cookery. Guided tours not only emphasize colonial skills and trades but the architecture of this very early home and its period furnishings. Maintained by the Norwich Historical Society, it is open May 15–Labor Day, Tuesday–Sunday 10:00–5:00, and by appointment. Admission.

## *Dr. John D. Rockwell House (1818)*

## *Nathanial Backus House (1750)*

42 and 44 Rockwell Street
203-887-8737

The imposing, two-story, 12-room Dr. John D. Rockwell House was constructed of native gray stone blocks quarried on the property by its original builder and owner, Joseph Perkins. His daughter Mary married John A. Rockwell, and the house was enlarged several times and lived in by several generations of the Rockwell family. It is furnished in early American and Victorian period pieces, along with displays of costumes, rare crewel work, fans, children's clothing, and toys. Next to it is the Nathanial Backus House, a fine example of Greek Revival domestic architecture built by a descendant of one of the founders of Norwich and containing some of its original furnishings. Both houses, owned and maintained by the DAR, are open July and August, Wednesday 1:30–4:30. Free.

## Leffingwell Inn (1675)

348 Washington Street
203-889-9440

This inn started out as a small saltbox home in 1675, built by Stephen Backus, son of one of the founding fathers of Norwich, and was later sold to Ensign Thomas Leffingwell. Leffingwell "joined" another old saltbox to it in 1701 to make an inn, and later, Christopher Leffingwell enlarged the inn by adding yet another saltbox to it in 1760. Christopher, a prosperous industrialist and ardent patriot, held revolutionary war conferences here. It has been carefully restored and furnished in seventeenth- and early eighteenth-century pieces. Special features are the George Washington Parlor, where Leffingwell entertained Washington, The Tavern Room, with its early pewter collection, and the Great South Parlor, furnished with elegant Queen Anne pieces. The inn is operated by the Society of the Founders of Norwich and is open May 15–October 15, Tuesday–Saturday 10:00–12:00, Sunday 2:00–4:00, and by appointment. Admission.

# Old Lyme

## Florence Griswold House (1817)

96 Lyme Street
203-434-5542

This beautiful, late Georgian house with a grand portico and central Palladian window, was purchased in

1841 by Robert Griswold, a prosperous captain of a packet boat that traveled from New York to England. Around the turn of the century and after her father's death, Florence, a musician, began taking in artists as boarders to help with the upkeep of the house. The house was to become one of America's first and best known art colonies. Many well-established artists were attracted to the colony by its pastoral setting and the camaraderie of their fellow artists, as well as the encouragement of "Miss Florence." Childe Hassam, William Metcalf, Walter Griffin, and Gifford Beal were among the early boarders. Some of them painted scenes on the doors and walls that have been carefully preserved. Many fine New England antiques and a rare china collection are on display, and there are changing exhibits in American Impressionism. Owned and operated by the Lyme Historical Society, it is open June–October, Tuesday–Saturday 10:00–5:00 and Sunday 1:00–5:00; November–May, Wednesday–Sunday 1:00–5:00. Gift shop and herb garden. Admission.

# Old Saybrook
*General William Hart House (1767)*

350 Main Street
203-388-2622

The Georgian-style home of General William Hart, an officer in the Continental Army during the Revolution, is an example of the home of a well-to-do New England settler. On the first floor two large parlors, a drawing room, and a library all boast corner fireplaces, while the original kitchen features a walk-in fireplace with a dutch oven. The library fireplace is decorated with an exceptional set of Staffordshire tiles, manufactured in Liverpool between 1765 and 1799 illustrating *Aesop's Fables*. Antique furnishings, costumes, and artifacts complement the original paneling and wainscoting throughout the house. Maintained by the Old Saybrook Historical Society, it is open late May–mid-September, Friday–Sunday 1:00–4:00. Herb and flower gardens and gift shop. Donation.

# Ridgefield
*Keeler Tavern Museum (1733)*

132 Main Street
203-438-4519

This two-and-one-half-story frame landmark was home to several families over the years, most notably, the renowned architect Cass Gilbert, who lived here from 1907 until 1955. But its history as a tavern during the revolutionary war has given it its special status. At that time bullets and ammunition were made in the cellar, making it a target for the British. It earned its nickname as the "Cannonball House," when it was fired upon in 1777 and a cannonball became lodged in the northeast corner of the house. It is still there. The tavern is filled with eighteenth-century furnishings, and guides are dressed in colonial costumes to recreate the atmosphere of an early inn. It is maintained by the Keeler Tavern Preservation Society and is open year-round, Wednesday, Saturday, Sunday, and Monday 1:00–4:00 (closed in January). Flower gardens and gift shop. Admission.

KEELER TAVERN MUSEUM (1733)

# Sharon

## Gay-Hoyt House (1775)

Main Street
203-364-5688

Located on the long, narrow green, the pink-hued Gay-Hoyt House is a fine example of a brick center-hall colonial. It was built during the Revolution by Lieutenant Colonel Ebenezer Gay, a prominent resident of Sharon who supplied provisions to the Continental Army. There are many exhibits on display throughout the house, including furniture, costumes, china, farm tools, guns, and records of local history. It is operated by the Sharon Historical Society and is open year-round, Saturday 2:00–5:00. Donation.

# Simsbury

## Captain Elisha Phelps House (1771)

800 Hopmeadow Street
203-658-2500

This gambrel-roofed, center-chimney colonial house is the centerpiece of Massacoh Plantation, a complex of early buildings along historic Hopmeadow Street in Simsbury that represent three centuries of local history. Built by Captain Phelps, a commissary in the Continental Army, the house was continuously occupied by his descendants until it became the property of the Simsbury Historical Society. During the nineteenth century the house was used as a hotel, and the north parlor has been restored to the original Tavern Room as it then appeared. The rest of the house is furnished with a fine collection of antiques and historical objects relating to local history. Among the many other buildings in the complex is Simsbury's first meetinghouse (1683), its first schoolhouse (1740), and the **Hendricks Cottage** (1795). The plantation is open May–October, Sunday–Friday (Saturday by appointment) with guided tours 1:00–3:30. The Phelps House is open year-round Monday–Friday 1:00–4:00, closed holidays. Admission.

CAPTAIN ELISHA PHELPS HOUSE (1771)

# Southington

## Barnes Museum (1836)

85 North Main Street
203-628-5426

This lovely, old, 15-room house is architecturally significant because it provides a clear and unusual record of the development of a structure through three distinct styles: Greek Revival, Italianate, and neoclassical Revival. The framework of the house is that of the original dwelling and is of solid oak. Many of the timbers were handhewn and put together with wooden dowel pins. The house was lived in by three generations of the same family and is filled with their furnishings, mementos, diaries, photographs, clothing, and collections. Owned by the town of Southington, it is open year-round, Monday–Friday 9:00–11:00 and 1:00–2:30. Herb and flower gardens. Donation.

# Stamford

## Hoyt-Barnum House (1699)

713 Bedford Street
203-329-1183/322-1565

HOYT-BARNUM HOUSE (1699)

Surrounded by the skyscrapers of downtown Stamford, this small, seventeenth-century, three-room cottage with a center chimney looks quite out of place. It was built by Samuel Hoyt, a blacksmith and farmer, who, with his first wife, Susannah, and later his second wife, Mary, raised 13 children here. The large kitchen still retains its original hand-hewn floor boards and wall paneling of vertical boards. Its furnishings are from the 1738 inventory of the original owner and feature some very early collections of Connecticut pottery and lighting fixtures. Also on display is a charming collection of nineteenth-century dolls and antique toys. The house is maintained by the Stamford Historical Society and is open by appointment.

# Stonington
## Whitehall (1771–1775)

Route 27
203-536-2428

Built as a country mansion by Dr. Dudley Woodbridge, a prosperous physician of Old Mystic, this house was moved to its present site during the building of Route I-95 in the early 1960s. At that time it was given to the Stonington Historical Society and painstakingly restored and furnished. Gambrel-roofed with three-foot cedar shingles, the house has twelve-over-twelve windows on the first and second stories. Most of the paneling is original, and the huge kitchen has an unusual fireplace with a rare brick "trimmer arch." The house is furnished in seventeenth- and eighteenth-century antiques, and on the second floor the society maintains a genealogical and historical library. The house is open from June 1–mid-September, daily except Monday 2:00–4:00 and by appointment. Herb garden. Admission.

# Stratford
## Captain David Judson House (c. 1750)

967 Academy Hill
203-378-0630

Nine generations of Judsons lived in this sturdy Georgian colonial, which has been restored to its original eighteenth-century condition. Some of its unusual features are the curved pediment over the central entrance door with its bulls-eye glass, fine paneling and moldings, three oversize fireplaces, and a slave cellar. Also, two beautifully detailed corner cupboards in the dining room display a superb collection of Canton ware. The house is furnished with eighteenth-century antiques, including a piano belonging to W. S. Johnson, signer of the Declaration of Independence. Owned and maintained by the Stratford Historical Society, the house is open April 15–October 31, Wednesday, Saturday, and Sunday 11:00–4:00. Admission.

# Suffield

## Dr. Alexander King House (1764)

232 South Main Street
203-668-5286/668-2533

Dr. King, a prominent doctor and activist in local and state political affairs, was born in Suffield in 1737. He built this house for his bride-to-be, Experience Hitchcock, a year before their marriage in 1764. A fine example of a conventional center-chimney plan, it has a most unusual feature, however; a long open porch on the south side of the house. The interior details and furnishings reflect the gracious, well-to-do lifestyle of this family. The house is furnished in period pieces, and there are several interesting collections, including Bennington pottery, old bottles, early tinware, and, in the doctor's office, a collection of Civil War surgical instruments. A rare collection of cigar and tobacco memorabilia in the rear ell reflects the fortunes made from the area's tobacco industry. Owned and maintained by the Suffield Historical Society, the house is open May–September, Wednesday and Saturday 1:00–4:00. Admission.

## Hatheway House (1761/1794)

55 South Main Street
203-247-8996

Regarded by some as one of New England's most important architectural landmarks, this stately frame dwelling reflects three distinct periods in Connecticut architecture and furnishings. The main portion of the house was built in the 1760s; while the ell, or wing, was built in 1794 and contains one of the only signed and dated rooms in early America. The rooms in the wing are still decorated with their original eighteenth-century French wallpapers of brightly colored elabo-

rate patterns. The rooms are furnished with fine period antiques, and the attractive grounds with formal
flower beds are set off from the street with an ornate
fence. The house is maintained by the Antiquarian &
Landmarks Society, Inc., and is open from May
15–October 15, Wednesday, Saturday and Sunday
1:00–4:00 and in July and August, Thursday and
Friday 1:00–4:00. Admission.

HATHEWAY HOUSE (1761/1794)

# Tolland

## Benton Homestead (c. 1720)

Metcalf Road
203-875-7559

This center-chimney colonial, for more than 200 years
the ancestral home of the Benton family, four of
whom served in the American Revolution, has an
intriguing history. Hessian mercenaries were quaran-
tined in the cellar here during the war after surren-
dering at the Battle of Saratoga. The house, "renovated but not remodeled," still retains the original
paneling, floors, five stone fireplaces, and small
handmade window panes, and has candlestick fixtures throughout. The furnishings, while not of any
special period, are interesting. More than 20 acres of

woodland surrounding the property have been developed with nature trails and recreation areas. The house is maintained by the Tolland Historical Society and is open May–October, Sunday 1:00–4:00. Donation.

## Hicks-Stern House (1795)

42 Tolland Green
203-875-7552

Located on the historic Tolland Green, this house is an interesting example of the architectural development of a home from the simple utilitarian design of the mid-eighteenth century to the highly ornate style of the Victorian period. It has served as a tavern ("Sign of the Yellow Ball"), and the first post office in Tolland, but is known best as the home of a very prominent local family, the Hicks. The house is furnished with family heirlooms. Concerts are held here in the summer, and during December, a Christmas open house. Maintained by the Tolland Historical Society, it is open mid-May–mid-October, Saturday and Sunday 1:00–4:00. Admission.

HICKS-STERN HOUSE (1795)

# Torrington
*Hotchkiss-Fyler House (1900)*

192 Main Street
203-482-8260

Long a landmark in Torrington, this large Victorian home, with a rosy-red slate and brick exterior, is distinguished by a large tower, elaborately decorated dormers, and a porte-cochere. It is an excellent example of the gracious, comfortable living of a wealthy family at the beginning of the twentieth century. Orsamus R. Fyler, who built this house, was a prominent Torrington industrialist and a dominant political figure in Connecticut. Today, the house remains furnished as it was when occupied by its last resident, Mrs. Edward Hotchkiss, the only daughter of Fyler. The interior of the house, with its mahogany paneling, parquet floors, handpainted ceilings, and stenciled walls, as well as its rich furnishings of

French antiques and rare glass, reflects the lavish lifestyle of the family that lived here. Maintained by the Torrington Historical Society, it is open year-round, Monday–Friday 9:00–4:00, and Saturday 10:00–3:00. Free.

# Wallingford
## Samuel Parsons House (1759)

180 South Main Street
203-294-1996

Located on the original main street of Wallingford, where the first settlers lived, this eighteenth-century, gambrel-roofed house retains much of its early construction. There are six fireplaces built around the two large chimneys at each end of the house. It is furnished with some fine eighteenth-century pieces, paintings by Wallingford artists, silver and pewter made by local craftsmen, early maps, tools, toys, and clothing. There is also a Civil War room displaying military memorabilia. The house is owned and maintained by the Wallingford Historical Society, Inc., and is open during July and August, Sunday 2:00–4:30. Herb garden. Donation.

# Washington
## Gunn Historical Museum (Willis House, 1781)

Wykeham Road at the Green
203-868-7756

This historical museum seeks to illustrate the "spirit and way of life" of early Washington residents. The house it occupies, donated for this purpose by a local resident, Mrs. June Willis, who lived in the house for many years, has seen significant changes. Originally built with a gambrel roof and two chimneys, it is typical of the late eighteenth-century central-hall design. It is filled with interesting collections of early Americana, such as silver, pewter, china, quilts and needlework, tools and kitchenware, toys, dolls and dollhouses, vintage clothing, paintings of local people by local artists, and military relics and autographs of revolutionary war heros. Operated by the Gunn Memorial Library, it is open year-round, Thursday, Saturday, and Sunday 12:00–4:00. Free.

# West Hartford

*Noah Webster Birthplace (c. 1700)*

227 South Main Street
203-521-5362

Begun early in the eighteenth century as a two-room structure with a side chimney, this house was expanded to a two-over-two Connecticut plan house at the time the Websters lived here. In these humble surroundings, Noah Webster (1758-1843), "Father of the American Language," wrote his famous books *Blue-Back Speller* and the first *American Dictionary.* Guided tours by costumed docents, offering visitors an opportunity to weave on an antique loom or take part in a kitchen demonstration, are part of the daily program. The house is furnished with period pieces and Webster memorabilia. Operated by the Noah Webster Foundation and Historical Society of West Hartford, it is open year-round, Monday–Thursday 10:00–4:00, and Sunday 1:00–4:00. Special events throughout the year. Gift/book shop. Admission.

## *Sarah Whitman Hooker House (1720)*

1237 New Britain Avenue
203-523-5887

This house began as a one-room structure with chamber above and later saw the addition of a tavern room and ell. It was purchased in 1773 by Thomas Hart Hooker, who died just two years later while serving in the Revolutionary Army. His widow, Sarah Whitman Hooker, remarried and lived here for 62 years. Many of the original features of the house, such as exterior siding, heavy hand-hewn beams, and gunstock posts, can be seen. A special detail is the wallpaper and stenciling, the former reproduced from fragments found on the original walls. The house contains a collection of eighteenth-century and Federal furniture. It is owned and operated by the Sarah Whitman Hooker Foundation, Inc., and is open year-round, Monday and Wednesday 1:30–3:30. Colonial herb and flower gardens. Admission.

# Wethersfield

Wethersfield, "the most ancient town in Connecticut," is an excellent example of a colonial riverport town

SOLOMON WELLES HOUSE

with an unusual amount of fine old homes still lining the main street and rimming the half-mile-long town green. There are nearly 150 homes built before 1850, all carefully restored and preserved, forming one of the largest and most interesting historic districts in Connecticut. The Wethersfield Historical Society, located in **The Keeney Memorial**, a renovated schoolhouse, administers several buildings and houses that are open to the public at certain times during the year and by appointment. These include the **Hurlbut-Dunham House**, built in 1804 by Captain John Hurlbut with the proceeds from a three-year voyage around the world; the **Captain James Francis House**, built in 1793, which traces a single family through 170 years; and the **Solomon Welles House**, begun in 1774 by carpenters who had to leave their work to go off to war. When the war was over the men picked up their tools and completed the house, and it is a tribute to their fine craftsmanship. The following houses are open to the public:

## Buttolph-Williams House (c. 1692)

249 Broad Street
203-529-0406

The oldest museum house in town, this well restored, four-room "mansion" with excellent period furnishings vividly depicts seventeenth-century life in Wethersfield. It is massively built in the English Tudor style, with the upper floor overhanging the lower floor. Of special interest is the large kitchen with its enormous fireplace, brass spit, and an exceptional collection of pewter and treenward. "Ye great kitchen," as it is called, is said to be the most authentic and completely furnished of its type in New England. Owned and operated by the Antiquarian & Landmarks Society, Inc., it is open May 15–October 15, daily 1:00–5:00. Admission.

## The Webb-Deane-Stevens Museum (1752–1789)

203–215 Main Street
203-529-0612

These three beautifully restored eighteenth-century houses, standing side by side on Main Street, owned and maintained by the National Society of the Colonial Dames of America in the State of Connecticut, are furnished with decorative arts spanning the years 1690 to 1840. The **Joseph Webb**

THE JOSEPH WEBB HOUSE (1752)

**House** (1752), the core of the museum, was home to a prominent family of merchants and patriots. Washington met here with Rochambeau in 1781 for an important conference that led to the British defeat at Yorktown. The **Silas Deane House** (c. 1766), with its elegant stairway and carved brownstone fireplace, reflects the prominence of its owner, a merchant, lawyer, and patriot. The **Isaac Stevens House** (1788), built for a leather worker and his bride, remained in the same family for more than 170 years. It contains many family artifacts, including antique toys, games, dolls, clothing, and nineteenth-century needlework. The houses and their landscaped grounds are open year-round, March–December, Tuesday–Saturday 10:00–4:00; January–February, Friday and Saturday 10:00–4:00, and Sunday 1:00–4:00. Additional hours: May 15–October 15, Sunday 1:00–4:00. Closed holidays. Herb garden. Admission.

## Sloan-Raymond-Fitch House (1756)

(Wilton Heritage Museum)
249 Danbury Road
203-762-7257

The headquarters of the Wilton Historical Society is located in a distinguished example of a mid-eighteenth-century gentleman's farmhouse. Built by Clapp Raymond, captain of the Wilton Militia, it is a classic central-chimney colonial house. Its period rooms are furnished to show the evolution of style between 1750 and 1850 and contain furniture and decorative accessories suitable to their time and place. The museum also houses a large costume collection, a permanent exhibit of dolls, toys, and dollhouses, and a study library. The museum features special exhibits throughout the year, as well as a full schedule of entertaining and educational activities for adults and children. It is open year-round, Tuesday, Wednesday, and Thursday 10:00–4:00 and Sunday 1:00–4:00 for special programs. Gift shop. Admission.

# Windsor

## Lt. Walter Fyler House (1640)

96 Palisado Avenue
203-688-3813

Built by Lieutenant Walter Fyler on land that was given to him for his services in the Pequot War, this gambrel-roofed colonial house (one section is Cape-style) was later purchased by Nathanial Howard, a sea captain. When Captain Howard returned to Windsor from his long sea voyages he brought back with him choice silks and cottons. His wife used a small room in the house for selling these treasured fabrics to the women of the town. The Windsor Historical Society has restored this two-story frame dwelling of the seventeenth and eighteenth centuries and kept intact the original entrance doors, the keeping rooms, the inside shutters, old random-width pine floorboards, and original paneling. The house is furnished as a living museum and contains many fine pieces of period furniture. Joined to the house is **The Wilson Museum**, built between 1961 and 1962, which houses a fine historical and genealogical library containing rare documents from many of Connecticut's earliest families. The house is open April 1–November 30, Tuesday–Saturday 10:00–12:00 and 1:00–4:00. Admission.

# Winstead

## Solomon Rockwell House (1813)

Prospect Street
203-379-8433

Built by Solomon Rockwell, a pioneer in the iron industry, this Greek Revival–style house with tall Ionic columns was fondly dubbed "Solomon's Temple" by the townspeople. It took two-and-a-half years to complete the building (woodwork in the main hall was carved with a jacknife), which includes a woodshed, a carriage house, and a nearby privy. The latter is also decorated with carved Ionic columns and dentils to match the house. The house was lived in by the Rockwell family and their descendants until 1912, and although few of their personal belongings remain in the house, it is furnished with many fine period pieces and paintings. One room is used for archives housing local documents and photographs. It is owned by the Winchester Historical Society and is open June 15–September 15, Thursday–Saturday 2:00–4:00. Admission.

# Woodbridge

## Thomas Darling House (c. 1765)

1907 Litchfield Turnpike
203-387-2823

Thomas Darling, a Congregational minister, Yale tutor, judge, and merchant, operated a tavern and cattle driver's stopover in his home on the early Litchfield Turnpike. This one-and-one-half-story, gambrel-roofed, frame house was occupied by the same family until 1973. It is furnished with early pieces pertaining to its tavern days, including cooking implements, account books, clothing, and furniture. It is maintained by the Amity and Woodbridge Historical Society and is open year-round, Sunday 2:00–5:00. Free.

# Woodbury
*The Glebe House (1740)*

Hollow Road
203-263-2855

This eighteenth-century, gambrel-roofed farmhouse is called "The birthplace of the Episcopal Church in America." It became a minister's farm, or glebe, in 1771, when Woodbury's first Anglican minister, John Rutgers Marshall, moved there with his wife and nine children. In 1783, just weeks after American independence was secure, a group of clergy met secretly here and elected the first American bishop of the Episcopal Church, Samuel Seabury. The Glebe House was restored between 1923 and 1925 and has some interesting features, such as an entrance to a secret tunnel, eighteenth-century graffiti done by children, and much of its original paneling and furnishings. It is owned by the Seabury Society for the Preservation of the Glebe House, Inc., and is open April–October, daily 1:00–5:00 (except Tuesday), November 1:00–4:00, and by appointment December 1–March 25. Gertrude Jekyll Garden (one of only three in this country) and gift shop. Donation.

# Woodstock
*Roseland Cottage (1846)*

On the Common (Route 169)
203-928-4074

This bright pink, restored Gothic Revival "cottage" was built as a summer home by successful merchant and publisher, Henry Bowen. His Fourth of July parties became legendary, attracting such important guests as Presidents Grant, Hayes, Harrison, and McKinley. The house is still furnished as it was when the Bowen family lived there, with specially designed furniture that is massive and ornate, and heavily embossed wallpaper resembling tooled leather. The grounds are beautifully landscaped with a parterre garden dating from 1850. One of several outbuildings contains the oldest indoor bowling alley in the country. It is owned and maintained by SPNEA and is open mid-May–mid-September, Wednesday–Sunday 12:00–5:00, and mid-September–mid-October, Friday–Sunday 12:00–5:00. Admission.

ROSELAND COTTAGE (1846)

# Additional Houses
## (Area code 203)

**ANSONIA**
 The Mansfield House, 33 Jewett Street, 734-1908

**BRIDGEPORT**
 Capt. John Brooks House, 199 Pembrook Street, 372-3521

**COLECHESTER**
 Foote House, The Green, 537-2378

**COVENTRY**
 Strong House, South Street, 742-7207

**EAST HARTFORD**
 Huguenot House, 307 Burnside Avenue, 568-6178/0716

**ELLINGTON**
 Nellie McKnight House, 70 Main Street, 875-1131

**ENFIELD**
 Martha A. Parsons House, 1387 Enfield Street, 754-6064

**FAIRFIELD**
   The Burr Homestead, 739 Old Post Road,
      255-8495/8200

**HARTFORD**
   Armsmear, 80 Wethersfield Avenue, 246-4025

   Katharine S. Day House, 77 Forrest Street,
      525-9317

**LEBANON**
   Jonathan Trumbull Jr. House, West Town Street,
      642-6040

   Dr. William Baumont House, West Town Street,
      642-7247

**LITCHFIELD**
   Chase House, Topsmead State Forest, 566-2304

**MADISON**
   Deacon John Grave House, 581 Boston Post
      Road, 245-4798

**MIDDLETOWN**
   Alsop House, Davison House, Russell House,
      301–327 High Street, (Wesleyan U.)
      347-9411/Ext. 2401

**NEW HAVEN**
   James Dwight Dana House, 24 Hillhouse
      Avenue, Othniel C. Marsh House, 360 Prospect
      Street (Yale U.) 432-2300

**NEW LONDON**
   Deshson-Allyn House, 613 William Street,
      443-2545

**SCOTLAND**
   Edward Waldo House, Walso Road, 456 0077

**WATERBURY**
   The Mattatuck Museum, Hillside Avenue,
      753-0381

**WATERFORD**
   Harkness Mansion, Harkness Memorial Park,
      443-5725

**WEST HARTLAND**
   Gaylord House, Main Street, 379-9722

**WILLIMANTIC**
   Jillson House, Main Street, 456-2316

**WILTON**
   Lambert House, 150 Danbury Road, 762-7257

# RHODE ISLAND

## Bristol

*Blithewold (1907)*

101 Ferry Road
401-253-2707

Built in the style of a seventeenth-century English manor house, this stone and stucco 45-room mansion is decorated and furnished much as it was when the original owner, Augustus Van Wickle, and his family lived there. Van Wickle, a Pennsylvania coal magnate, built it as a summer home, but his wife and eldest daughter are credited with turning the 33 acres of landscaped grounds into a showplace. The turn-of-the-century designed gardens include many exotic plants and shrubs not usually found in New England. The interior furnishings of the stately house include many rare antiques spanning several centuries, fine china, and crystal. The property, owned and operated by the Heritage Trust of Rhode Island, is open mid-April–October 10:00–4:00 (closed Mondays and holidays). The grounds are open year-round 10:00–4:00, and many special events and horticultural programs are held here throughout the year. Admission.

## Charlestown

*The General Stanton Inn (1667)*

Boston Post Road
401-364-8888

This is one of the oldest continuously run inns in America, but it began as a one-room, gambrel-roofed house, won in a lottery by Thomas Stanton. Stanton, a successful fur trader, had the house moved to this site, where it first served as a schoolhouse for the tutoring of Indian children and Negro slaves before becoming a residence. Many nationally known names are in the guest book, including future presidents, generals, socialites, and theater people. The inn still embraces some of the old original atmosphere, with low ceilings, large fireplaces, brick ovens, and hand-hewn timbers. Rooms are available year-round by the day or week, and breakfast, lunch, and dinner are served daily. Owners, Janice and Angelo Falcone.

# Coventry

## General Nathanael Greene Homestead (1774)

50 Taft Street
401-821-8630

This simple, two-and-one-half-story, clapboard house, with a handsome pedimented doorway, was built by Nathanael Greene in the small village of Anthony (now part of Coventry) in 1774. A year later, when he joined the Continental Army and went off to war (becoming Washington's second in command), his wife turned their home into a hospital for officers recuperating from smallpox. The interior of the house (which is presently undergoing extensive renovation) still retains its original paneling and hand-wrought hardware, the latter said to have been forged at the Greene family iron works in Warwick. Four rooms on each floor contain period furnishings and exhibits of articles connected with the revolutionary war and the Greene family. Operated by the Nathanael Greene Homestead Association, the house is open March 1–November 30, Wednesday, Saturday, and Sunday 2:00–4:00, and by appointment. Donation.

## Paine House (c. 1668)

7 Station Street
401-231-9492

PAINE HOUSE (C. 1668)

This nicely restored, two-and-one-half-story, gable-roofed house began as a one-room structure built by Francis Brayton sometime before 1748. In 1785 his son incorporated the old portion of the house into the southeast corner of the present house and enlarged it considerably. He opened an inn here with 22 rooms, and a tavern in the stone cellar at ground level. Located on a busy corner, on what was then the main artery linking Providence to Hartford, Connecticut, it soon became a popular stopping place for travelers and continued as such well into the nineteenth century. The house was purchased and restored by the Western Rhode Island Civic Historical Society in 1952, keeping to the original interior and furnished with period pieces. It is open from June–mid-October, Saturday 1:00–5:00 and by appointment. Donation.

# Cranston

## *The Sprague Mansion (1790)*

1351 Cranston Street
401-944-9226

THE SPRAGUE MANSION (1790)

This 28-room mansion with a gabled roof and large bay windows was the ancestral home of one of Rhode Island's most prominent families of the 1800s. In 1808 William Sprague converted a small gristmill on his property into one of the first cotton mills in

New England, thus launching the "Sprague Empire." The family produced two governors who also became United States senators, and their home was for many years the center of social life in the community. With a weakening economy following the Civil War, and heavily in debt, the family empire began to crumble and the home was sold. In 1968 the Cranston Historical Society purchased the property and restored it to much of its original elegance. It is furnished throughout by gifts and items on loan, including some original Sprague family pieces and an impressive collection of Oriental art objects. The large carriage house on the grounds holds a famous collection of vintage carriages, sleighs, and wagons. The mansion is open from July 1–Labor Day, Tuesday and Sunday 2:00–5:00. Gardens. Children's programs. Admission.

## Joy Homestead (1778)

156 Scituate Avenue
401-944-9226

Three generations of the Joy family lived in this cozy-looking red farmhouse, which is an excellent example of eighteenth-century construction. The red-painted, one-and-a-half-story homestead, with a gambrel roof, 10 rooms, and a deep cellar, has a central chimney with a most unusual feature: it rests in a wooden cradle. The Joy family, who were shoemakers as well as farmers, built a small industrial complex around their homestead and became so prosperous that at one point their area was called Joytown. The house, simply furnished in early American period pieces, is open by appointment and is available for rent to small groups. Children's programs. Admission.

# East Greenwich

## The General James Mitchell Varnum House Museum (1773)

57 Pierce Street
401-884-4110

General James Mitchell Varnum, the first commander of the Kentish Guards (one of the oldest military units in the country, still meeting in their 1842 headquarters just down the street), built this handsome, two-story, Georgian-style mansion in 1773. Located on one of the highest points in town, it commands a

fine view of the bay. It contains 13 rooms, eight fire-places, and two central chimneys. Much of the original interior hardware and beautiful paneling have been preserved. It is furnished with distinctive period antiques, highlighted by colonial and Victorian children's playrooms. There is also an extensive marine exhibit, a colonial garden, and a coach-house museum in the rear. Owned by the Varnum Continentals, it is open from Memorial Day to Labor Day, Tuesday–Saturday 1:00–4:00 and by appointment. Admission.

# Hopkinton
### The General Thurston House (1763)

496 Main Street
401-377-2460/377-9049

This large, square, two-story colonial, with an ell and an immense chimney, is built of heavy oak timbers with oak clapboard sides. It was built by Joseph Brayman as a half-house in 1741 and later purchased and enlarged by General George Thurston. Thurston, a distinguished soldier in the revolutionary war, was a member of one of Hopkinton's most prominent families. Throughout the years this house has been home to three lieutenant governors of Rhode Island: General Thurston's son, his grandson, and his nephew. Much of its original colonial charm has been preserved, and it is now operated as a seven-room bed and breakfast by the Thurman Silks family. Interested people may tour the house by prior arrangement (no charge).

# Johnston

## *Clemence-Irons House (c. 1680)*

38 George Waterman Road
617-227-3956

One of the oldest dwellings in the state, this "stone-ender" characterizes one of Rhode Island's seventeenth-century regional house forms. Thomas Clemence, a friend of Roger Williams, bought this property from the Indians in 1654. It is believed that the original house built here in 1650 was burned during King Philip's War of 1676, and the new house was constructed around the stone-end chimney about 1680. The four-room, one-story house is entered through an off-center plank door that has its original knob-headed nails. The interior is paneled in vertical sheathing with beveled and beaded edges, and there are two huge fireplaces placed side by side. This was home to five generations of the Irons family, and it is now restored and maintained by SPNEA. It is open by appointment by calling the society.

# Kingston

## *Fayerweather House (c. 1820)*

Mooresfield Road
401-789-9072

This modest, one-and-a-half-story, shingled frame house was built by the village blacksmith around 1820. George Fayerweather was the son of one of the many slaves who labored on the surrounding plantations here in the seventeenth century. His descendants continued to run the business and occupy the house for many years. The house is now owned by the Fayerweather Craft Guild. Weekly demonstrations and exhibits of various arts and crafts are held here during the summer months. Fayerweather House is open May–December, Tuesday and Saturday 10:00–4:00. Free.

HELME HOUSE (1802)

## Helme House (1802)

139 Kingstown Road
401-783-2195

Bernon Elijah Helme, for whom this house and gallery are named, was a descendant of the Huguenot Gabriel Bernon, and James Helme, Rhode Island Supreme Court chief justice in 1767. The two-and-one-half story, double-chimney farmhouse also functioned as Mr. Helme's store. He was a philanthropic and civic-minded businessman and a patron of the arts. When he died in 1944 the financial generosity of his will enabled the South County Art Association to purchase the property and some of its contents. The house is now their headquarters, and throughout the year workshops and classes in pottery, drawing, and painting are held. It is open during shows (12 per year), Wednesday–Sunday 1:00–4:00. Donations.

# Lincoln

*Eleazer Arnold House (c. 1687)*

449 Great Road
617-227-3956

Another characteristic Rhode Island stone-end house (see Clemence-Irons House in Johnston), and one of the few remaining in the state, features a massive pilaster-top stone chimney. Known for years as the "splendid mansion of Eleazer Arnold," a prosperous farmer, it has a simple plank door placed off-center on the front of the house, six small leaded windows, great corner posts, and a chamfered summer beam. The rough interior walls of the house, covered with paneled boards having beveled and beaded edges, reflect the wealth of Arnold at that time. Restored and maintained by SPNEA as a "study house," it is open by appointment only.

# Little Compton

*Wilbor House (1680)*

West Main Street
401-635-4559

WILBOR HOUSE (1680)

When this house was built by Samuel Wilbore (original spelling) in the seventeenth century, it had only two rooms, one above the other, a cramped stairway, and a small attic. Eight generations of the same family continued to live here, making several changes and additions as time went by. The architecture of the house reflects the evolution of tastes throughout these years, and when it was restored in 1955 by the Little Compton Historical Society, the original details were kept intact. The house is furnished with gifts from Wilbor descendants and local residents representing items used in Little Compton during the periods in which the house was occupied. The old barn has a display of farm tools, carriages, sleighs, and a Wilbor coach. The house is open late June–September 1, Tuesday–Saturday 2:00–4:30. Admission.

# Middletown
## *Prescott Farm (c. 1715)*

2009 West Main Street
401-847-6230/849-7300

PRESCOTT FARM (C. 1715)

This re-creation of a colonial Rhode Island farm is an important revolutionary war landmark. General Richard Prescott, commander of the occupying British

Army, was captured here by a band of daring patriots on the night of July 9, 1777. The main house is not open to the public, but the surrounding buildings are open to visitors and offer a unique look at a typical early Rhode Island farm. Owned and operated by the Newport Restoration Foundation, it is open April–November, daily 10:00–4:00. Admission.

## Whitehall (1729)

311 Berkeley Avenue
401-846-3790/846-2911

Built by the eminent Irish philospher and Anglican churchman, George Berkeley, during his three-year stay here (1729–1732), this frame hipped-roof house with a kitchen ell incorporates some unusual features for a New England farmhouse of the period. Berkeley named it Whitehall, and members of the clergy and other scholars gathered here regularly, forming a philosophical society that was the basis for the famed Redwood Library in Newport (the oldest library building in the country in continuous use). The house is furnished throughout with antiques appropriate to the period of the house. Owned and operated by the National Society of the Colonial Dames in Rhode Island (who have shown the house since 1900), it is open daily July–Labor Day 10:00–5:00. An eighteenth-century garden adjoining the house is maintained by the Newport Garden Club. Admission.

# Newport
## The Astors' Beechwood (1855)

580 Bellevue Avenue
401-846-3772

This large, white stucco mansion, with Palladian windows and an elaborate porte-cochere, was built in 1855 by John Jacob Astor for his family as a summer residence. It was here that his wife, *The* Mrs. Astor (as she insisted on being called), reigned as queen of Newport society. Because her ballroom would hold only 400 people, she compiled a list of just that number, from which the expression "Society's 400" originated. A feature of a visit here is being entertained by costumed actors and actresses, who take on the roles of servants and guests as they escort you through the house. Many of the elaborate furnishings are original

THE ASTORS' BEECHWOOD (1855)

to the house. Operated by the Beechwood Foundation, it is open daily, year-round 10:00–4:00. Admission.

## Belcourt Castle (1892)

Bellevue Avenue
401-846-0669

The finest craftsmen and artists of Europe were employed to create this opulent 60-room château in the style of King Louis XIII's hunting lodge at Versailles. Built for Oliver Hazard Perry Belmont, scion of the wealthy New York Belmonts (Belmont Park) and who married a Vanderbilt, the castle has a

large Gothic ballroom, the scene of many fabulous balls during Newport's Gilded Age. The ballroom, with its vaulting stained-glass windows and tapestries, is now the perfect backdrop for a large exhibit of armor. The castle contains a priceless collection of art treasures and antiques (including a coronation coach) acquired from palaces and castles of 33 countries. It is the only privately owned mansion that is open to the public by the family in residence. It is open year-round, daily 10.00–5.00, and groups can arrange for catered affairs here. Admission.

BELCOURT CASTLE (1892)

## The Breakers (1895)

Ocre Point Avenue
401-847-1000

In the style of a Renaissance Italian villa, this 70-room "cottage" was designed by famed architect Richard Morris Hunt, for Cornelius Vanderbilt. It is the most stunning and opulent of all the Newport mansions. The rooms are arranged around a two-story Great Hall, rising more than 45 feet and filled with intricate carvings, marble columns, ornate chandeliers, and a lavishly gilded ceiling. The dining room features a ceiling painting of Aurora at Dawn, overlooking a

THE BREAKERS (1895)

spacious room surrounded by massive red Numidian marble columns. Many artists, craftsmen, and laborers, as well as materials, were imported from Europe to complete the mansion, which contains all the original furnishings. Situated on Ocre Point, overlooking the Atlantic Ocean, the mansion offers spectacular views from the ornate windows and balconies. A children's cottage is also located on the beautifully landscaped grounds (designed by Olmsted). Maintained by the Preservation Society of Newport County, it is open April–October, daily 10:00–5:00. Admission.

## Chateau-Sur-Mer (1852)

Bellevue Avenue
401-847-1000

One of the earliest summer "cottages" to be built along Bellevue Avenue, Chateau-Sur-Mer (castle-on-the-sea), is also one of the best examples of lavish Victorian architecture in America. Noted architect Richard Morris Hunt designed this granite castle with its high mansard roof for William S. Wetmore, who made his fortune in the China trade. A striking feature of the house is the central hallway, an atrium

that rises 45 feet, surrounded by balconies on each floor, to a glass ceiling. The Italian decorator Frulini designed much of the interior, such as the Renaissance-style walnut library with elaborate carvings, and the dining room, with its walls and ceilings decorated with bacchanalian carvings denoting the sensual pleasures of eating and drinking. The elaborate Victorian furnishings are particularly enhanced at Christmastime, when the house is draped in holiday decorations. Maintained by the Preservation Society of Newport County, it is open May 1–November 2, daily 10:00–5:00, and during the winter months, Saturday and Sunday 10:00–5:00. Admission.

CHATEAU-SUR-MER (1852)

## The Elms (1901)

Bellevue Avenue
401-847-1000

Modeled after the Château d'Asnieres near Paris, this eighteenth-century, classic French château was built for Edward J. Berwind, the Pennsylvania coal magnate. The interior, quite in contrast to its somber facade, is exquisite. The grand staircase is made of white marble and limestone, and the rooms, with their lavishly decorated ceilings and walls, were the work of the renowned House of Alavoine of Paris. The furnishings and objets d'art, while not original, are authentic Louis XIV and XV pieces. The grounds on the estate are particularly beautiful, with rolling terraces and lawns bedecked with statuary, flower gardens, fountains, and a wide variety of beautiful trees. Maintained by the Preservation Society of Newport County, it is open May 1–November 2, daily 10:00–5:00, and during the winter months on Saturday and Sunday 10:00–5:00. During December it is decorated for the holiday season. Admission.

## *Hammersmith Farm (1887)*

Ocean Drive
401-846-0420/846-7346

This beautiful, 28-room Victorian farmhouse, with its silver-gray shingle-style construction, is more typical of southern New England summer cottages. The house would have most likely stayed a private residence had it not been the scene of a famous wedding reception. It was built by John W. Auchincloss

HAMMERSMITH FARM (1887)

and later owned by his nephew, Hugh D. Auchincloss, Jr., stepfather of Jacqueline Bouvier. When Jackie married John F. Kennedy in Newport in 1953, she held her wedding reception here. Later, President Kennedy and his family spent part of each summer here, making Hammersmith Farm a summer White House. The interior furnishings are informal and casual, typical of the era and without distinction, except for the Kennedy memorabilia. The broad lawns and meadows reach to the bay, where the presidential yacht once docked, and a children's play-house (now a gift shop) is on the grounds. Hammersmith is privately owned but open to the public daily April–October, weekends in March and November. Spring and fall 10:00–5:00; Memorial Day weekend–Labor Day 10:00–7:00. Admission.

## Hunter House (1748)

54 Washington Street
401-847-1000

This National Historic Landmark was built in 1748 by Jonathan Nichols, deputy governor of Rhode Island. During the American Revolution it served as the headquarters of Admiral de Ternay, commander of the French naval forces. Considered one of the 10 best examples of residential colonial architecture in America, it is an extremely handsome house. Of particular note is the doorway, with its segmented pediment enclosing a pineapple—the symbol of hospitality in colonial Newport. The interior is elaborately paneled and furnished with Townsend and Goddard pieces, Newport silver, china, and period portraits and paintings. Owned by the Preservation Society of Newport County, the house is open May 1–November 2, daily 10:00–5:00. Admission.

## Kingscote (1839)

Bellevue Avenue
401-847-1000

This Gothic Revival summer cottage was originally built by architect Richard Upjohn for George Noble Jones, a wealthy plantation owner from Savannah, Georgia. At the outbreak of the Civil War, Jones sold the house to William King, a shipbuilder engaged in the China trade. Gothic Revival features carry through to the interior of the house, with intricately carved woodwork, arches, and columns, and rooms of vari-

KINGSCOTE (1839)  ous sizes. The ornate dining room, with its mahogany paneling, Tiffany glass-tile walls, and cork ceiling, is by far the most dramatic room in the house. The house contains many pieces by the famous Newport cabinet makers Townsend and Goddard, and some outstanding Chinese export paintings and porcelains. Owned by the Preservation Society of Newport County, it is open April, Saturday and Sunday 10:00–5:00; May 1–October 31, daily 10:00–5:00. Admission.

## Marble House (1892)

Bellevue Avenue
401-847-1000

It took four years to complete this fabulous house, which takes its name from the many kinds of marble used in its construction and decoration. Considered by many to be not only the most sumptuous, but the most beautiful of all Newport mansions, it was built for William K. Vanderbilt and designed by Richard Morris Hunt. A two-story porte-cochere, supported by Corinthian columns, dominates the exterior of the house. Huge ornamental columns surround the house, which is circled by a rooftop balustrade. The

MARBLE HOUSE (1892)

interior rooms of the mansions are faced in marble, and the ceilings, pilasters, and trim elements are gilded. The French firm of J. Allard was responsible for most of the interior decoration, including the ironwork on the Grand Staircase, and the bronze chairs and stools (believed to be the only examples of bronze furniture in the world) in the dining room. The Vanderbilts entertained lavishly here until their divorce in 1896, which shocked Newport society, and the mansion was closed for many years thereafter. Now completely restored, it is furnished throughout with its original elaborate furnishings and artwork, and there is an interesting Chinese teahouse on the grounds. It is owned by the Preservation Society of Newport County and is open April–October 31, daily 10:00–5:00, and November–March, Saturday and Sunday 10:00–4:00. Admission.

## Rosecliff (1902)

Bellevue Avenue
401-847-1000

Modeled after the Grand Trianon at Versailles, by the architectural firm of McKim, Mead, and White, this elegant, white terracotta mansion was built for Mr. and Mrs. Hermann Oelrichs. Mrs. Oelrichs ("Tessie") was one of Newport's great hostesses, and her home was designed for entertaining on a grand scale. The ballroom, the largest in Newport, dominates the lower level of the house, with large French windows opening onto a terrace overlooking the formal gardens and the sea. The 40-room mansion features an eighteenth-century Court of Love designed by Augustus Saint-Gaudens and patterned after one built for Marie Antoinette. The rose gardens for which the estate is named are in bloom all summer and were the setting in 1973 for the motion picture *The Great Gatsby*. Owned by the Preservation Society of Newport County, the house is open April–October 31, daily 10:00–5:00. Admission.

## Samuel Whitehorne House (c. 1811)

416 Thames Street
401-847-2448

This three-story, solid brick house on the waterfront is a fine example of the Federal period. Its austerity is broken by a prominent rounded portico with a Palladian window and oculus above. It was built for Samuel Whitehorne, a prosperous Newport merchant, and when it was built it was one of the finest houses in Newport. The house contains an outstanding collection of eighteenth-century furniture made by the Newport craftsmen Goddard and Townsend. Much of the silver and pewter collection in the house was also fashioned by early Newport artisans. The house and its eighteenth-century garden are owned by the Newport Restoration Foundation and are open

May–October, Friday 1:00–4:00, Saturday, Sunday, and Monday 10:00–4:00, and other days by appointment.

### Wanton-Lyman-Hazard House (c. 1690–1700)

17 Broadway
401-846-0813

This National Historic Landmark, descended through several prominent Newport families, is the oldest house in Newport and one of the few seventeenth-century houses left in the city. It was originally the home of Richard Ward, the stamp master of Newport, charged with enforcing the hated Stamp Act. He was run out of town in 1765 by an angry mob during the Stamp Act Riot. The house has been carefully restored by the Newport Historical Society, and shows the evolution of several architectural tastes during the early American period, such as the exposed heavy chamfered beams and massive gunstock corner posts. It is furnished throughout with period Newport pieces, and the kitchen features an exhibition of eighteenth-century cookery. Behind the house is a colonial herb garden. It is open mid-June–August, Tuesday–Saturday 10:00–5:00. Admission.

# North Kingston
### Smith's Castle (1678)

41 Richard Smith Drive
401-294-3521

This New England landmark, built by Richard Smith, Jr., as a blockhouse, was the site of trading centers established by Richard Smith and Roger Williams in 1637. When Smith died in 1692 he left the property to his nephew, Lodowick Updike, who turned it into a plantation maintained by slave and Indian labor. It is called "America's oldest plantation house," and is the only house still standing where Roger Williams, the founder of Rhode Island, visited and preached. On the grounds is the mass grave of 40 colonial soldiers killed in 1675 in the Great Swamp Fight with the Indians. Adjacent to the house is a replica of an eighteenth-century flower and herb garden. Operated by the Cocumscussoc Association at Smith's Castle, the house is open daily (except Monday), June, July, and August, and Thursday–Sunday in May and

SMITH'S CASTLE (1678)   September. Hours: 11:00–4:00 Tuesday–Saturday, and 1:00–5:00 Sunday. Admission.

# Pawtucket
## Daggett House (1685)

Slater Memorial Park
401-722-2631/333-1268

Eight generations of Daggetts lived in this two-and-a-half-story, frame colonial house, which has a gabled roof and central chimney. The Daggetts (two members of the family fought in the revolutionary war), were farmers and slaveholders and cultivated a 195-acre farm here, now known as Slater Memorial Park. The house is furnished throughout with an outstanding collection of eighteenth- and nineteenth-century antiques and Rhode Island memorabilia, including colonial pewter and tools, and china owned by General and Mrs. Nathanial Green. The house is administered by the Pawtucket Chapter DAR, and tours are conducted every Saturday and Sunday, June–September, 2:00–5:00. (Bus tours, April–October.) Admission.

## Slater Mill Historic Site

Roosevelt Avenue
401-725-8638

Called the "birthplace of the American industrial revolution," the mill, built by Samuel Slater in 1793, was the first cotton spinning mill in the United States with a fully mechanized power system. The mill now houses operating machinery used to illustrate the process of converting raw cotton to finished cloth, as well as a slide theater, classrooms, and museum shop. The site has been restored to its appearance in the early 1800s, to depict the development of factory production and life in a nineteenth-century industrial village. Guided tours include visits to the Sylvanus Brown House, the Wilkinson Mill (built in 1810), the Slater dam and power canal, and a two-acre riverfront park. The **Sylvanus Brown House**, a small, red, gambrel-roofed house, was built in 1758 and owned by millworker Sylvanus Brown, and is furnished as an early nineteenth-century artisan's home. Operated by the Slater Mill Historic Site, it is open June 1–Labor Day, Tuesday–Saturday 10:00–5:00, Sunday 1:00–5:00, and March 1–May 31 and September–mid-December on Saturday and Sunday 1:00–5:00. Admission.

# Portsmouth
## Brayton Estate (c. 1800)

(Green Animals)
Cory's Lane
401-847-1000

This small country estate overlooking Narragansett Bay, now known as Green Animals, was purchased in 1872 by Thomas E. Brayton as a summer residence for his family. It consisted of seven acres of land, a handsome, white clapboard, two-story house, farm outbuildings, a pasture, and vegetable gardens. Mr. Brayton's love of horticulture led him to turn the grounds into a showplace of formal gardens complete with 80 pieces of topiary (many shaped like animals). The first floor of the main house contains a small Victorian toy museum, and there is a plant and gift shop on the property. A brochure with a guide to the garden beds is provided. Maintained by the Preservation Society of Newport County, it is open June 1–September 30, daily (weather permitting) 10:00–5:00, and on weekends and holidays in October. Admission.

# Providence
## Betsy Williams Cottage (c. 1785)

Roger Williams Park
950 Elmwood Avenue
401-785-9450

This small, red, gambrel-roofed house was last owned by Betsy Williams, great-great-great-granddaughter of the founder of Rhode Island, Roger Williams. The 430-acre park (140 acres of which are lakes and ponds) where the house is located was developed by the city of Providence after an initial gift by Betsy Williams of her family's 100-acre farm in 1871. The cottage, recently renovated and reopened, contains colonial furniture and items of historical interest. It is maintained by the Department of Public Parks in Providence and is currently open mid-April–mid-June, Sunday 1:30–4:00. Free.

## Governor Stephen Hopkins House (1707/1785)

15 Hopkins Street
401-751-1758

"My hand trembles, but my heart does not," were the words spoken by Stephen Hopkins as he signed the Declaration of Independence. Hopkins, a member of the first and second Continental Congresses, 10 times governor of Rhode Island, chief justice of the Rhode Island Superior Court, and first chancellor of Brown University, was one of Providence's most distinguished citizens. He was a Quaker, and his modest house reflects his simple tastes. The two-and-a-half-story colonial, with a gabled roof and two chimneys, has most of its original interior woodwork, and it is furnished with period antiques. An eighteenth-century parterre garden is adjacent to the house. Owned by the state of Rhode Island, it is administered by the National Society of Colonial Dames in America in the State of Rhode Island. It is open April 1–December 15, Saturday and Wednesday 1:00–4:00. Free.

GOVERNOR STEPHEN HOPKINS HOUSE (1707/1785)

## Governor Henry Lippitt House (c. 1862–1865)

199 Hope Street
401-751-2110

This large, handsome, three-story Italianate mansion was home to two Rhode Island governors, Henry Lippitt and his son Charles Warren Lippitt (whose grandson, John H. Chafee, became a recent governor of the state). Considered the finest mid-nineteenth-century house in Providence, it represents traditional Providence forms, with its brick exterior, low roof with overhanging eaves, and a dramatic semicircle front entrance porch with slim Ionic columns topped with a balustraded balcony. The interior, an example of Renaissance Revival with skillfully crafted paneling, inlaid woods, and stenciling, is exceptionally well maintained. Much of the original furniture belonging to the Lippitt family remains in the house. Now owned and maintained by the Heritage Trust of Rhode Island, it is open during the summer months at specific times and by appointment other months. Donation.

## John Brown House (1786)

52 Power Street
401-331-8575

John Brown was one of the most powerful and wealthy men in Providence in the second half of the eighteenth century, and his elegant three-story brick Georgian mansion reflected his wealth and position. He began the China trade in Providence and, as an ardent patriot, used his money and influence for the American cause during the Revolution. The house remains an outstanding showpiece today just as it did in the eighteenth century, when such distinguished guests as Washington and Adams visited here. The mansion has been well restored, with careful attention to historical accuracy. The interior is filled with elaborately carved woodwork and French wallpapers, which serve as a tasteful backdrop for an extensive collection of fine Rhode Island furniture and decorative arts. Many of the pieces are original to the house. It is considered one of the 10 finest historic houses in America. Owned by the Rhode Island Historical Society (headquarters), it is open Tuesday–Saturday 11:00–4:00, and Sunday 1:00–4:00, closed Mondays and holidays. From January to February, it may be viewed by appointment only. Admission.

# Saunderstown
## Gilbert Stuart Birthplace (1751)

815 Gilbert Stuart Road
401-294-3001

This small, red, two-and-one-half-story, gambrel-roofed homestead on the banks of the Mettatuxet River was the humble birthplace of America's premier portraitist of the eighteenth century, Gilbert Stuart. In his lifetime he painted over a thousand faces, immortalizing Presidents Madison, Jefferson, Monroe, and Adams, but he is best known for his famous portrait of George Washington. The house, built by Stuart's father, is an authentically restored and furnished eighteenth-century working man's home and the site of the first snuff mill in America. Throughout the house are more than two dozen reproductions of Stuart's work—the originals now hang in galleries all over the world. A restored water wheel in the basement of the house is on display, as well as the original fine-grained granite stones first used in the manufacture of snuff and later to grind corn for the famous Rhode Island Jonny Cakes. Maintained by the Gilbert Stuart Memorial, Inc. Association, it is open mid-

CASEY FARM (C. 1750)   March–mid-November, daily except Friday, 11:00–5:00. Admission.

## Casey Farm (c. 1750)

Boston Neck Road (Route 1A)
617-227-3956

This mid-eighteenth-century homestead in a very picturesque setting still functions as a working farm with an assortment of animals and outbuildings. Surrounded by fields, barns, and high stone walls, the main house overlooks Narragansett Bay and Conanicut Island. It was the home of General Thomas Lincoln Casey, supervising engineer for the completion of the Washington Monument and the construction of several buildings in the nation's capital, including the Library of Congress. The two-story, clapboard "mansion house" with a gable-on-hip roof was built and continuously occupied by the Casey family until it was acquired by SPNEA. The house contains family paintings, prints, china, furniture, and political and military documents from the eighteenth through the twentieth centuries. It is open June 1–October 15, Tuesday, Thursday, and Sunday 1:00–5:00. Donations.

# Smithfield

## Smith Appleby House (c. 1696)

Stillwater Road, Pole 67
401-231-7363/231-5920

The original structure of this 12-room farmhouse was a one-room stone-ender with a loft above. It was built by Elisha Smith, grandson of John Smith, who was one of the original party of six men, headed by Roger Williams, which formed the first settlement in Rhode Island. Smith was given 40 acres of land by Roger Williams that increased to more than 600 acres during Elisha's lifetime. Now consisting of only seven acres and named for the two families who lived in the house from 1696 to 1958, the property is the headquarters of the Historical Society of Smithfield. Furnishings are early American and Victorian, and some of the original stenciling done in 1830 can still be seen. The house is open May 1–December 30 for many special events, and tours are given by appointment.

# Tiverton

## Chase-Cory House (c. 1730)

Main Road at Tiverton Four Corners
401-624-4013/624-8881

CHASE-CORY HOUSE (C. 1730)

This simple, gambrel-roofed, five-room structure with a central chimney was the ancestral home of the Chase family, early settlers in Tiverton. The original twelve-over-twelve windows with pegged frames were restored with old glass from a demolished building. The 1730s kitchen has a seven-foot-wide fireplace with two large parallel beams that extend on either side, and vertical oak paneling. The house was acquired and restored in 1816 by Andrew Cory, a whaling captain. The south parlor exhibits a fine Federal-style mantelpiece, and the house is furnished throughout with period antiques. The grounds include a nineteenth-century wash house, outhouse, and corn crib, which serve to illustrate colonial living. Owned by the Tiverton Historical Society, it is open from the end of May to September, Sunday 2:00–4:30 and by appointment. Free.

# Warren

## *James Maxwell House (c. 1743)*

59 Church Street
401-245-7652

The oldest house in the historic waterfront district of Warren is the restored two-and-one-half-story brick home of James Maxwell. Maxwell, a merchant and privateer, was captured by the British during the Revolution and held prisoner on a ship in New York harbor. Upon his safe return after the war he became one of the town's leading citizens. This house, in which he was born, is made of soft handmade bricks of variegated colors and bonded in the Flemish style. Maxwell had nine daughters, and, as a token of his affection for them, he gave each one a new house as a wedding present. Five of these "wedding present houses" remain standing today, but all are privately owned. The Maxwell house, still undergoing some interior restoration, is used for colonial demonstrations in cooking, candle-dipping, and eighteenth-century crafts. It is open June–September, on first Friday, 5:00–8:00 P.M. and by appointment. Donation.

# Warwick
## John Waterman Arnold House (c. 1800)

11 Roger Williams Avenue
Roger Williams Circle
401-467-7647

This simple, two-and-one-half-story, gabled-roof structure is set on a stone foundation and built on land that was purchased from the Indians in 1660. The house was built by Stephen Arnold, one of the first settlers in the area, and passed down from father to son for six generations. Typical of rural eighteenth-century Rhode Island residences, it has a basic central-chimney plan with five rooms on each floor, two rooms on either side of the chimney and three small rooms across the back. By the nineteenth century it had acquired a two-story ell and a Greek Revival entrance. Many of the early features still remain. It is operated by the Warwick Historical Society. Call for schedule. Donation.

# Westerly
## Babcock-Smith House (c. 1732)

124 Granite Street
401-596-4424/596-3330

Dr. Joshua Babcock, Westerly's first physician and postmaster, lived in his early two-story, wooden-frame, gambrel-roofed house with a central stone chimney. He was appointed to this post by his friend, Benjamin Franklin, who was a frequent visitor to the house. In 1848 the house was purchased by Orlando Smith, who discovered granite on the property. This resulted in the largest granite quarry in the United States being founded here, making Westerly one of the most important granite centers in the world by the end of the nineteenth century. The house is nicely furnished with a wide variety of antiques, mostly from the Smith family. Owned and maintained by the Orlando R. Smith Trust under the auspices of the Westerly Historical Society, it is open May–October, Sunday 2:00–5:00, and during July and August, Sunday and Wednesday 2:00–5:00. Admission.

# Additional Houses
*(Area code 401)*

**BRISTOL**
>Coggeshell Farm, Colt State Park, 253-9062
>
>Linden Place, 500 Hope Street, 253-0390

**JOHNSTON**
>Dame Farm, 29 Brown Avenue, 277-2632

**KINGSTON**
>Watson House, University of Rhode Island, 789-3309

**NEWPORT**
>Griswold House, 76 Bellevue Avenue, 847-0179
>
>Edward King House, Spring Street, 846-7426
>
>Ochre Court, Bellevue Avenue, 847-6650

**PROVIDENCE**
>Aldrich House, 110 Benevolent Street, 331-8575
>
>Jeremiah Dexter House, 957 North Street, 274-8005
>
>Pendleton House (Rhode Island School of Design), 224 Benefit Street, 331-3511
>
>Woods-Gerry House, (Rhode Island School of Design), 62 Prospect Street, 331-3511

# MASSACHUSETTS

## Acton

*The Faulkner House (1707)*

5 High Street
508-263-7503

For 202 years (1738–1940) this two-and-a-half-story, white frame farmhouse, with a large central pilastered chimney and overhanging gables, was the homestead of six generations of the Faulkner family. On the nineteenth of April, 1775, Colonel Francis Faulkner (1728–1805), one of Acton's most distinguished citizens, mustered Acton's provincial militia from the front yard here and marched his troops down to the Concord fight. The house represents many alterations and styles from its original construction. Many early decorative details of the house remain, and it is furnished with period pieces. The house is owned by the Iron Work Farm in Acton, Inc., and is open from Patriots' Day to October, the first Sunday of each month, 2:00–5:00 and by appointment. Admission.

## *The Hosmer House (1760)*

300 Main Street
508-264-0690

A restored saltbox farmhouse, the Hosmer House is actually two houses in one. The original eastern section was built for Jonathan Hosmer and his bride, Submit, in 1760. The addition to the west was built for their son Simon and his bride, Sarah, in 1797. The Hosmers were a prominent Acton family; Jonathan was a bricklayer and deacon, and Simon, also a deacon, started a music school in Acton. An unusual feature of the house is the plaster painted to resemble brick on the exterior end walls. One of the two original parlors of the house is restored and furnished to its early 1800s fashion, while the other, The Wedding Room, is furnished in the 1860 fashion. Owned and maintained by the Acton Historical Society, Inc., the house is open May–November, on the last Sunday of the month 2:00–4:00, and by appointment. Donation.

# Amesbury

## John Greenleaf Whittier Home (c. 1830)

86 Friend Street
508-388-1337

When Whittier moved to this white clapboard, gable-roofed house in 1836 it was a simple four-room cottage. The expansions were financed by his public speaking tours on behalf of the abolitionist movement and his prolific writings. The Garden Room, on the second floor (so called because it overlooked the garden), where the poet and author composed his works and entertained his literary friends, remains the same as when he left it. Here he penned some of his most famous works, including "Snow Bound," "The Barefoot Boy," and over 100 hymns. The house contains original furnishings, portraits, engravings, manuscripts, and a large portion of Whittier's library. Operated by the Whittier Home Association, it is open May–October, Tuesday–Saturday 10:00–4:00, and by appointment. Admission.

# Amherst

## The Dickinson Homestead (c. 1813)

280 Main Street
413-542-8161

This large, square brick house with a cupola atop the roof was built by Samuel Fowler Dickinson, one of the chief founders of Amherst College and grandfather of one of America's foremost poets, Emily Dickinson. Emily was born here in 1830 and spent most of her life in this house. The house is now an Amherst College faculty residence, but the Emily Dickinson Room, restored in exacting detail by the curators, contains her original furnishings and memorabilia. Arrangements must be made in advance for tours that are given at 1:30, 2:15, 3:00, and 3:45. In March and April, tours are on Wednesday and Saturday; May–October, Wednesday through Saturday; and November–December 15, Wednesday and Saturday. Donation.

## Strong House (1744)

67 Amity Street
413-256-0678

Nehemiah Strong, a Northampton farmer, moved to Amherst in 1740 and built one of the first homes in town. It was originally constructed as a saltbox around a huge central chimney with two-over-two-rooms. Strong's son, Simeon, a Tory lawyer, enlarged the house and added decorative interior woodwork, and succeeding owners made additional period changes, but the basic eighteenth-century Connecticut architecture is still quite visible. With the exception of an eighteenth-century bedroom, almost all of the furniture and artifacts on display date from the nineteenth century, giving the interior a strong Victorian flavor. An ornamental eighteenth-century garden is to the east of the house. Owned and maintained by the Amherst Historical Society, the house is open June–October, Wednesday and Sunday 2:00–4:00. Admission.

STRONG HOUSE (1744)

# Andover

## *Amos Blanchard House (1819)*

97 Main Street
508-475-2236

This handsome three-story Federal house is a typical New England mansion of the early 1800s. Built by Amos Blanchard, a middle-class Andover merchant and deacon, it contains period rooms filled with early American and imported furnishings and household artifacts. The mantels and stair rails are finely carved, and Blanchard kept careful records showing the exact cost for nails, lumber, and everything that went into the house. (The total cost of the mansion was $4100.) The barn contains an extensive collection of nineteenth-century farm and woodworking tools. The house is owned by the Andover Historical Society and is open year-round, Monday–Friday 1:00–3:00 and by appointment. (Research library and office 9:00–5:00). Admission.

# Arlington

## *Jason Russell Farmhouse (1740)*

JASON RUSSELL FARMHOUSE (1740)

7 Jason Street
617-648-4300

This wooden two-story dwelling, with pitched roof and central chimney, was built by Jason Russell, a farmer and descendant of one of the founders of Arlington. The house began, as so many New England farmhouses did, with two rooms, one above the other, with the chimney and stairs at the north end. As his family grew in size, Jason doubled the house, and later, descendants added an ell and lean-to. Many early features of the house remain, including the unplastered ceiling in the kitchen, which is whitewashed and has black sponge painting. The house is furnished with eighteenth-century furniture and artifacts, some original to the house. The house is particularly famous as the site of the bloodiest battle on the first day of the American Revolution, April 19, 1775, and several bullet holes can still be seen in the walls. Smith Museum, adjacent to the farmhouse, has exhibits detailing local history from before the revolutionary war until World War II. Both are owned by the Arlington Historical Society and open to the public April–October, Tuesday–Saturday 2:00–5:00 and by appointment. Admission.

# Ashley Falls
## *Colonel John Ashley House (1735)*

Weatogue Road
413-298-3239

Built by a prominent businessman and leading citizen, this two-and-one-half-story, center-chimney, oak-frame house is the oldest dwelling in Berkshire County. It was considered the finest house in Sheffield, with craftsmen coming from near and far to fashion the gracefully curved staircase, beautiful paneling, sunburst cupboard, and broad fireplaces. In the colonel's paneled study the Sheffield Declaration of Independence, a response to British tyranny by an 11-man committee led by John Ashley, was written in 1773. Also here, Mrs. Ashley's black servant, Mumbet, overhearing these liberal ideas for the first time, brought suit and won her freedom, being the first slave to do so. The house is furnished in eighteenth- and early nineteenth-century period pieces and household items, including many from the Ashley family. It is owned by the Trustees of Reservations and is open Memorial Day–Columbus Day; guided tours are given Wednesday–Sunday 1:00–5:00. Admission.

# Bedford

*The Job Lane House (c. 1729)*

295 North Road
617-275-8503

The Job Lane House, the oldest structure in Bedford, was built on land originally belonging to Governor John Winthrop, the first governor of Massachusetts. Lane originally built a small half-house for himself and his family, adding to it as his family grew. The other "half" of the house was added after 1800 with an ell and lean-to, producing the old saltbox that is seen today. Restored by the town of Bedford as a living museum of rural farm life in the colonial period, it features murals by the inventor-artist Rufus Porter. Open house is held the second Sunday of the month from May–October 2:00–4:00. Colonial gardens. Free.

# Belchertown

*The Stone House Museum (1827)*

THE STONE HOUSE MUSEUM (1827)

20 Maple Street
413-323-7502

Jonathan Dwight, a prosperous businessman, built this lovely fieldstone house for his daughter, Julia Diantha, as a wedding present in 1827. The Federal-style structure, with a Greek portico, is constructed entirely of stone, a most unusual material for a Connecticut valley home. The interior is well restored and filled with nineteenth-century antiques. Besides a large and varied collection of Staffordshire china, glass, and pottery, the house contains one of the largest collections of Rogers Group sculptures in New England. Owned and operated by the Belchertown Historical Society, the house and grounds are open May–October, Wednesday and Saturday 2:00–5:00 and by appointment. Admission.

# Beverly

The following three house museums are owned and maintained by the Beverly Historical Society, incorporated in 1891, and represent the development of architecture, art, and decorative arts during several periods of American history. The Balch and Cabot houses are open June 1–Labor Day, Wednesday–Saturday 10:00–4:00 and Sunday 1:00–4:00. The Hale House is open on weekends only (same hours). Guided tours are given at all three sites. There is an admission fee with a special three-house ticket available. For further information call 508-922-1186.

## *Balch House (1636)*

448 Cabot Street

This is one of the two oldest wood-frame houses in America and contains many interesting original structural features. The house was built for John Balch, one of the earliest settlers in this region, and one of the first "Old Planters" from England. The house was given to the Beverly Historical Society by the remaining descendants of John Balch, and every other year the many descendants, now numbering in the hundreds, gather here for a family reunion. It was also the home of the first male child born in the Massachusetts Bay Colony. The oldest section of the house, decidedly English in flavor, has a steep roof with a two-gabled corner. It is carefully furnished in the simple, early colonial style with authentic pieces, and in the old kitchen spinning and weaving equipment used for demonstration purposes is on display.

BALCH HOUSE (1636)

## Cabot House (1781–1782)

117 Cabot Street

This three-story brick home is considered one of the finest mansions of the revolutionary era. It was built for John Cabot, a wealthy merchant, owner of numerous revolutionary war privateers and cofounder of America's first cotton mill. Now headquarters for the Beverly Historical Society, the house was once home to the tenth oldest bank in America. It has now been restored to period rooms with some original furnishings and several Gilbirt Stuart portraits of family members. It also contains an extensive library on local history and genealogy.

## Hale House (1694)

39 Hale Street

This house had been home to nine generations of Hale descendants. Its original owner, Reverend John Hale, was the first minister of Beverly and had been active in the witchcraft trials. When a charge of witchcraft was brought against his own wife, who was above reproach, the accusation served to break the spell, and the witchcraft hysteria died away. In the mid-eighteenth century the house was enlarged by Hale's grandson, Dr. Robert Hale. It is furnished to reflect the many generations who lived here and includes artifacts from the witchcraft trials. Several additions and alterations to the house over a period of years have made this a valuable study house.

# Boston

## Fenway Court (1903)

Isabella Stewart Gardner Museum
280 The Fenway
617-566-1401
617-734-1359 (concert information)

This magnificent Venetian palazzo, filled with priceless treasures, was built for "Mrs. Jack," one of Boston's most interesting and colorful women of the mid-nineteenth century. She left it as a museum to be kept exactly the way she had decorated it with her extensive European and American art collection. The exterior of the four-story building (the top floor for living quarters, the lower floors for the museum) is of a somber gray marble, but the interior opens up to a large glass-enclosed courtyard, filled with blooming flowers throughout the year. Many of the architectural features—doors, archways, pillars, and railings, as well as large pieces of sculpture—were imported from European castles and churches. The walls are adorned with a rich collection of paintings by Raphael, Rembrandt, Manet, Degas, Whistler, and her favorite artist, John Singer Sargent. The museum is open Tuesday–Sunday 12:00–5:00 in July and August, Tuesday 12:00–6:30 and Wednesday–Sunday 12:00–5:00 the rest of the year. Concerts are performed in the music room on Tuesday at 6:00, Thursday at 12:15, and Sunday at 3:00, September–June. Donations.

## Gibson House (1859)

137 Beacon Street
617-267-6338

One of the first houses to be built in Back Bay, this Victorian brownstone and red brick town house was designed by noted Boston architect Edward Clark Cabot. It was built for Catherine Hammond Gibson following the death of her husband, a wealthy sea merchant, who had died at sea. When her only son, Charles, died in 1954, he left the house intact "to preserve his home as both a monument to the age and to his family." It offers a unique glimpse into the world of opulence and tastes of the quintessential upper middle class Victorian Boston family. It is elegantly decorated with silks, tapestry, frescoes, rich wallpapers, imported carpets, and elaborately ornamented and overstuffed furniture. Owned and operated by the Gibson Society and headquarters for the Victorian Society in America, it is open May 1–October 31, Wednesday–Sunday; November 1–April 30, Saturday and Sunday. Tours are promptly at 2:00, 3:00, and 4:00, and visitors must be on time. Admission.

## Harrison Gray Otis House (1796)

141 Cambridge Street
617-227-3956

This handsome, three-story, Federal-style house, the first of three houses in Boston designed by the noted architect Charles Bulfinch, is the headquarters of the SPNEA. Founded in 1910 and the largest regional preservation organization in the country, SPNEA is devoted to preserving New England domestic buildings and artifacts. It owns 43 properties in five states, 34 of which are open to the public. The Otis House, built for a prominent lawyer, member of Congress, and third mayor of Boston, architecturally reflects the proportions and delicate detail that Bulfinch introduced to Boston during the period from 1796 to 1820. It is beautifully restored and furnished, and some pieces are original to the house. It also contains an extensive visual archives (open by appointment) of historic photographs and other material relating to New England domestic life. Open year-round, Tuesday–Friday 12:00–5:00, and Saturday 10:00–5:00. Tours on the hour; last tour at 4:00. Admission.

## Nichols House Museum (c. 1803–1804)

55 Mt. Vernon Street
617-227-6993

Almost at the top of Mt. Vernon Street, on Boston's famous Beacon Hill, stands this proud sentinel of nineteenth-century Boston. A four-story, Federal brick house, designed by Charles Bulfinch, it was home to the Nichols family. The eldest daughter of Dr. and Mrs. Arthur Nichols, Rose Standish Nichols, willed the house to be used as a museum. Rose was an extremely talented woman, being a landscape architect, world traveler, author of books on gardening, and founder of intellectual clubs for women. Her home was a salon where many important international visitors gathered for discussions. It is furnished just as she left it, with many interesting period pieces and artifacts, and particularly, her own fine examples of needlework. Guided tours are given throughout the year, June–September, Tuesday–Saturday 1:00–5:00. (Check for winter schedule.) Admission.

PAUL REVERE HOUSE (C. 1680)

## Paul Revere House (c. 1680)

19 North Square
617-523-2338

This is the oldest wooden building in Boston proper and an official Freedom Trail site. It was purchased by Paul Revere in 1770, and he lived here with his large family (eight children by his first wife and another eight by his second wife) until 1780. It was his home at the time of his famous midnight ride through the countryside on horseback to warn the patriots that the British troops were coming. Originally a two-story house, it has undergone many changes over the years, and its steep gabled roof, clapboards, and casement windows with diamond panes are largely a reproduction of the original. It is considered a good example of the domestic architecture of its time, and is furnished to reflect the style of the colonial period when the Reveres lived there. Exhibits of Revere memorabilia, including some of his silver pieces, are on display. It is owned and maintained by the Paul Revere Memorial Association and is open year-round, April 15–October 31, 9:30–5:15 daily; November 1–April 14, Tuesday–Sunday 9:30–4:15. Admission.

## Pierce-Hickborn House (c. 1711)

29 North Square
617-523-1776

Because there were a great many destructive fires in the city of Boston in the early days, the General Court of Massachusetts Bay Colony enacted a law in 1683 that all buildings and houses should henceforth be made of stone or brick. Moses Pierce, a glazier, built this English Renaissance-style brick house in compliance with the law, and it remains the earliest brick structure in Boston. It was sold to Nathaniel Hickborn, a shipbuilder and cousin of Paul Revere (who lived next door), in 1781. A typical colonial period town dwelling, with six rooms, fashioned into a narrow, three-story structure, it is furnished with seventeenth- and eighteenth-century antiques. Along with the Revere House next door, it is now owned and maintained by the Paul Revere Memorial Association. Inquire at Revere House for days and hours of tours, which emphasize the architectural features of the house. (Closed holidays.) Admission.

# Braintree

## The General Sylvanus Thayer Birthplace (1720)

786 Washington Street
617-848-1640

Known as the Father of West Point, Sylvanus Thayer was born in 1785, in this house which had been built by his great-great-grandfather. The original house consisted of only four rooms, and numerous alterations over the years covered up many interesting old features. Today, after an excellent job of restoration, the house looks very much as it did in 1785. The furnishings have been carefully selected to represent those used by a well-to-do New England farmer and landlord of the period. The large eighteenth-century barn contains sleighs, farm tools, and other historical items. Owned and operated by the Braintree Historical Society, the house is open April 19–October 12, Tuesday, Thursday, Friday, and Sunday 1:30–4:00, and Saturday 10:30–4:00; October 13–April 18, Tuesday and Saturday 1:30–4:00. Admission.

# Brockton

## The Homestead (c. 1808)

216 North Pearl Street
508-583-1039

The Homestead, facing the old Boston-Taunton Turnpike (now Pearl Street) was built around 1808 for Jeremiah Beals, Jr. It was attached to an eighteenth-century (c. 1768) house owned by Jeremiah Beals, Sr., and remained in the family until 1867. Later, the house served as the "Solid Rock Inn," where stagecoaches stopped while traveling the turnpike. The Federal-style house with hipped roof has two floors and is two rooms deep. The interior is furnished with a mixture of authentic pieces and some reproductions. The second floor, along with furnished bedchambers, has a room devoted to Rocky Marciano (a local celebrity) and the Thomas A. Edison Electric Light Bulb Documentary. The attached Shoe Museum Wing (1981) traces the story of shoemaking, an important Brockton industry. Owned and operated by the Brockton Historical Society, the house is open year-round on Sunday 2:00–4:00 and by appointment. Donation.

# Brookline

*John F. Kennedy Birthplace (1909)*

83 Beals Street
617-566-7937

This simple, green clapboard, three-story frame house, with a wide front porch, looks like a fairly ordinary suburban Boston house of the early 1900s. An American flag flying over a marker in the small enclosed front yard, however, distinguishes it as the birthplace of the thirty-fifth president of the United States. An audiotape tour of the home, presented by the president's mother, Rose Kennedy, recalls JFK's early childhood and describes life with the Kennedy family in the early part of this century. Each of the seven rooms is filled with original furnishings and personal memorabilia. The house had several owners

JOHN F. KENNEDY BIRTHPLACE
(1909)

after the Kennedys sold it in 1921, but in 1961 the family purchased it, and Rose Kennedy supervised the restoration and refurnishing of the house to its appearance in 1917 (the year of JFK's birth). It was donated to the National Park Service in 1969 and is open year-round, daily 10:00–4:30, with tours every 30 minutes on the hour and half-hour. Admission.

## The Longyear Museum (1890)

120 Sever Street
617-277-8943

This house is billed as "The house that rode on a train." It took 190 railroad cars to move the carefully marked pieces of what was in 1903 a 60-room mansion from Marquette, Michigan, to the top of Fisher Hill in Brookline, Massachusetts. This beautiful stone and brick mansion was moved over 1300 miles from its original site by its owner, John Munro Longyear, a self-made millionaire, geologist, and railroad entrepreneur. When it arrived, it took more than three years to reassemble, and Longyear made some changes, adding a wing and increasing the size of the mansion to 100 rooms. Mrs. Longyear devoted herself to many humanitarian projects, but particularly to collecting, establishing, and maintaining the effects of Mary Baker Eddy and the Christian Science movement. The estate, with eight acres of formal and informal gardens, is owned and immaculately maintained by the Longyear Historical Society and Museum. It is filled with original furnishings and historical exhibits pertaining to the life of Mary Baker Eddy and is open year-round (except February), Tuesday–Saturday 10:00–4:15, and Sunday 1:00–4:15. Admission.

# Cambridge
## Hooper-Lee-Nichols House (c. 1685–1690)

159 Brattle Street
617-547-4252

This house, one of the oldest houses in Cambridge, shows elements that date from the 1600s. Built for physician Richard Hooper, the original house was a small medieval farmhouse with a steeply pitched roof and massive chimney. In 1716, Hooper's son, also a physician, had another building moved to the site and butted against the existing west half. He rebuilt

HOOPER-LEE-NICHOLS HOUSE
(C. 1685–1690)

the chimney and added a one-and-a-half-story lean-to with a fireplace. Joseph Lee, a wealthy merchant, purchased the house in 1758 and made additional changes, as did its next owner, George Nichols. Some of the rooms are furnished with period pieces, while some are mainly illustrative of the various architectural details of the several different building periods of the house. It is owned and maintained by the Cambridge Historical Society and is open year-round, Tuesday and Thursday 2:00–5:00 (Monday–Friday for tour groups) and Sunday 2:00–5:00 June–September. Admission.

## Longfellow National Historic Site (1759)

105 Brattle Street
617-876-4491

This large, yellow, Georgian colonial-style house was lived in for 45 years (1837–1882) by one of America's foremost poets, Henry Wadsworth Longfellow. The house was built in 1759 for Major John Vassall, a wealthy Tory who fled Cambridge on the eve of the Revolution. It was then used by George Washington as his headquarters during the siege of Boston. He and his wife Martha celebrated their seventeenth wedding anniversary here in January 1776. The present furnishings and decorations are those of Longfellow and his family, and his study, where he wrote such immortal poems as "The Wreck of the Hesperus," "The Village Blacksmith," "The Song of Hiawatha," and "The Children's Hour," is filled with mementos of his famous contemporaries and friends, who often visited here. The house is owned and maintained by the National Park Service, U.S. Department of the Interior, and park rangers take visitors on half-hour guided tours of the house throughout the year (except major holidays) 10:00–4:30 (last tour at 4:00). Visitors can tour the gardens on their own. Admission.

# Centerville
*Mary Lincoln House (c. 1840)*

513 Main Street
617-775-0331

Now called the Centerville Historical Society Museum, this typical rambling Cape Cod–style house was built for Clark Lincoln, a local tinsmith who willed it to his daughter, Mary Ellen. Two modern additions were added by the historical society to house their extensive exhibition galleries and a historical research library. Along with rooms furnished in eighteenth- and nineteenth-century antiques, the society has a 300-piece collection of quilts and costumes dating from 1650 to 1950. This active society sponsors many special exhibitions, lectures, school programs, and publications throughout the year. The museum is open mid-June–mid-September for guided tours Wednesday–Sunday 1:30-4:30 (last tour at 3:30). Admission.

# Chatham
*Atwood House (1752)*

Stage Harbor Road
508-945-2493

This is one of Cape Cod's oldest homes and the first to feature a gambrel roof, a compromise between the need for second-story space and a steep roof's protection against the weather, which became a popular roof style on the Cape. This lovely, old weathered-shingle sea captain's house is furnished with Captain Joseph C. Atwood's period antiques. The interior has

ATWOOD HOUSE (1752)   fine paneling and much of the original hardware. One wing of the house is dedicated to the memorabilia of Joseph C. Lincoln, who was a summer resident of Chatham and known for his popular books (now collector's items) on Cape Cod. The barn in back contains the nationally known murals painted by Alice Stallknecht-Wight. Owned and operated by the Chatham Historical Society, the house is open mid-June–September 30, Monday, Wednesday, and Friday 2:00–5:00. Admission.

# Chelmsford

## Barrett-Byam Homestead (c. 1663)

40 Byam Road
508-256-7180/256-5554

The Barrett-Byam Homestead was built sometime prior to 1663 by James Parker, one of the founders of Chelmsford. Originally a saltbox, the house was constructed around a central chimney opening into five fireplaces and two dutch ovens. The house was enlarged in the late 1800s and is a good example of a farmhouse that expanded periodically to meet the growing needs of its occupants. Its seven rooms now house the Chelmsford Historical Society's extensive collections. It is used as a teaching resource for the local school system and offers a valuable source of genealogical information for researchers. It is open June–September on the second and fourth Sunday 2:00–4:00. Admission.

## Garrison House (1690)

Garrison Road
508-256-2311

One of 19 original garrisons in Chelmsford that protected its people against the Indians, this lovely old house, the only one surviving, remains practically unspoiled. Among its prominent features are the great central chimney built entirely of fieldstone, set on a 12-foot-square base; an original fieldstone fireplace; a chamfered summer beam almost 17 inches wide; gunstock posts; 33-inch-wide paneling; and hand-split laths. The "Old Chelmsford" Garrison House Association was formed in 1959, when it received the house as a gift, and has since repaired and restored it, removing "much that impaired its authenticity." It is used mainly for educational pur poses and demonstrating old crafts. It is open on special occasions and from June–September on Sundays 2:00–4:00. Donation.

# Chelsea
## The Governor Bellingham-Cary House (1659)

34 Parker Street
617-884-4407 (Town Clerk)

This rare old landmark is the only house now in existence that was built by one of the founders of the Massachusetts Bay Colony. It was visited by many of the most prominent and distinguished leaders of colonial times, including General Washington, Lafayette, Stark, and others. Governor Bellingham was deputy governor of Massachusetts for 13 years, and governor for 10 years (1635–1658). Succeeding owners added greatly to the original building, particularly when it became the property of Samuel Cary, a prosperous plantation owner. It is now a fine example of an eighteenth-century house with a hipped roof, gables, and a central hall dividing two pairs of rooms, and some of its original features are still intact. It has been owned by the Governor Bellingham-Cary House Association since 1908 and is open year-round, on Thursdays 2:00–4:00 and by appointment. Admission.

# Cohasset
## Wilson-Historic House (1810)

Elm Street
No telephone

This modest frame house, with hipped roof and chimneys at each end, is a typical and charming old New England village home. It has been preserved in its original condition and furnished with a rare collection of antique furniture and artifacts to recreate an early American dwelling. It was built in 1810 for Captain John Wilson and remained in the family ownership for over a century. It is now owned and maintained by the Cohasset Historical Society, which also operates the Maritime Museum adjacent to the house. Both the house and museum are open mid-June–September, Tuesday–Sunday 1:30–4:00. Admission. Write Cohasset Historical Society, 14 Summer Street, Cohasset, MA 02025.

# Concord
## Ralph Waldo Emerson House (1835)

Lexington Road
508-369-2236

This large, Federal-style clapboard house with hipped roof was home to one of America's leading poets, essayists, and spokesmen of transcendentalism. Ralph Waldo Emerson, a major figure in American literature, lived here from 1835 until his death in 1882. His personal belongings, mementos, and photographs of contemporaries fill his study and library, and the house contains the original furnishings throughout. It is owned by the Ralph Waldo Emerson Memorial Association, and 30-minute tours are given mid-April–mid October, Thursday–Saturday 10:00–4:30, and Sunday 2:00–4:30. Admission.

## The Old Manse (1769–1770)

Monument Street
508-369-3909

The Old Manse was built by the Reverend William Emerson, pastor of the Church of Concord and, later,

chaplain of the American forces. On April 19, 1775, the Reverend Emerson witnessed, from the fields behind his house, the battle at the North Bridge, giving encouragement to the minutemen and militia and helping those who fled to the manse for safety. His famous grandson, Ralph Waldo Emerson, lived here for a while and during that time wrote his first book of essays, *Nature*. In 1842 Nathaniel Hawthorne brought his bride, Sophia, here, where they spent three "blissful years." You can still see a whimsical note, etched by Sophia with her diamond ring, on the window in her husband's study. This red clapboard house with gambrel roof, twin chimneys, and a pedimented doorway, has changed little since it was built. Now owned by the Trustees of Reservations, it was owned and lived in continuously by members of the Emerson-Ripley family since 1770. It is furnished with period furnishings, many original to the house. It is open mid-April–May 31, Saturday 10:00–4:30, Sunday and holidays 1:00–4:30; June–October, 10:00–4:30 (closed Tuesday and Wednesday). Admission.

THE OLD MANSE (1769–1770)

## Orchard House (1690–1720)

399 Lexington Road
508-369-4118

When Bronson Alcott, philosopher, writer, and educator, purchased 12 acres of land in Concord in 1857 there were two early seventeenth-century houses on the property. He joined them together, forming a large, oddly shaped clapboard house with several eaves and a large central dormer over the front door. The Alcotts named it The Orchard House (later dubbed "Apple Slump" by Louisa May) and lived here for 20 years. Bronson Alcott founded the Concord School of Philosophy on the hillside behind the house, which flourished as a summer school of adult education and is still today the site of many educational programs. But the house is probably best known as the setting for the book *Little Women* and for the woman who wrote it, Bronson's daughter, Louisa May. Many of the furnishings are original to the house, including the piano, children's toys, paintings, Louisa May's bedroom furniture, and some sketches on doors and walls by Amy Alcott. It is owned and maintained by the Louisa M. Alcott Memorial Association and is open early April–mid-September, Monday–Saturday 10:00–4:30, Sunday and holidays through late October, weekends in November and March, and by appointment. Admission.

## The Wayside (c. 1717)

455 Lexington Road
508-369-6975

Now known as "the house of four authors," The Wayside was originally the small, primitive seventeenth-century home of Nathaniel Ball. Later, Samuel Whitney, muster master for the Concord minutemen, purchased it and made it into a substantial square colonial house. When the first of the "authors," the Alcotts, moved here in 1842, it was remodeled with gables and bay windows. The Hawthornes owned the house next, from 1852 to 1870, adding a tower for Nathaniel's study and naming it The Wayside. The Lothrops owned it from 1883 to 1965, adding the broad piazza. Harriet Lothrop, under the pen name Margaret Sidney, wrote a series of books about the Five Little Peppers and was a leader in the historic preservation movement. Her husband, Daniel, head-

THE WAYSIDE (C. 1717)

ed one of the first publishing companies devoted to children's literature. Their daughter, Margaret Lothrop, who wrote a book about The Wayside, left the house to the National Park Services with all the original furnishings, including pieces belonging to both the Alcotts and the Hawthornes. It is open mid-April–October 9:30–5:30 (closed Wednesday and Thursday), with guided tours on the hour (last tour at 5:00). Admission.

# Cummington
*William Cullen Bryant Homestead (1785)*

Bryant Road
413-298-3239

The Homestead was the boyhood home and later summer residence of one of America's foremost literary figures, William Cullen Bryant (1794–1878). Built by his maternal grandfather and set on a peaceful hillside with superb views of the Hampshire Hills beyond, this lovely, white clapboard house with a wraparound porch was where Bryant found inspiration for some of his finest verse. The house contains many of Bryant's personal effects and souvenirs of travels in Europe and the Near East, as well as furniture of several different periods and styles. The barn behind the house contains a collection of old farm tools. It is the property of the Trustees of Reservations and is open from the end of June to Labor Day, Friday, Saturday, Sunday, and holidays; guided tours 1:00–5:00. Admission.

# Danvers
## Glen Magna (c. 1814–1890)

Ingersoll Street
508-774-9165

Originally a farm with a dwelling house and outbuildings, this property was purchased in 1814 by Joseph Peabody, a wealthy Salem merchant, to keep his family safe from coastal bombardments by the British during The War of 1812. His descendants enlarged and improved the house and gardens, turning the old farm into an elegant country estate. During the 1890s the house was reconstructed in the colonial Revival style, and in the 1930s William Crowninshield Endicott, Jr., a grandson, upgraded the house and grounds into the magnificent showplace it is today. The lovely interior woodwork and paneling are set off by some of the original furnishings belonging to the Peabody and Endicott families, who occupied the house for 144 years. The grounds were laid out by the renowned landscape architect Frederick Law

GLEN MAGNA (C. 1814–1890)

Olmsted, and throughout the summer, gardens bloom in profusion and plants are sold in the greenhouse. The **Derby Summer House**, a Federal-style summer house built by architect Samuel McIntire in 1793, was moved to the estate grounds in 1901. The property is owned and maintained by the Danvers Historical Society and is open June–September, Tuesday and Thursday 10:00–4:00. Tea is served on Tuesdays 2:00–4:00, and the greenhouse is open Monday and Wednesday 8:00–1:00. Admission.

## Jeremiah Page House (1754)

11 Page Street
508-777-1666

This handsome gambrel-roofed house with dormer windows was home to three generations of the Page family. Jeremiah Page, a brickmaker, prospered in the clay fields of the town and built his house here in 1754. On the roof of this house Madam Page held her infamous tea party in response to her husband's edict that "no British-taxed tea be served under his roof." Page was a captain in the militia, and when the alarm came to Danvers on April 19, 1775, he left the house to lead his company to the Lexington battlefield. The last member of the Page family to live here was Ann Page. Active in the kindergarten movement of the late nineteenth century, she conducted a kindergarten in the house. It is furnished with period antiques and with mementos of the Page family and town history. Owned by the Danvers Historical Society, it is open June–Labor Day, Wednesday 2:00–4:00. Donation.

## Rebecca Nurse Homestead (1678)

149 Pine Street
508-771-1661

An old dirt road leads to this ancient saltbox house, giving the visitor a visible link to the famous and infamous events of Salem village during the witchcraft trials. The frame dwelling, situated on a small knoll surrounded by deserted fields, pasture, and woods, was home to Francis and Rebecca Nurse and their eight children in the winter of 1691, when their troubles began. Young girls in the neighborhood began to fall into horrid fits, and a village doctor concluded that they were being afflicted by witchcraft. Rebecca Nurse was unjustly accused of being a witch and was dragged from her home,

REBECCA NURSE HOMESTEAD
(1678)

adamantly protesting her innocence, and hanged. Nearby is her grave and a monument with an inscription written by the poet Whittier. The house is owned by the Rebecca Nurse Homestead Preservation Society and is open June–September, Wednesday and Sunday 1:00–5:00. Admission.

# Dedham
## Fairbanks House (c. 1636)

511 East Street
617-326-1170

Considered one of the oldest wood-frame buildings in America and one of the few that can claim to have been lived in by one family for eight generations, this ancient landmark has weathered many storms. It was built with oak timbers, tiles, bricks, and windows brought from England by the Fayerbankes (now Fairbanks) family to build their new home in America. The house grew from a simple, two-story, central-chimney, one-room-deep dwelling, to the rambling structure with steeply pitched roof that you see today. It is filled with antiques and furnishings reflecting over three centuries of American life. Every

summer, the descendants of the Fayerbanks, now numbering in the hundreds, hold a reunion on the property. It is owned and operated by the Fairbanks Family Association and is open May 1–October 31, 9:00–12:00 and 1:00–5:00 daily, Sunday 1:00–6:00. Admission.

FAIRBANKS HOUSE (C. 1636)

# Deerfield

413-774-5581

When the village of Deerfield was settled around 1669, it was the last outpost on New England's frontier. It was devastated twice by Indian attacks, the Bloody Brook Massacre of 1675, and the Deerfield Massacre of 1704. The settlers persevered, and the beautiful homes you see today, gracing the famous mile-long main street, give evidence of the wealth and gracious living that came to dominate this once lonely outpost. Historic Deerfield was founded in 1952 by Mr. and Mrs. Henry N. Flynt to carry on the tradition of historic preservation in this picturesque western Massachusetts village. It maintains 12 house museums, a research library, and an active education program, all devoted to the study of the history of Deerfield, the culture of the Connecticut valley, and the arts in early American life. The Center for Information and Visitor Orientation is located in The Hall Tavern, in the center of the village, where you can purchase a ticket for guided museum house tours and guided walking tours of The Street (weather permitting). House tours last about 30 minutes and are given year-round, daily 9:30–4:30 (except on major holidays). Admission.

## The Allen House (c. 1720)

This handsome saltbox with feather-edge paneling was the residence of Mr. and Mrs. Henry N. Flynt, the founders of Historic Deerfield. Their fine collection of Connecticut Valley furniture, neddlework, and other decorative arts remains in the house.

## Ashley House (c. 1730)

ASHLEY HOUSE (C. 1730)    This weathered, unpainted clapboard house with a

gambrel roof in front and a saltbox sweep behind was the home of Deerfield's eighteenth-century Tory minister and illustrates the lifestyle of a community leader. The house was later moved from its foundations and used as a tobacco barn for 75 years. During the early restoration of the village it was painstakingly restored to its original site and appearance.

## Dwight-Barnard House (c. 1775)

Moved here from Springfield, this eighteenth-century, gambrel-roofed house was completely rebuilt and restored on this site in 1954. Several of the rooms have the original fine paneling. A doctor's office on the first floor (both Dr. Thomas Williams and his son, William, who lived here for almost a century, were prominent doctors in Deerfield), an eighteenth-century kitchen, and bedchambers upstairs display furniture and accessories made in Boston and the Connecticut valley, that belonged to the Williams family.

## The Ebenezer Hinsdale Williams House (1816)

This large, two-story, white clapboard house has had many additions and remodelings through the years. It is presently a "restoration-in-progress," featuring the methods that historians use to restore early buildings. The styles and furnishings to be added will reflect the 1816–1838 period. Tour leaders discuss and show the technical and decision-making processes that create a historic house museum.

## The Frary House/Barnard Tavern (c. 1740/c. 1795)

One of the few remaining structures in Deerfield to survive the fire and massacre of 1704, this was the home of Samson Frary and his family, who were killed in that infamous Indian raid. It was bought by Major Seelah Barnard, who enlarged it and made it into a tavern, adding an elegant ballroom. In 1890 it was saved from demolition by Miss C. Alice Baker, a Frary descendant, and faithfully restored in the spirit of colonial times. Many notables, including Benedict Arnold, were guests here.

## The Sheldon-Hawks House (1743)

This large, timber-frame house with narrow windows, capped with pediments on the facade, and a fine old Connecticut Valley doorway is classic Deerfield architecture. It was the birthplace of George Sheldon, a

THE SHELDON-HAWKS HOUSE
(1743)

colorful local historian and founder of the historical society. It is filled with fine period antiques, including New England furniture, English ceramics, European brass, and excellent examples of needlework.

## The Stebbins House (1799/c. 1810)

This was the first brick house to be built in Deerfield, by Asa Stebbins, a wealthy farmer and businessman. It was considered one of the showplaces of the village. Inside the imposing structure are a free-flowing stairway (attributed to the architect Asher Benjamin), French wallpapers, freehand wall painting, decorative plasterwork, Chinese porcelain, and fine New England furniture of the Federal period.

## The Wells-Thorn House (1717/1751)

An early pioneer, Ebenezer Wells, built himself a simple, two-room, "split-level" house on this sloping lot. As he became more successful as a farmer, tavern keeper, and merchant, he was able to add, in 1751, the front section of the house, designed in Federal style. By 1801 the property passed to Hezekiah Wright Strong, who made some interior changes, particularly adding a law office. The house is furnished completely with Connecticut Valley furniture and needlework, English ceramics, and an unusual collection of rugs.

## The Wright House (1824)

This handsome brick house was originally built by Asa Stebbins for his son, Asa, Jr., and his bride, but eventually took the name of its second owner. The house is filled with some of the most outstanding antiques in Deerfield—the Cluett and Watson collections of Chippendale and Federal furniture (including an elaborate pianoforte once belonging to Queen Maria Louisa of Spain), and American paintings and Chinese export porcelain from the Historic Deerfield collections.

# Dennis

## Jericho House Museum (1801)

Trotting Park Road
508-394-0907

Although built by a sea captain, Theophilus Baker, in 1801, it got its name in 1955 from Cape Cod authoress Elizabeth Reynard, who wrote *The Narrow Land*. The "walls were a-tumblin down," when she began her restoration of the property, and so she named it "Jericho." It is a classic Cape Cod–style house, with clapboard siding, shingled roof, center chimney, and twelve-over-twelve windows. It is home to the Dennis Historical Society and is furnished with nineteenth century antiques, including some from the Fairbanks Collection. The enlarged barn behind the house is a museum containing the society's many and varied collections. It is open from July 1–Labor Day, Wednesday, Friday, and Saturday 2:00–5:00. Donation.

## Josiah Dennis Manse (1736)

77 Nobscusset Road
508-385-2232

Another typical Cape Cod–style house, this shingled saltbox was the home of the beloved minister of Dennis, the Reverend Josiah Dennis, for whom the town was named. Featured within are wide floorboards, wainscoting, five fireplaces, gunstock corner posts, and the original roof rafters. Exhibits include the reverend's own "portable pulpit," writing desk, large collection of old Cape Cod books and manuscripts used for research, and many fine period antiques. The oldest existing Dennis schoolhouse has been moved to the grounds. Owned and operated by the town of Dennis, it is open July and August, Tuesday and Thursday 2:00–4:00. Donation.

# Dorchester

617-436-8367

The Dorchester Historical Society, originally founded in 1843 as the Dorchester Historical and Antiquarian Society, owns and operates three early houses that are open for tours year-round on the second and fourth Saturday of each month and by appointment. Admission.

## Blake House (c. 1648)

Richardson Park (Edward Everett Square)

The relocation and restoration of this house in 1895 marked one of the very earliest preservation efforts in America. It is believed that the Blake House, built by James Blake, is one of the few remaining buildings in America that was built by a first generation immigrant. Though not an absolutely precise historic or architecturally accurate restoration, the house is a continuing source of interest to scholars and visitors and of great pride to the residents of Dorchester. The two-and-one-half-story, shingled cottage with steeply pitched roof and leaded glass diamond-patterned windows, has the original hand-hewn beams and is furnished with period antiques.

## Captain Lemuel Clapp House (c. 1710–1765)
## The William Clapp House (1806)

199 and 195 Boston Street

In 1945, the society acquired the William Clapp House, a two-story clapboard house, considered a fine example of a country neoclassical mansion. William Clapp made his livelihood in the tannery business and was followed into the business by his son, Lemuel. Lemuel built his handsome brick and clapboard house on the family land just next door to his parents' house. The Clapp estate, comprising the

larger brick and clapboard mansion of Lemuel Clapp, a carriage house, and two barns (one now demolished), was purchased by the society in 1953. This house now serves as headquarters for the society. Both houses are furnished with period antiques, and the William Clapp House features a particularly interesting kitchen.

THE WILLIAM CLAPP HOUSE (1806)

# Duxbury
## *Captain Gershon Bradford House (1808)*

931 Tremont Street (Route 3A)
617-934-6106

Only one family, four generations of Bradfords, lived in this large clapboard house over a period of 160 years. It is a spacious, comfortable captain's house, typical of a successful shipmaster, with much attention to fine detail in the woodwork. Original colors have been maintained throughout, particularly in the painstakingly reproduced wallpaper in the four museum rooms. The house contains many fine antiques, paintings, books, and memorabilia of the Bradford family. It is owned and maintained by the Duxbury Rural and Historical Society, Inc., and is open mid-

June–September, Wednesday 1:00–4:00 and by appointment. Admission.

## The John Alden House (1653)

105 Alden Street
No telephone

The only house still standing that was actually occupied by *Mayflower* Pilgrims, this simple, weathered-shingle dwelling, with a large center chimney, was home to John and Priscilla Alden during their later years. It was built by John Alden and his third son, Jonathan, and some of the interesting features are the powdered clam and oyster shell ceiling in the "great" room, the camber panels in the "best" room, and the gunstock beams found in the chambers. Characteristic of such an early house, the ceilings and doorways are very low, the stairs and steprisers are steep, shallow, or narrow, and the floors pitch. Both John and Priscilla died in this house, and it continued to be owned and lived in by the Alden family until the early 1900s. It is furnished with seventeenth-century furniture and artifacts and is now owned by the Alden Kindred of America, Inc. It opens the last Saturday in June and closes the day before Labor Day. Daily (except Monday) 10:00–5:00. Admission.

## King Caesar House (1808–1809)

King Caesar Road
617-934-6106

Ezra Weston II, like his father, was known as "King Caesar" for his remarkable ventures in shipbuilding and shipping during the early part of the nineteenth century. Lloyd's of London recognized his enterprises as the largest in America. The house is a fine example of Federal architecture, sturdy and four-square, built with careful attention to detail, characteristic of skilled ships carpenters. The front rooms, both downstairs and upstairs, remain practically unchanged, and especially notable are the rare French wallpapers in the two front parlors. The house is decorated and furnished in fine antiques and exhibits relics of maritime history. The house overlooks Duxbury Bay, and the massive stone wharf at which the Weston ships were once rigged and fitted can still be seen. It is owned and maintained by the Duxbury Rural and Historical Society and is open mid-June–Labor Day, daily except Saturday and Monday, 1:00–4:00. Admission.

# East Sandwich

## Nye Homestead (1685)

Old County Road
508-888-2368

This house was built by Benjamin Nye, one of the
first 50 men to settle in Sandwich and one of the first
settlers to build a gristmill in the country. The tradition of milling lasted for six generations in the Nye
family, until the mill was torn down in 1867.
Originally a small peaked-roof structure with a central
chimney, the house took on a saltbox shape with the
addition of more rooms and eventually became the
full colonial-style house we see today. The house, of
braced frame construction, retains many interesting
old features, such as early paneling and hand-stenciled walls, interior window shutters, and eighteenth-
century wallpaper reproduced from an early sample
found in the house. Owned and operated by the Nye
Family of America Association, Inc., it is authentically
furnished, mostly with Nye family heirlooms. It is
open June 15–October 15, weekdays 12:00–4:30
(closed Saturday, Sunday, and holidays). Admission.

## The Wing Fort House (1641)

Spring Hill Road
508-833-1540

This house was traditionally called the Fort House
because of its possible use as a refuge from Indian
attack. In 1646 it became the home of Stephen Wing,
one of the early settlers of Sandwich, and has
remained in the family ever since. Recently restored,
it is furnished with Wing family antiques showing the
different periods of its 300-year history. In the old
Fort Room can be seen, through a movable panel,
the original walls, and the long keeping room with its
huge fireplace displays many primitive cooking and
baking utensils. Upstairs are an early bedroom, a children's playroom, and a nineteenth-century Victorian
parlor. The house is owned and operated by the
Wing Family of America, Inc., and is open mid-
June–Sept 30, Monday–Friday 10:00–4:00 and by
appointment. Admission.

# Eastham

*Swift-Daley House (1741)*

Route 6 (next to Post Office)
508-255-4968

This small Cape-style house with a bowed roof is characteristic of houses built when Cape Cod carpenters were also shipbuilders. Nathanial Swift, one of the brothers who started the Swift meat packing company, lived in the house in the early 1860s. The second part of its name comes from the Daley family, who restored the house in the early 1940s and gave it to the Eastham Historical Society in 1974. The house is furnished with antiques ranging from colonial to Victorian, reflecting the many generations who lived there. It is open July and August, Wednesday and Friday 1:30–4:30, and by appointment. Admission.

# Edgartown

*Thomas Cooke House Museum (1765)*

Cooke Street
508-627-4441

This two-and-one-half-story, shingled house, with central doorway and chimney, was built for Squire Thomas Cooke, collector of customs and justice of the peace. The four corners of the house slant away from the chimney in the same way that the decks of a ship slant away from the mast. The 12 rooms of the house are furnished with authentic pieces gathered from other homes on Martha's Vineyard, including a rare scrimshaw collection. A lens tower, a carriage shed, the Gale Huntington Library of History, and the Frances Foster Museum are also on the grounds. This complex is owned and operated by the Dukes County Historical Society and is open mid-June–mid-September, Tuesday–Saturday 10:00–4:30 (admission), and from mid-September–mid-June, Wednesday–Friday 1:00–4:00 (no admission).

# Falmouth

*Conant House Museum (c. 1794)*

Falmouth Village Green
508-548-4857

This eighteenth-century, wood-frame house is now a

CONANT HOUSE MUSEUM (C. 1794)

museum filled with furnishings and objects relating to Falmouth's historic whaling and maritime past. On display is a large collection of china, silver, and glass. A military exhibit includes items from the revolutionary war to World War I. A shell collection and rare examples of "sailors' valentines," as well as some "mourning" samplers, are on display. One room is devoted to Katharine Lee Bates, author of "America the Beautiful" and one of Falmouth's most famous citizens. The house also includes a genealogical and historical library for research (open year-round). Owned and operated by the Falmouth Historical Society, it is open mid-June–mid-September, Monday–Friday 2:00–5:00. Admission.

## The Julia Wood House (c. 1790)

Falmouth Village Green
508-548-4857

This elegant, hipped-roof colonial, with a widow's walk, was constructed in 1790 as the home of Dr. Francis Wicks, one of Falmouth's early physicians, who served as a medical corpsman in the Revolution and was the impetus behind Cape Cod's first hospital. In 1923 it was bequeathed to The Falmouth Historical Society by Mrs. Julia Wood for their headquarters. Interesting exhibits include the original eighteenth-century scenic wallpaper, brought from Paris by a sea captain for his bride, period furniture, portraits, and toys. The adjacent Hallett Barn displays early tools and farm implements and houses the old town pump and the society's gift shop. The house is open mid-June–mid-September, Monday–Friday 2:00–5:00. Admission.

# Georgetown
## Captain Samuel Brocklebank Museum (c. 1660)

108 East Main Street

This classic center-entrance colonial, with a large chimney and lean-to, was built by Captain Samuel Brocklebank, a local surveyor. He was killed during King Philip's War when he led a contingent of men to Sudbury to fight the Indians. The house continued as a residence for the next 100 years, then became a tavern for the following 100 years, then a parsonage, and then a residence once again until 1971. There are a few intriguing mysteries surrounding the history of the house—the haunted meal chest, the slave hole, and an old tavern sign with a ghostly face appearing from beneath the painting on the bullet-pierced wood. The house contains many Georgetown artifacts and memorabilia. It has one of the largest fireplaces in Essex County and shows how a beehive oven was constructed. It is owned and maintained by the Georgetown Historical Society, Box 376, Georgetown, MA 01833, and is open from July–Columbus Day, Sunday 2:00–5:00. Donation.

# Gloucester
## Beauport (1907)

Eastern Point Boulevard
508-283-0800

Using the paneling from an eighteenth-century farmhouse, Henry Davis Sleeper, a prominent collector of antiques and a leading interior designer of the 1920s, built himself a three-room house. As his vast collection of antiques grew, he employed a local architect to come up with a workable plan to add on to his house. He continuously added rooms until, at the time of his death in 1934, the house contained over 40 rooms. Mr. Sleeper painstakingly assembled an impressive collection of American and European decorative arts. In every room light, color, shape, and texture are brilliantly combined to demonstrate his interpretation of America's history. A stream of famous artists, writers, actors, businessmen, and statesmen were entertained here over the years, including such names as Helen Hayes, F. Scott Fitzgerald, Eleanor Roosevelt, and President William Howard Taft. Beauport, the name Samuel de Champlain gave to Gloucester harbor when he charted it in 1604, was chosen by Sleeper as the name for his unique home. Owned by SPNEA, it is open mid-May–mid-October, Monday–Friday 10:00–4:00 (tours on the hour); mid-September–mid-October, Saturday and Sunday 1:00–4:00. Admission.

## Hammond Castle (1926–1929)

80 Hesperus Avenue
508-283-2080

This medieval-style castle overlooking the sea was designed by John Hays Hammond, Jr., an electronics genius and inventor, to reflect the style and beauty of a European castle. In addition to an interesting col-   HAMMOND CASTLE (1926–1929)

lection of Roman, medieval, and Renaissance objects, the building houses a magnificent 8600-pipe organ, which was also designed by Mr. Hammond. In the Great Hall, where the organ is located, is a nave of a cathedral, providing a backdrop for the collection of medieval religious objects, and an enormous fifteenth-century fireplace. This room is used throughout the year for changing exhibits and many types of concerts. An unusual courtyard is surrounded by . . . marbled columns, Romanesque and Gothic doorways, and fifteenth-century French house facades, creating the ambiance of a European village square. Changing exhibits occupy three floors of galleries in the tower and there is a rooftop cafe. Hammond Castle Museum is open May–October, daily 10:00–4:00, and November–April, Thursday–Saturday 10:00–4:00, Sunday 1:00–4:00. Gift shop. Admission.

## Sargent House Museum (late eighteenth century)

49 Middle Street
508-281-2432

This three-story, gray clapboard structure, originally built just one room deep and then added to in later years, was built for feminist author Judith Sargent by her father, Winthrop Sargent III. Its terraced lawn leads down to Main Street, which in colonial times, called Front Street, bordered Gloucester harbor. Today the house presents a view of life in Gloucester from 1760 to 1830 and contains works of art by prominent painters and sculptors, unique collections of silhouettes and miniatures, fine examples of eighteenth- and nineteenth-century needlework, and period furniture, china, silver, ceramics and, glass. The house is operated by the Sargent-Murray-Gilman-Hough House Association and is open June–September, Tuesday, Thursday, and Saturday 1:00–5:00 and by appointment. Admission.

# Grafton

## Willard House (1718)

Willard Street
508-839-3500

The Willard House and Clock Museum, Inc., is the birthplace of the famous clockmakers Benjamin, Simon, Ephraim, and Aaron Willard, born between 1743 and 1757. Joseph Willard, the first settler of Grafton, built a one-room house in 1718 that evolved into the saltbox farmhouse and workshop you see today. He was the first white settler, and his daughter was the first white child born in Hassanamesit, later named Grafton. His son Benjamin was the father of the four famous clockmakers. These men possessed great mechanical aptitude and skillfully crafted their fine shelf, wall, and tall case clocks, which attracted the attention of Presidents Jefferson and Madison during the early nineteenth century. One of the brothers was commissioned to create three clocks for the U.S. Capitol. The homestead is furnished with period pieces, and there are many Willard clocks on display. It is owned and maintained by the Willard House and Clock Museum, Inc., and is open year-round, Tuesday–Saturday 10:00–4:00 and Sunday 1:00–5:00. Admission.

# Hadley
*Porter Phelps Huntington House (1752)*

130 River Drive
413-584-4699

This large, Dutch colonial house (also called "Forty Acres") is neither a restoration nor a reproduction, but has been lovingly cared for by the same family for more than 10 generations. It was built by Moses Porter on a tract of land, known as "Forty Acres and its Skirts," outside the then stockaded town of Hadley. The house was enlarged and refined by Charles Phelps who married Moses Porter's only child, Elizabeth, in 1770. Since then there have been no structural changes. The rooms remain much as they were when lived in and contain many personal mementos of the families that have lived here. Concerts are held here on Wednesday evenings throughout the summer and picnickers are welcome. The house is owned by the Porter Phelps Huntington Foundation and is open mid-May–mid-October, Saturday–Wednesday 1:00–4:30 and by appointment. Admission.

# Harvard
*Fruitlands Museums*

Prospect Hill
508-456-3924

This collection of buildings includes the **Fruitlands Farmhouse**, **Shaker House**, **American Indian**

Museum, **Picture Gallery**, and several administrative buildings. It was founded by Miss Clara Endicott Sears, a prominent Bostonian novelist and poet. The Fruitlands Farmhouse is a historic, early eighteenth-century farmhouse, where Bronson Alcott established in 1843 a community under a new social and religious order known as the Con-Sociate Family. Thus, the building serves as a museum of the transcendental movement and contains memorabilia of the leaders—Alcott, Emerson, Thoreau, Margaret Fuller, Lane, and others. The Shaker House, built in the 1790s, was originally used as an office by the members of the Harvard Shaker Society, which flourished from 1791 to 1918. It now offers a setting for a wide range of Shaker handicrafts and products of community industries. A tea room (serving light lunches), research library, museum shop, nature trails, and picnic facilities are available. Fruitlands is open mid-May–mid-October, Tuesday–Sunday, and Monday and holidays 10:00–5:00. Admission.

# Haverhill
*The Buttonwoods (1814)*

240 Water Street
508-374-4626

This large, hipped-roof colonial house with high chimneys was named for the buttonwood trees planted on the grounds in 1739. It is headquarters for the Haverhill Historical Society and is furnished with Haverhill heirlooms, old glass, china, period furniture, and exhibits of Haverhill's nineteenth-century shoe industry. It also houses a small museum containing an early lighting collection, revolutionary and Civil War relics, and Haverhill historical items. Also located on the property is **The John Ward House**, the oldest frame house in the city. It was built for the Reverend John Ward, an early settler of the town, and is furnished in primitive and early American furniture. An early cobbler shop and Tenny Hall, with its large display of Indian artifacts, are additional buildings to be seen here, and all are included in the admission fee. The Buttonwoods is open year-round, Wednesday, Thursday, Saturday, and Sunday 2:00–4:30 and by appointment. Admission.

## John Greenleaf Whittier Birthplace (1688)

305 Whittier Road
508-373-3979

This fine example of an early New England farm-house is the birthplace of the famed poet John Greenleaf Whittier. It was built by his great-grandfather, Thomas Whittier, an early pioneer, who built the house beside a bubbling brook that furnished enough water for his farm needs and to turn his mill wheel. The farm has been in continual operation since the days of Thomas, and with few exceptions (although a fire in 1901 nearly destroyed it), the house remains as it was when it was built. Its massive hearth still dominates the keeping room, and the borning room is elevated because a rock below it was too large to move. Many of the original furnishings remain, including the desk on which the poet Whittier wrote his poems. The house and its environs are the setting for Whittier's beloved poem "Snowbound," and other works. It is owned and maintained by the Trustees of the Birthplace and is open Tuesday–Saturday 10:00–5:00, Sunday 1:00–5:00; Columbus Day–Patriots' Day, it is open Tuesday–Friday 1:00–5:00. Admission.

# Hingham
## *The Old Ordinary (1680)*

21 Lincoln Street
617-749-0013

The Old Ordinary is considered one of the finest examples of an early wayside inn in New England. The original structure dates from 1680 and was built as a "one-room" house, meaning one ground floor room, one room above, and an attic. Additions were made in 1740 and 1760, and special exhibition rooms have been added in recent years. During its history the house has had many owners; several were tavern keepers. Thus, the name the Old Ordinary, for a tavern that provided an ordinary meal of the day at a fixed price. The tap room and many other hospitable features are still preserved. This 14-room house museum contains an extensive collection of period furniture, export porcelain, glass, paintings, textiles, tools, and artifacts of Hingham history. The design of the beautiful garden, maintained by the Garden Club of Hingham, is attributed to Frederick Law Olmsted, Jr. The house is the property of the Hingham Historical Society and is open Mid-June–Labor Day,

THE OLD ORDINARY (1680)

Tuesday–Saturday 1:30–4:30 and by appointment. Admission.

# Holyoke
*Wistariahurst Museum (1848)*

238 Cabot Street
413-534-2216

This elegant, 26-room Victorian mansion, with 16 fire-places and nine bathrooms, which is now the Wistariahurst Museum of natural history and art, was the home of renowned silk manufacturer William Skinner and his family from 1874 to 1958. The museum is ornamented with leather wall coverings, parquet floors, coffered ceilings, marbleized columns, elaborate woodwork, and etched glass, and its permanent collections include period rooms, paintings, prints, decorative arts, textiles, and an archive of family and Holyoke history. On the three acres of grounds are landscaped gardens, dinosaur footprints, and other fossil marks. The Education Center, in the Carriage House, displays the history, culture, and art of the native people of North America and the natural and social history of Holyoke and the region. The museum is governed by the Holyoke Historical Commission and is open year-round, Wednesday 1:00–5:00, Saturday and Sunday 12:00–5:00, and by appointment. Admission.

# Ipswich
*The Great House (1925–1927)*

Argilla Road
508-356-4351

This 59-room Stuart mansion overlooking Crane Beach was built for Richard T. Crane, Jr., heir and President of Crane Company, the highly successful manufacturers of plumbing fixtures and valves. The Great House, designed to reflect the grand residences of England during the seventeenth century, took more than two years to complete. It is distinguished by a facade of pink Holland brick, a stone lunette hood over the entrance, and a cupola resembling the one on Sir Christopher Wren's Belton House in Lincolnshire, England. Interior features include a 63-foot-long gallery with a 16-foot ceiling, a library with ornamental wood carvings by seventeenth-century English craftsmen, bedrooms with panels that were

THE GREAT HOUSE (1925–1927)

shipped piece by piece from the London residence of William Hogarth, and 10 bathrooms embellished with sterling silver fixtures and soft-hued Italian marble. Castle Hill is a property of the Trustees of Reservations, a state-wide land conservation organization, which maintains the house and grounds. House tours are offered to the public four times each year and to groups by reservation. Facilities are available for private functions. A Summer Music Festival is held annually and picnicking is permitted prior to the concerts on the Grand Allee—a magnificent half-mile sweep of landscaped lawns overlooking the ocean. Call Castle Hill for function information, a schedule of summer events, and house tour dates.

## *John Heard House and Museum (1795)*

40 South Main Street
508-356-2641

This handsome, Federal-style house, built by John Heard and lived in by his descendants until 1936, reflects the wealth of his successful China import trade business. Notable features include the Palladian window over the entrance and a lovely Chippendale-style staircase in the wide central hall. The house is furnished with American antiques, with an emphasis on many Oriental treasures that were brought back during the China trade period. The museum on the third floor contains collections of china, fans, tools, Indian relics, and toys. The formal garden in the courtyard adds to the charm of the house. Operated by the Ipswich Historical Society, the house is open mid-May–mid-October, Tuesday–Saturday 10:00–5:00 and Sunday 1:00–5:00. Admission.

## *John Whipple House (1640)*

53 South Main Street
508-356-2641

Ipswich is renowned for its collection of pre-Revolution houses, and perhaps its finest example is the Whipple House. Of medieval design, with a steeply pitched roof and casement windows, it is reminiscent of Elizabethan England. It was built by John Fawn as a two-story, two-room structure and sold to Elder John Whipple soon after. The house was enlarged several times to accommodate his growing family. His descendants remained there for some 200 years, until the house became the property of the Ipswich Historical Society. It has some unusu-

JOHN WHIPPLE HOUSE (1640)

ally fine seventeenth-century interior details, such as a rare handcarved ogee molding, chamfered oak and tamarack beams, gunstock posts, pine sheathing, and an enormous fireplace. It is furnished in seventeenth- and eighteenth-century style with many rare pieces. The flower and herb garden is filled with plants grown in the colony during the seventeenth century. The house is open mid-April–October 31, Tuesday–Saturday 10:00–5:00, and Sunday 1:00–5:00. Admission.

# Kingston
## Major John Bradford House (1674)

Landing Road
617-585-6300

Another old, weatherbeaten, shingled frame house, constructed in the medieval style favored by the early settlers, was built by the grandson of Governor William Bradford. Major John Bradford brought his bride, Mercy Warren, also the grandchild of a *Mayflower* Pilgrim, to this house in 1674, and they lived here for more than 60 years. A wonderful old kitchen, with a huge fireplace and dutch oven, features furniture, pewter, wooden ware, and utensils similar to those used during the Bradfords' occupation. The rest of the house is furnished in similar style. It is operated by the Jones River Village Historical Society and is open July and August, Friday–Sunday 12:00–4:00. Admission.

# Lenox
## The Mount (1901–1902)

Plunkett Street
413-637-1899

"On a slope overlooking the dark waters and densely wooded shore of Laurel Lake we built a spacious and dignified house to which we gave the name of my great-grandfather's place, The Mount." So wrote the famed author and the first woman novelist to receive a Pulitzer Prize, Edith Wharton, on the completion of her classical American summer residence. The estate is modeled after an English manor house and has 50 acres of landscaped lawns, gardens, and woodlands. Its three stories of rooms, along with the gardens, are now undergoing restoration. Owned by the Edith Wharton Restoration, Inc., The Mount is now used

throughout the summer by Shakespeare & Company, a theater group, which co-offers with the Restoration plays centering on Wharton's life and writings. Hourly tours of the house are given Memorial Day–Labor Day, Tuesday–Friday 10:00–5:00, and Saturday and Sunday, 9:30–5:00; Labor Day–October 31, Thursday–Sunday 10:00–5:00. Admission.

THE MOUNT (1901–1902)

# Lexington
## Hancock-Clark House (1698)

36 Hancock Street
617-861-0928

The original part of this house was the small gambrel-roofed ell, built as a parsonage for the First Church by the Reverend John Hancock, grandfather of the famous patriot and signer of the Declaration of Independence. The main part of the house, a two-and-one-half-story colonial, was added in 1734. It was here that John Hancock and Samuel Adams were sleeping on the night of April 18, 1775, when Paul Revere arrived to warn them of the impending British attack. This eight-room house is now a museum with an extraordinary collection of period furniture and objects of great historical interest. The house is owned and maintained by the Lexington Historical

BUCKMAN TAVERN

Society and is open April 18–October 31, Monday–Saturday 1:00–5:00, and Sunday 1:00–5:00. Admission.

## Buckman Tavern

Lexington Battle Green

## Munroe Tavern

1332 Massachusetts Avenue
617-861-0928

**Buckman Tavern** (facing the Battle Green), the rendezvous point for the minutemen, and **Munroe Tavern** (one mile east of the green), which served as the British headquarters and hospital during the Lexington battle, have been restored and have furnishings of the revolutionary war period. Guided tours of these two buildings are given from mid-April–October 31, Monday–Saturday 10:00–5:00, Sunday 1:00–5:00. Admission.

# Lincoln
## *The Grange/Codman House (1735–1741)*

Codman Road
617-259-8843

Used primarily as a summer residence by several
generations of the Codman family for over 200 years,
the mansion and estate reflect the Codmans' fondness
for decorating, collecting, and gardening. Preserved
now as it was when the last two generations lived
here, the house contains a fascinating array of furniture, paintings, books, china, toys, and personal
effects of a family with the resources and leisure time
to pursue personal interests and hobbies. Originally a
two-story, ell-shaped Georgian mansion, built by the
politically prominent Russell family, it passed to a rel-
ative, John Codman, a Federal merchant, who more
than doubled the size of the house from 1797 to
1798. The grounds, with an Italian Renaissance villa
garden, incorporate such elements as multilevel ter-
racing, wall fountains, a reflecting pool, classical statuary, and marble colonnades. In 1968 it was
bequeathed by Sarah Codman to SPNEA. It is open
June 1–October 15, Wednesday–Sunday 12:00–5:00

THE GRANGE/CODMAN HOUSE
(1735–1741)

(tours on the hour). Afternoon tea is served by reservation. Admission.

## Gropius House (1937–1938)

68 Baker Bridge Road
617-227-3956

Walter Gropius, director of the Bauhaus School in Germany from 1919 to 1928, and known as one of the chief innovators of modern architecture, designed this home for himself upon his arrival in the United States in 1937. His two-story, wood-frame house used the proven and familiar building materials of the region, but handled them in an entirely new way. The building materials were all purchased from catalogs or building supply stores in America, and were adapted to the Bauhaus principles of function and simplicity. The house is furnished as it was when the Gropius family lived there, with furnishings made in the Bauhaus workshops and brought from Germany, as well as objects acquired in this country. It is now owned by SPNEA and is open June 1–October 15, the first Saturday and Sunday of the month, 12:00–5:00. Admission.

GROPIUS HOUSE (1937–1938)

# Longmeadow

*Storrs House (1786)*

697 Longmeadow Street
413-567-3600

Also called the Storrs Parsonage, this large, white clapboard, twin-chimney house was built by Richard Storrs, the second pastor of the First Church of Christ, in Longmeadow. Three generations of the Storrs lived here until it was bequeathed to the town in 1907. During restoration work the original paint colors of the rooms, typical of the Connecticut valley in the eighteenth century, were discovered and the redecorated rooms were painted accordingly. It is furnished with seventeenth- and eighteenth-century antiques, and some particularly interesting pieces include Chippendale chairs and desk, seventeeth-century William and Mary chairs and table, a refectory table used for communion in the old church, a four-poster, cherry canopy bed, and a Chickering piano and stool. The Longmeadow Gardeners have restored the garden and attend to its upkeep. The house is the headquarters of the Longmeadow Historical Society, which maintains it, and is open year-round Wednesday and Thursday, 9:00–12:00 and by appointment. Donation.

# Lynn

*Hyde-Mills House (c. 1838)*

125 Green Street
617-592-2465

This white frame, Greek Revival, "double" nineteenth-century house was built by two local carpenters, Daniel Hyde and William N. Mills, about 1838. The interior has been changed over the years to accommodate the Lynn Historical Society's collection of local history and memorabilia. Period furnishings, a library, and changing exhibits can be seen here. A special feature of the museum is an early shoe shop, filled with items relating to this trade and highlighting Lynn's important contribution to the shoe industry. The house is open Monday–Saturday 1:00–4:00. (Check for summer/winter schedule.) Admission.

TRASK HOUSE (1814)

# Manchester

*Trask House (1814)*

12 Union Street
617-526-7230

This is a late Federal house with extensive Empire renovations, such as the spiral staircase and large living room, which were added in 1834. It was the home of Captain Richard Trask, who, with his partner, Samuel Train, was engaged actively in Russian trade. His wife, Abigail, ran a shop at one end of the house in which she sold hats and other items brought back from England by her husband. The house was acquired by the Manchester Historical Society in 1924 and is filled with the society's extensive collection of furniture, pictures, books, toys, dolls, textiles, and artifacts relating to local history. Included are many Empire and early Victorian furnishings made in Manchester, as well as a number of Hepplewhite and Sheraton pieces. The house is open July and August, Wednesday 2:00–5:00. Free.

# Mansfield

*The Fisher-Richardson House (1704)*

354 Willow Street
508-339-4704/339-8748

Originally a small, gambrel-roofed frame, half-house with a single chimney, this building was added to in 1800, doubling its size to the full house seen today. It was purchased in 1760 by the Reverend Ebenezer White, the town's first minister, and lived in by his descendants for well over 150 years. It was deeded to the town in 1929 as a historical landmark. The restoration of the house in 1930 has been carefully documented by SPNEA. The house is furnished with period antiques and displays exhibits of early American industries. Operated by the Mansfield Historical Society, it is open mid-June–mid-September, Saturday and Sunday 2:00–5:00. Free.

# Marblehead

*The Jeremiah Lee Mansion (1768)*

161 Washington Street
617-631-1069

THE JEREMIAH LEE MANSION
(1768)

This magnificent Georgian-style house, with a rusticated wooden facade, Ionic entrance portico, and a cupola on its hipped roof, was built for Colonel Jeremiah Lee, a leader in the commerce of Marblehead and one of the wealthiest men in the colonies. Materials to decorate the house were brought from all over the world on Lee's ships. Handsomely carved woodwork throughout the house, English handpainted tempera wallpaper, the richly decorated main stairway, and the carved chimney piece in the great hall are only a few of this home's outstanding features. It is furnished with many rare period pieces, and the walls are hung with portraits of early residents of Marblehead. Operated by the Marblehead Historical Society, it is open mid-May–mid-October, Monday-Saturday 10:00–4:00. Admission.

## King Hooper Mansion (1728)

8 Hooper Street
617-631-2608

This handsome house was built in two historic stages. The original house of Greenleaf Hooper dates from about 1728. Three stories high, with gambrel roof and beautiful cellar brickwork, it was set back from the street. In 1747 Mr. Hooper's son Robert (called "King" by his devoted seamen) added the Georgian mansion in front. He built a facade of wide-grooved clapboards to simulate stone blocks, topped with a fine dentil cornice, and finished the corners with quoining. The entrance hall is dominated by a magnificent staircase with carved balusters of three differing twists to each step. The hall has high wainscoting of horizontal panels. The house, furnished throughout with period antiques, also contains a brick wine cellar, pine kitchen, bedrooms, and a ballroom on the third floor that is the main gallery of the Marblehead Arts Association. The house is now owned by the association, which holds a series of art exhibits throughout the year. It is open daily (except Monday) 1:00–4:00.

# Marshfield

## Isaac Winslow House (1699)

Careswell Street
617-826-2295

This large, gable-roofed, central-chimney frame house

was built by the Honorable Isaac Winslow, grandson of Governor Edward Winslow, Pilgrim founder of Marshfield and thrice governor of Plymouth Colony. It remained in the Winslow family for three generations until 1820. Restored in 1920, it represents one of the best examples extant of an old Plymouth Colony home. It is furnished with fine period antiques. The **Daniel Webster Law Office** is also on the property, moved here from the Webster estate in 1966. This small frame building contains furnishings and artifacts belonging to Webster. Operated by the Marshfield Historical Society, the house is open July 1–Labor Day, daily (except Tuesday) 10:00–5:00, and the law office is open July and August, Wednesday–Saturday 1:00–4:00. Donation.

# Medfield
## *The Peak House (1677–1680)*

347 Main Street
508-359-6488

During King Philip's War (1675–1676), the most devastating Indian war in New England, more than half the village of Medfield was burned to the ground. Benjamin Clark's original house was among those burned, and the one now standing is the one he built in its place. Called the Peak House because of the extreme pitch to the roof, it is a one-and-one-half-story cottage with three levels and a dirt cellar. The house underwent alterations in the mid-1800s and suffered from neglect in the early 1900s. When it became the property of the Medfield Historical Society in 1924, it was completely restored to its original style. It is furnished with many early artifacts and items of local interest and is open for special events during the year and also by appointment. Donation.

# Medford
## *Isaac Royall House (1732)*

Corner of Main and George streets
617-396-9032

In the mid-seventeenth century, Governor John Winthrop built a farmhouse on this property. In 1732 it was bought by Colonel Isaac Royall, Sr., a wealthy rum merchant from the West Indies. He rebuilt the house as a three-story Georgian-style mansion, together with quarters for his 27 slaves brought from

ISAAC ROYALL HOUSE (1732)

the islands. In 1775, the estate was confiscated by the colonists, and General John Stark made it his headquarters. The interior woodwork is finely detailed with paneled walls and doors and elegant hand-carved balustrades, providing an excellent backdrop for the beautiful antique furnishings throughout. It is owned and maintained by the Royal House Association and is open May 1–October 1, daily (except Monday and Friday) 2:00–5:00. Admission.

# Milton

## *Captain Robert Forbes House (1833)*

215 Adams Street
617-696-1815

This handsome, three-story Greek Revival country mansion was built, according to Boston architect Isaiah Rogers' plans, for Captain Robert Bennet Forbes, a wealthy sea captain prominent in the China trade. Forbes became head of the China trade firm of Russell and Company in the 1840s and accumulated an outstanding personal collection of Chinese porcelain, lacquerware, silver, and textiles. The house served as the Museum of the American China Trade for many years, but recently the vast collection of treasures was transferred to the Essex Institute, in Salem. Forbes' own collection, however, remains in the house and is beautifully displayed among the Chinese, Empire, and Victorian furnishings. Also on the grounds is the Lincoln Cabin, a replica of Lincoln's birthplace in Hodgenville, Kentucky, built in 1923 for Mary Bowditch Forbes, granddaughter of Robert Bennett Forbes. Operated by the Museum of the American China Trade, the house is open year-round, on Wednesday and Sunday 1:00–4:00. Admission.

# Monterey
*The Bidwell House (c. 1750)*

Art School Road
413-528-6888

This Georgian saltbox with added ells is set on 190 acres of what was once prosperous agricultural land acquired by the Reverend Adonijah Bidwell in the eighteenth century. The Reverend Bidwell was the first minister of Township Number I, which included both Monterey and Tyringham at that time. Many original features of the house remain, such as the large, symmetrically placed rooms that open off the small front stair hall, four fireplaces (two with beehive ovens), elegant yet simple paneling in faithfully re-created colors, and the dining room corner cupboard with its collection of delft and redware dishes. It is furnished with an impressive collection of eighteenth- and early nineteenth-century furniture and decorative arts "assembled under the guidance of Reverend Bidwell's 1748 estate inventory." The house is open late May–mid-October, Tuesday–Sunday 11:00–4:00. Admission.

# Nantucket

508-228-1894

The first four houses listed here (as well as several other historical buildings) are owned and operated by the Nantucket Historical Society and are open daily in season, mid-June–mid-September, 10:00–5:00. (Inquire for off season hours.) A discounted visitor's pass entitles the holder to one admission for all the buildings.

GREATER LIGHT (1930)

## Greater Light (1930)

8 Howard Street

This most unusual house reflects the penchant for summer visitors to convert any possible building into a vacation retreat. In the early 1930s two Quaker sisters from Philadelphia converted an old, gray-shingled livestock barn into a summer home of eclectic charm. In marked contrast to the simple tastes of Quakers, these two distinctly individual and creative women fashioned a striking, even funky, architectural delight. It is embellished with fascinating finds bought at auctions from all over the world—wrought-iron gratings, balconies, stained-glass windows, large doors, tapestries, and unusual furniture—exhibiting the theatrical and artistic interests and talents of the occupants. Paintings by one of the sisters, Hannah Monihan, adorn the walls.

## Hadwen House (1845)

96 Main Street

This handsome, white-columned, Greek Revival mansion, with a huge portico, captures the full elegance of Nantucket's whaling prosperity in the mid-1800s. It was built for William Hadwen, co-owner of a spermaceti works (now the Whaling Museum). Hadwen married Eunice Starbuck, daughter of Jason Starbuck, who built the Three Bricks (private homes) for his three sons on the opposite side of the street. The house is appointed with Federal, Empire, and nineteenth-century Revival furnishings and features a carved Italian marble fireplace, large sliding doors, silver doorknobs, molded plaster cornices, and ceiling rosettes. Portraits, needlework, canopied beds, and mid-nineteenth-century decorative objects fill the house. There is an 1850s garden maintained by the Nantucket Garden Club.

## Jethro Coffin House (1686)

Sunset Hill

Built as a wedding present for Jethro and Mary Gardner, this dwelling is also known as the oldest house on Nantucket. It is a restored example of a weathered-cedar-shingle New England saltbox, with a long, rear-sloping roof. The inverted horseshoe in raised brick on the huge central chimney was to discourage witches from entering the house. In 1978, a

JETHRO COFFIN HOUSE (1686)

massive bolt of lightning struck the house, causing severe damage but fortunately, no fire. Restoration has recently been completed, and the charming little house, once again furnished in period antiques, is on view.

## 1800 House

10 Mill Street

This simple, white clapboard house with a central chimney was the home of Jeremiah Lawrence, hatter and high sheriff of the county. It has changed little over the years and exhibits details of both the Georgian and Federal styles. Nantucket-made furniture, samplers worked at island schools, copper wares, and other furnishings and household goods depict domestic life in the early nineteenth century. Notable features of this house are the large round cellar (exposed for viewing) and the dooryard garden.

## Maria Mitchell Birthplace (1790)

1 Vestal Street
508-228-2896

Another simple Quaker house with a widow's walk is this one built by Hezekiah Swain in 1790. It has been preserved, however, in honor of its last owner, Maria Mitchell, who was born here in 1818. Mitchell was the country's first woman astronomer, the first woman to be elected to the American Academy of Arts and Sciences, Vassar College's first professor of astronomy, and the discoverer of Mitchell's comet. As a fitting memorial to her, the Maria Mitchell Association, which owns and operates the house, has established a complex of buildings here, including Mitchell's house and small observatory, an aquarium, and a library devoted to educational programs in the natural sciences. Classes and lectures for both children and adults are held here from mid-June–August, Tuesday–Saturday 10:00–4:00. Admission.

# New Bedford

## The Rotch-Jones-Duff House (1834)

398 County Street
508-997-1401

This handsome, large, Greek Revival house, its clapboards painted yellow with white trim and its shutters a dark green, has recently undergone extensive restoration. Wide porches surround the house, and a lovely gazebo highlights the beautifully landscaped grounds and formal gardens. The house and gardens reflect the three families who resided there and their periods of residence: Wiliam Rotch, Jr. (1834–1851), a prominent whaling merchant, for whom the house was built; Edward Coffin Jones (1851–1934), another successful whaling merchant; and Mark M. Duff (1934–1981), an important New Bedford businessman. Restoration and acquisition of furnishings is ongoing, and the Rotch-Jones-Duff House and Garden Museum, Inc., seeks to interpret "the special quality of life which existed in New Bedford during the whaling era." The house is open during April and May, Sunday 1:00–4:00; June–August, Tuesday–Saturday 10:00–4:00; and September and October, Saturday and Sunday 1:00–4:00. Admission.

# Newbury

## Coffin House (c. 1654)

14–16 High Road
617-227-3956

This picturesque, weathered house, with a steep roof and high chimneys, is one of the best examples in New England of early pioneer life. It started as a small cottage, but with the growth of Tristram and Judith Coffin's family of 10 children (and many distinguished descendants), it was enlarged considerably over the years, which more than tripled its original size. The house represents the continuous story of eight generations of Coffins, who lived here for well over two centuries. Of special interest is the kitchen and buttery, virtually unchanged, with an excellent display of early pewter and utensils, and the parlor, with early nineteenth-century American wallpaper. It is owned by SPNEA and is open June 1–October 15, Tuesday, Thursday, Saturday, and Sunday 12:00–5:00. Admission.

# Newburyport

## Cushing House Museum (1808)

98 High Street
508-462-2681

CUSHING HOUSE MUSEUM (1808)

This 21-room, three-story, Federal-style mansion is the headquarters for The Historical Society of Old Newbury. Built for a local sea captain in 1808, it later became the home of a prominent diplomat, Caleb Cushing, who was the first mayor of Newburyport, a minister to Spain, and the first U.S. Ambassador to China. The house is kept partly as a historic house and partly as a museum, and its exhibits tell the story of the seaport town and the many industries that flourished there. Period furnishings, silver, clocks, glass, china, toys, paperweights, and military items are on display, as well as a collection of paintings by local and itinerant artists. An eighteenth-century French garden, carriage house, and cobblestone courtyard add to the dignity of the house. It is open May 1–November 1, daily (except Sunday and Monday) 10:00–4:00. Admission.

# Newton
## *The Jackson Homestead (1809)*

527 Washington Street
617-552-7238

This impressively large, clapboard Federal-style house, with brick ends, a low, hipped roof, and four

THE JACKSON HOMESTEAD
(1809)

chimneys, was partly constructed from an earlier 1679 saltbox that stood on the property. Many of the original beams, handcarved mantels, and doorways from the earlier house were skillfully utilized in the nineteenth-century home that now serves as the Newton City Museum. The museum is furnished to convey a sense of early nineteenth-century life in Newton, and its collections include period rooms, costumes, farming and household implements, toys, maps, photographs, and an extensive repository of research material relating to local history. An interesting feature of the house is the exposed root cellar, where William Jackson hid runaway slaves during the 1850s. Owned by the city of Newton, and headquarters of the Newton Historical Society, it is open October–June, Monday–Friday 10:00–4:00, on the first Sunday 2:00–5:00; July and August, Tuesday–Friday 10:00–4:00; September, Monday–Friday, 10:00–4:00. Admission.

# Northampton

## *The Isaac Damon House (1813)*

46 Bridge Street
413-584-6011

Isaac Damon, an architect and bridge designer, built this house for himself upon coming to Northampton to build the fourth meetinghouse for the First Congregational Church. He also constructed many other buildings and covered bridges in the Connecticut River valley while living in this house. It is now headquarters for the Northampton Historical Society and contains the society's considerable collection of nineteenth-century dresses, bonnets, accessories, and textiles. It also features the Caleb Strong room, with mementos of this 11-term governor of Massachusetts, and a Hadley-type dower chest belonging to his daughter, Sarah Strong. The Damon Educational Center, used for workshops, lectures, exhibitions, school programs, and meetings, was added to the house in 1986. It is open year-round (except for January and February and holidays) Wednesday, Saturday, and Sunday 2:00–4:00 and by appointment. (Office open Monday–Friday 9:00–5:00). Admission.

## Parsons House (c. 1712)

58 Bridge Street
413-584-6011

This is the oldest house in town, built by the grandson of the first settler, Joseph Parsons, a fur trader and explorer. Originally consisting of only four rooms arranged around a massive central chimney, this center-entrance colonial has undergone many alterations over the years, and an interesting exhibit traces these architectural changes. Semipermanent exhibits include an 1840s parlor, a 1930s bedroom (from the last owner), plus changing displays on subjects such as the Damon House archaeological dig and mementos of visits and concerts by Jenny Lind, the "Swedish Nightingale." One of the three houses in town owned by the Northampton Historical Society, it is open for tours year-round Tuesday–Sunday 12:00–4:00. (Closed January, February, and holidays.) Admission.

## Shepherd House (c. 1798)

66 Bridge Street
413-584-6011

Another one of the three colonial houses that line Bridge Street, and owned by the Northampton Historical Society, the Shepherd House contains the nineteenth-century furnishings of one of Northampton's former distinguished families. The Shepherds traveled extensively in Europe, the Orient, and North Africa, and the furnishings and heirlooms reflect this. Exotic Near Eastern textiles, ornamental workboxes, Korean brasses, Japanese prints, diaries, and portraits are among the collections in the period rooms. The Shepherd Barn, built in the early nineteenth century, houses the society's fascinating collections of early plumbing, trade signs, and weathervanes. It is open for tours Tuesday–Sunday 12:00–4:00. Admission.

# North Andover
## Johnson Cottage (1789)

153 Academy Road
508-686-4035

This is one of the two North Andover Historical Society's sites that give visitors a sense of the lives and times of eighteenth- and nineteenth-century New Englanders, from prominent citizens to artisans and farmers. A simple, white clapboard, one-story building accentuated with black shutters and trim, the cottage contains part of the Samuel Dale Stevens collection of early New England furniture, lighting devices, pewter, tools, woodenware, ironware, and local artifacts, displayed in period rooms. Stevens, a descendant of the first American woolen manufacturer and a successful local textile merchant, founded the North Andover Historical Society in 1913. He was particularly interested in showing everyday life in the period from 1690 to 1830. The house is open year-round Tuesday–Friday 10:00–12:00 and 2:00–4:00. Admission.

## Stevens-Coolidge Place (c. 1800)

Andover Street
508-682-3580

For many years, author and diplomat John Gardner Coolidge and his wife, Helen Stevens Coolidge, summered at Ashdale Farm, a magnificent 90-acre estate. The colonial Revival-style mansion, called "Home Place," is filled with the Coolidges' collections of souvenirs of their travels around the world. Chinese porcelain, Anglo-Irish cut glass, Oriental rugs, and fine hangings are mixed with American decorative arts. Particularly noteworthy are the landscaped grounds and garden, as well as the acres of pastures

STEVENS-COOLIDGE PLACE
(C. 1800)

and woodlands. There is also a greenhouse and an unusual serpentine brick wall on the property. The estate is administered by the Trustees of Reservations, and is open April 15–October 31, Sunday 1:00–5:00. Admission.

# North Oxford

## *Clara Barton Birthplace (1805)*

Clara Barton Road
508-987-5375

This small, white clapboard, Cape Cod–style cottage was the birthplace of Clara Barton, founder of the American Red Cross. A school teacher in this rural town, she was moved by the plight of the wounded soldiers in the Civil War and began her lifelong career to improve medical conditions on the battlefield. The house tells the story of Clara, who became known as the "Angel of the Battlefield," and her field desk and other personal items are among the furnishings. Also, there are many early items, letters, and documents pertaining to the American Red Cross. Now owned by the Unitarian Universalist Women's Federation, the house serves as a centerpiece for a summer camp for diabetic children and a conference center. It is open April 1–October 31, Tuesday–Sunday 11:00–5:00. Admission.

# North Swansea
## *The Martin House Farm*

Stoney Hill Road
508-379-0066

In the small southern Massachusetts town where the first bloody battle between colonial militia and King Philip's Wampanoag Indians took place in 1675, a weathered gambrel-roofed farmhouse sits peacefully in its original setting of cornfields, woodlots, orchards, and barns, framed by dry stone walls. For more than 200 years, the Martin family farmed the land and added to the one-room dwelling built by John Martin in 1728. It contains many relics of the family's history, including Jacobean furniture, fine old pewter, documented bed hangings, and a loom that attests to John Martin's vocation as a weaver. An Old Shrub Rose Garden, featuring almost extinct varieties of roses brought to America by the early colonists, is on the grounds. The house is owned and maintained by the Colonial Dames of Massachusetts and is open May 1–October 31, Wednesday–Saturday 10:00–4:00, Sunday 2:00–5:00. Admission.

# Norwood
## *The Fred Holland Day House (c. 1859)*

93 Day Street
617-762-9197

This large, 17-room Tudor mansion, set on a hill overlooking the town of Norwood, was the home of one of the town's most famous and eccentric individuals. Fred Holland Day, the son of a wealthy leather merchant and his wife, was born here in 1864, rose to international fame as a bibliophile, publisher, and photographer, and died here in almost total obscurity in 1933. The house, with its richly paneled Great Hall and huge fireplace, is encircled on three sides by balconies on both the second and third floors. A split-level library on the second floor leads directly to Day's bedroom on the third floor. In these two rooms he spent the last 15 years of his life in a self-imposed seclusion. The house is filled with many original furnishings, paintings, photographs, and Day memora-

THE FRED HOLLAND DAY HOUSE (C. 1859)

bilia. It is maintained by the Norwood Historical Society and is open Memorial Day–Labor Day, Saturday and Sunday 1:00–4:00 and by appointment.

# Osterville

## Captain Jonathan Parker House (1795)

Parker Road
508-428-5861

This small, eighteenth-century shingled Cape was built by a local sea captain, and later additions were used to house the Osterville Historical Society's fascinating collections and exhibits. The museum now has 11 rooms with furniture of various styles from colonial times through the Victorian era, Sandwich glass, china, fans, paintings, and a large display of photographs and mementos pertaining to local history. A children's room features many early toys, dolls, and dollhouses. It is open July and August, Sunday and Thursday 2:00–5:00.

# Peabody

## General Gideon Foster House (1810)

35 Washington Street
508-531-0805

Originally built on a four-acre lot on Main Street in 1810 and moved to Washington Street in 1842, this three-story house with a shallow, hipped roof and graduated window openings was designed in the mode of Salem architect Samuel McIntire. In 1815 Gideon Foster, a prominent local mill owner, bought the property and lived there for many years. An outstanding patriot during the Revolution, he led a band of minutemen to Arlington to intercept the British and later participated in the Battle of Bunker Hill. He was elected major general by the state legislature in 1801. The house is now headquarters of the Peabody Historical Society, and seven rooms of this building— the Reference Library, the Parlor, Peabody Room, Tea Room, Costume Room, Children's Room, and Military Room—are filled with the majority of the society's collections. The house is open year-round, Tuesday evenings 7:00–9:00, and by appointment. Donation.

## The Felton Houses (1644, 1683)

Brooksby Farm
508-531-0805

The earliest settlers in this area were the Feltons, who built two houses (one of which is the oldest in Peabody) and developed more than 200 acres of orchards, pasture, and meadowland. Now known as Brooksby Farm, the property was purchased by the city of Peabody in 1976. The town maintains 200 acres of the orchard land as a productive farm and recreational area. The Peabody Historical Society maintains the two houses and barn, where guided tours are given June–September and by appointment. Admission.

# Pittsfield

## Arrowhead (1780)

780 Holmes Road
413-442-1793

Arrowhead is the headquarters of the Berkshire

County Historical Society, but is best known as the home of author Herman Melville from 1850 to 1863. Seeking a quiet place to write, Melville moved his family to this large colonial farmhouse in a peaceful country setting in 1850 and named it Arrowhead. He lived, farmed, and wrote at Arrowhead for 13 years, finishing his most famous novel, *Moby Dick,* and writing *Typee, Billy Budd,* and many others. The author's study, piazza, the original fireplace from his short story "I and My Chimney," and the restored barn in which he and his friend and neighbor, Nathaniel Hawthorne, spent hours discussing their writings are all open to the public. "The Berkshire Legacy," a film recalling the days in which many famous writers lived and worked in the Berkshires, is shown twice daily. There are nature trails and wildflower gardens on the property. It is open Memorial Day–October 31, Monday–Saturday 10:00–4:30, Sunday 11:00–3:30. (Closed Tuesday and Wednesday after Labor Day.) November 1–Memorial Day by appointment. Admission.

## Hancock Shaker Village (1790–1960)

Route 20
413-443-0188

Set among 1200 acres of meadows and woodlands, the followers of Mother Ann Lee, founder of the Shaker Movement in this country, called this village The City of Peace, and Hancock became the third of 18 Shaker communities to be established in the United States. At its peak, in 1830, 300 inhabitants made their living here. The Main Dwelling House, built in 1830, was a residence for more than 100 "brothers and sisters" and now contains period rooms of the Shaker occupancy. Beautifully restored and maintained, the village now comprises 20 buildings, a reproduction furniture workshop and salesroom, herb and vegetable gardens, farm animals, gift shop, lunch room, and picnic facilities. Craft demonstrations and guided tours take place daily. It is open Memorial Day–October 31, 9:30–5:00; April; May, and November 10:00–3:00. Admission.

# Plymouth

## Antiquarian House (1809)

126 Water Street
508-746-9697

Built in the Federal style, this large clapboard house with a shallow, hipped roof and four corner chimneys was the home of nineteenth-century merchant and ship owner William Hammatt. Overlooking the waterfront, it has several octagonal-shaped rooms filled with an excellent collection of China trade porcelains, quilts, samplers, children's toys, dolls, and costumes, and a fully equipped nineteenth-century kitchen. Daniel Webster was a frequent guest in the house, and a portrait of him hangs over the fireplace in the Keeping Room. Owned by the Plymouth Antiquarian Society, the house is open late May–mid-October, Monday–Saturday 10:00–5:00, Sunday 12:00–5:00. Admission.

ANTIQUARIAN HOUSE (1809)

## *Harlow Old Fort House (1677)*

119 Sandwich Street
508-746-9697

This story-and-a-half dwelling, with a gambrel roof, is a working museum that presents an intimate glimpse into the daily life of seventeenth-century settlers. Costumed guides explain and demonstrate the household activities of the early occupants, such as fireplace and beehive oven cooking, candle dipping, weaving, spinning, and yarn dyeing. The house was built in 1677 by William Harlow, and it derives its name from the beams and framework, believed to be from the old Pilgrim fort. The building stands on its original site and is furnished with artifacts of the period. It is owned by the Plymouth Antiquarian Society and is open mid-May–October, Wednesday–Saturday 10:00–5:00. Admission.

## Howland House (1667)

27 North Street
508-746-9590

This is the only remaining structure in Plymouth in which members of the original colony are known to have lived. The house, originally consisting of one large room with an immense chimney and a staircase leading to the second floor and attic, was built by Jacob Mitchell, who was later killed by the Indians. Jabez Howland, son of *Mayflower* Pilgrims John and Elizabeth Howland, bought the house and constructed a westerly wing for the use of his parents. It was purchased, repaired, and furnished by the descendants of John Howland in 1913. The furnishings are a collection of seventeenth- and eighteenth-century antiques, and some are family heirlooms. Owned by the Pilgrim John Howland Society, the house is open late May–mid-October, Monday–Saturday 10:00–5:00, Sunday 12:00–5:00. Admission.

## Mayflower Society House (1754, 1898)

4 Winslow Street
508-746-2590

This elegant, white clapboard house with black shutters, roof balustrades, and several "Tory" chimneys, was built by Edward Winslow, a prominent political figure in Plymouth and great-grandson of Governor Winslow. When Winslow, a Tory leader, fled to Canada, the house was purchased by the Jackson family. In 1842 Dr. Jackson made the house famous when he and his assistant Dr. Morton discovered ether here. His sister, Lydia Jackson, was married to Ralph Waldo Emerson in 1835 in the east front parlor. Many changes have taken place in the house, which now combines eighteenth-century architecture in the front portion and turn-of-the-century Victorian style in the rear. The house features a "flying staircase" in the front hall, tiled fireplaces, and an excellent collec-

tion of Queen Anne and early Chippendale furniture. It is the headquarters of the General Society of Mayflower Descendants and is open July–mid-September 10:00–5:00 daily; Memorial Day–June 30 and mid-September–mid-October, Thursday–Sunday 10:00–5:00. Also open Thanksgiving weekend. Admission.

MAYFLOWER SOCIETY HOUSE
(1754, 1898)

## Plimoth Plantation

Warren Avenue (Route 3)
508-746-1622

This 1627 Pilgrim village is a living museum re-creating life in the original colony. Costumed interpreters, impersonating known residents of Plymouth in 1627, explain daily chores and culture of the Pilgrims in authentic language and manners. Together with the Wampanoag Indian Settlement, which presents the history and culture of the native people whose support was so vital to the newcomers, Plimoth Plantation gives the visitor a unique opportunity to understand the life of the early settlers. The museum is open daily, April 1–November 30, 9:00–5:00. Admission.

### Richard Sparrow House (1640)

42 Summer Street
508-747-1240

Diamond-shaped casement windows and heavy red-oak timbers add to the medieval look of this dwelling, the oldest house in Plymouth. The first floor, with its original wide floorboards and exposed gunstock corner posts, remains virtually unchanged. It also contains the only known intact seventeenth-century fireplace. It was the home of Richard Sparrow, his wife, Pandora, and their son, Jonathan, who arrived in Plymouth in 1630. The house was substantially enlarged in 1750 and completely restored in the 1930s. Since then it has been noted for its dedication to the crafts. Demonstrations and classes in pottery making are given here, and many pieces are for sale in the gift shop. The house, furnished with period pieces, and the shop are open late May–mid-October, Thursday–Tuesday 10:00–5:00. Donation.

### Spooner House (1749)

27 North Street
508-746-9697

This well-maintained, solid clapboard house was home to five generations of the Spooner family, and was left as a museum with all of its furnishings intact. The house tells the authentic story of a Plymouth family from pre-Revolution days till the death of its last owner in 1954. The Spooners were prominent in local politics, in the church, and in business ventures. The house contains many interesting artifacts and furnishings. It is maintained by the Plymouth Antiquarian Society and is open late May–mid-October. Admission.

# Provincetown

### Seth Nickerson House (1746)

72 Commercial Street
No telephone

Typical of Cape Cod–style houses, this weathered-shingle cottage with a huge chimney has an interesting history. It was built by Seth Nickerson, a ship's carpenter, using timbers from wrecked ships, and is thought to be the oldest house in Provincetown. The house contains nine rooms filled with an eclectic array of antiques. Of particular note is the Keeping Room fireplace, one of three supported by the 16-ton chimney, containing a brick oven. The house is privately owned but open to the public June 1–mid-October, daily 10:00–5:00 for tours. Admission.

# Quincy
## Adams National Historical Site (1731)

135 Adams Street
617-773-1177

Originally built as a country villa by Leonard Vasall, a wealthy sugar planter from Jamaica, this handsome house gained historical prominence by being the home of two presidents, John Adams and John Quincy Adams. Purchased by John and Abigail Adams in 1787, "The Old House," as the family came to call it, was occupied by four generations of the Adams family for the next 140 years. During that time it became a large rambling house with various extensions and additions. It is furnished throughout with family heirlooms and a large collection of family portraits, among them some of the finest works of John Singleton Copley and Gilbert Stuart. The Stone Library, built by Charles Francis Adams (1807–1886), contains a collection of 14,000 volumes and is fronted by an eighteenth-century garden. The house is maintained by the National Park Service and is open April 19–November 10, daily 9:00–5:00. Admission.

## John and John Quincy Adams Birthplaces (1681)

133 and 141 Franklin Street
617-773-1177

John Adams was born on October 30, 1735, in a typical New England clapboard saltbox with a great central chimney, at 133 Franklin Street. He spent much of his early life in this house, attending a neighborhood school and then later going off to Harvard College. The adjacent house, of almost identical style, at 141 Franklin Street, which his father, Deacon John, had purchased in 1744, was bequeathed to John. It was to this house that he brought his bride, Abigail Smith, and on July 11, 1767, she gave birth here to their second child, John Quincy Adams. Both houses are furnished in simple period pieces, and National Park Service personnel provide interpretive guided

JOHN AND JOHN QUINCY
ADAMS BIRTHPLACES (1681) tours relating to the early colonial lifestyles of the second and sixth presidents of the United States. They are open April 19–November 10, daily 9:00–5:00. Admission.

## Josiah Quincy House (1770)

20 Muirhead Street (Wollaston)
617-227-3956

This former home of Colonel Josiah Quincy, a prominent patriot, wealthy merchant, and shipbuilder, is a large Georgian house with a pillared portico and a Chinese fretwork balustrade. Several generations of the Quincy family lived here, including Josiah Quincy III, who was the second mayor of Boston and president of Harvard. (Josiah is a favorite Quincy family name and an old saying is that the house "descended from `Siah to `Siah.") The rooms contain Georgian paneling and fireplaces with colorful English tiles, English and American furniture from Colonel Quincy's time, and objects added by later generations of the family. It is owned by SPNEA and is open June 1–mid-October, Tuesday, Thursday, Saturday, and Sunday 12:00–5:00. Admission.

## Quincy Homestead (1706)

34 Butler Road
617-472-5117

QUINCY HOMESTEAD (1706)

This early Georgian mansion with a gambrel roof, dormers, and balustrade, has a very dignified look. It was home to four generations of the Edmund Quincy family, but is often called the Dorothy Quincy Homestead, in honor of the celebrated "Dorothy Q," the high-spirited wife of John Hancock, who was born here. The kitchen is the oldest part of the house and, according to studies, it was built in the late seventeenth century (1686), moved from an unknown site, and attached to the house early in the eighteenth century. It contains many early pieces of furniture, pewter, and kitchen utensils, as well as Dorothy Quincy's spinning wheel. The rest of the house is a fine example of a family residence, with furnishings representing the changes in styles that occurred with each succeeding generation. Operated and maintained by the National Society of the Colonial Dames of Massachusetts, it is open May 1–October 31, Wednesday–Sunday 12:00–5:00. Admission.

# Reading
## The Parker Tavern (1694)

103 Washington Street
617-944-5051/944-7577

The oldest documented house in Reading is a saltbox with a large central chimney, built by Abraham Bryant in 1694. The house takes its name from its fourth owner, Ephraim Parker, who operated an inn here for 15 years during the revolutionary war period. Some of the prisoners of war from the Seventy-first Scotch regiment were quartered here. Since 1923 the house has been owned and maintained by the Reading Antiquarian Society and preserved as a typical early homestead, filled with a significant collection of materials such as woodenware, lighting devices, household furnishings, and children's toys. The house is open May–October, Sundays 2:00–5:00 and by appointment. Donation.

# Rockport
## Old Castle (1715)

Castle Lane
508-546-9533

This venerable old weathered-shingle house, with its central chimney, hewn overhang, and added lean-to, has been a local landmark for more than 200 years and the object of much speculation. One explanation of its name is that it derived from the fact that during the early days, the house was visible from far out at sea, reminding sailors of the castles along the coast of England. It is thought that many of its old timbers were salvaged from shipwrecks along the neighboring shores. The house is furnished with period pieces, kitchen utensils, and artifacts relating to Rockport's early history. It is maintained by the Sandy Bay Historical Society and is open July 1–Labor Day, daily 2:00–5:00. Admission.

## The Sewall-Scripture House (1832)

40 King Street
508-546-9533

Rockport has long been known for its high quality granite, so it is not surprising to find that this stately stone house is made from local granite. It was built by Levi Sewall, from granite taken from his own quarry, later to be known as the Pigeon Hill Granite Company. It is now the home of the Sandy Bay Historical Society and Museum, Inc. Interior features in several period rooms include a graceful flying staircase, French wallpapers, dentils, and many fine furnishings. In the Library and General Room many historic objects and documents from Cape Ann's early days are on exhibit, and The Cable Room attests to the fact that Rockport was once the American terminus of the Atlantic Cable. The museum is open July 1–Labor Day, daily 2:00–5:00. Admission.

# Rowley
*Platts-Bradstreet House (c. 1677)*

233 Main Street
508-948-2858

Restoration work is presently going on at this large, traditional central-chimney house with narrow clapboard siding and a lean-to. The house was built some time before 1677 by Samuel Platts, on land that was granted to William Bellingham, brother of the governor of Massachusetts Bay Colony, around 1643. It remained in the Platts family until 1771, when it was purchased by the Bradstreets, who lived there until 1906. Its seventeenth-century rooms are furnished with period pieces and many artifacts pertaining to Rowley's past. A small, eighteenth-century shoemaker's shop complete with benches and tools adjoins the house, and a re-created seventeenth-century English garden is on the grounds. The house is owned and maintained by the Rowley Historical Society, and guided tours are given May–September, Wednesday and Saturday 10:00–4:00 and by appointment. Admission.

# Roxbury
*Shirley-Eustis House (1747)*

33 Shirley Street
617-442-2275

This impressive mid-Georgian home was built in 1747 by the royal governor of Massachusetts, William Shirley. It was designed by Peter Harrison, the architect of King's Chapel in Boston, who gave it a high stone base, boxy profile, tall hipped roof, and a bold row of Corinthian pilasters across the front. Damaged

SHIRLEY-EUSTIS HOUSE (1747)

during the Revolution (it was used as a barracks and a hospital by the British), it was rebuilt in 1800 by James Magee, one of the early China trade captains. In 1819 it was purchased by a continental army surgeon, Dr. William Eustis, who later became governor of the Commonwealth. Many important visitors were entertained here, including the Marquis de Lafayette, George Washington, Benjamin Franklin, and Daniel Webster. In recent years it has been restored once again, and is now open as a museum, containing furnishings and artifacts pertaining to local history. It is owned by the Shirley-Eustis House Association and is open year-round, Wednesday 11:00–4:00. Free.

## Salem

Salem, the original capital of the Massachusetts Bay Colony, is a showcase for some of the richest early American homes in the country. Just 15 miles north of Boston, this once prosperous seaport has been left a legacy of handsome homes attesting to the great wealth made here during the days of the China trade. Most of these houses have been restored and are maintained by the Essex Institute (132 Essex Street).

This excellent museum, one of the earliest to display home furnishings, has been collecting arts and artifacts of Essex County for more than 150 years.

## Crowninshield-Bentley House (1727)

Essex Street
508-744-3390

This gambrel-roofed, Georgian colonial was built by Captain John Crowninshield, a shipmaster and fish merchant, who left it to his son, Jacob. When Jacob died at sea, his wife, Hannah, left with his insolvent estate, sold half of the house to her brother-in-law, and took in a boarder. The hyphenated name of the house commemorates both the family and their most celebrated boarder, the Reverend William Bentley. He was pastor of Salem's East Church and distinguished himself as a scholar, linguist, and historian. His second-floor combined study and bedroom retains its original furnishings. The most important decorative styles of the eighteenth century are featured throughout this beautifully decorated house. Maintained by the Essex Institute, it is open June 1–October 31, Tuesday–Saturday 10:00–4:00, Sunday 1:00–4:30. Admission.

## Derby House (1762)

168 Derby Street
508-745-1470

This handsomely detailed brick town house was a wedding gift to Elias Hasket Derby and his bride, Elizabeth Crowninshield, from his father, Richard Derby, a sea captain, shipowner, and merchant. Elias, starting out in his father's business as a bookkeeper and later expanding the shipping part to include trade with India and the Orient, became Salem's first millionaire. This richly decorated house, the oldest surviving brick house in Salem, is furnished throughout with eighteenth-century antiques and paintings, many of them original to the house. It is open to the public by the Salem Maritime National Historic Site, operated by the National Park Service. Call for tour reservations.

## Gardner-Pinegree House (1804)

128 Essex Street
508-744-3390

This three-story, red brick Federal house, with semi-circular portico supported by slender corinthian pillars, was designed by Samuel McIntire and has been called one of the finest neoclassical buildings in America. It was built for the well-to-do merchant John Gardner, and has been restored to reflect the elegant taste of the prosperous Federal era in Salem. McIntire's special talent as a wood carver is evident in the richness of the fine interior details in the mantelpieces, door frames, chair rails, and cornices. Most of the early nineteenth-century French and American wallpapers remain, and there are many excellent examples of eighteenth- and nineteenth-century window and bed hangings. The house is furnished throughout with flawless antiques. It is maintained by the Essex Institute and is open year-round, Tuesday–Saturday 10:00–4:00, Sunday 1:00–4:30. Admission.

## House of the Seven Gables (1668)

54 Turner Street
508-744-0991

HOUSE OF THE SEVEN GABLES (1668)

Captain John Turner, merchant mariner, built this dark, rambling multigabled house—considered quite luxurious for its time—on Salem Harbor in 1668. In

1851, Nathaniel Hawthorne, America's first internationally known man of letters, inspired by this house, wrote his classic Gothic novel *The House of the Seven Gables*. Today the house is the centerpiece of a unique historic site featuring three seventeenth-century houses and Nathaniel Hawthorne's birthplace (all moved to this site). With the exception of the old kitchen, which recalls the early Puritan days, the House of the Seven Gables is furnished very much as it would have been when Hawthorne visited it during the early part of the nineteenth century. Few pieces are original, but they are all authentic to the period. A secret staircase and the old garret add to the mystery of the house. It is open year-round (except on holidays and during the last two weeks in January) for a slide presentation and guided tours, 10:00–4:30, and from July 1–Labor Day, 9:30–5:30. Gardens, coffee and gift shops. Admission.

## John Ward House (1684)

132 Essex Street
508-744-0991

Another picturesque, late seventeenth-century house featuring the same Elizabethan cross gables and overhangs as the houses at The Gables historic site, this one was moved to the grounds of the Essex Institute in 1910. The house reflects the modest means of its builder, John Ward, who made a living softening leather. The old kitchen exhibits an early fireplace with brick ovens, mechanical spit, and utensils. Housed in a lean-to are an 1830s apothecary's shop, complete with equipment, and a "cent shop," the kind Salem wives kept while their husbands were away at sea. The house is open June 1–October 31, Tuesday–Saturday 10:00–4:00, Sunday 1:00–4:30. Admission.

## Ropes Mansion (c. 1727)

318 Essex Street
No telephone

Originally built for Samuel Barnard, a Salem merchant, this pre-Georgian-style house, its gambrel roof outlined by a railing, later became the home of Judge Nathaniel Ropes. The grounds are enclosed by a handsome white picket fence with intricately designed gate posts. The house was occupied by four generations of the prosperous Ropes family and is furnished entirely with their possessions. Of particular interest is a butler's pantry filled with the double set of Canton china and the rare table glass that were imported in 1817 for the wedding of Sally Ropes. The interior reflects several stylish remodelings, the last in 1894. The house and formal gardens were left to the Ropes Memorial and are maintained by the Essex Institute. It is open June 1–October 31, Tuesday–Saturday 10:00–4:00, Sunday 1:00–4:30.

## Stephen Phillips Memorial Trust House (c. 1800)

34 Chestnut Street
508-744-0440

This gracious, Federal-style house was moved to this site in two sections from Danvers in the mid-1800s. It was part of a large estate called Oak Hill, designed by McIntire, and its story is featured in an exhibit at the Museum of Fine Arts in Boston. Stephen Phillips, who bought the house in 1914, was a descendant of a prosperous mercantile family, whose ancestral home was at 17 Chestnut Street. Portraits of five generations of Stephen Phillipses (all of the male heirs were named Stephen Phillips) are to be seen in this elegant mansion. Family heirlooms and furnishings relating to the historic China trade include Chinese porcelain, Oriental rugs, rare pieces of furniture, and paintings. Owned by the Stephen Phillips Memorial Trust, the house is open May–October, Monday–Saturday 10:00–4:30. Admission.

## Witch House (c. 1642)

310½ Essex Street
508-744-0180

Jonathan Corwin built this house now popularly known as the Witch House, and it exemplifies the medieval architecture of seventeenth-century New England. It has a pilastered chimney, front gables, diamond-paned casements, and decorative pendants ornamenting the second-story overhang. The house stands as a reminder of the infamous witch trials that took place in Salem in the 1690s. Corwin was one of the judges in the witch trials, and here in his chambers on the second floor, the preliminary examinations took place. The house has been restored and furnished with such early artifacts as heavy oak furniture, old pewter ware, primitive lighting devices, and a one-hand clock to reflect its appearance in the

1690s. Operated by the city of Salem, it is open daily mid-March–June, 10:00–4:30; July and August, 10:00–6:00; Labor Day–December 1, 10:00–4:30. Admission.

# Sandwich

*Hoxie House (c. 1675)*

Sandwich Center
No telephone

This house is said to be the oldest on Cape Cod, actually built in 1637, only 17 years after the landing of the Pilgrims. A typical saltbox, built on a bluff overlooking Shawme Pond, it is named for Captain Abraham Hoxie, a whaling captain who bought the house in 1859. His neighbors called the place Fort Hoxie because the captain fired off a saluting cannon to mark Union victories on public holidays and other celebrations. The house has been restored to the period of 1680–1690 with many authentic features such as gunstock posts, chamfered beams, wide floorboards, leaded windows, and period furniture on loan from the Museum of Fine Arts in Boston. Maintained by the Sandwich Historical Society, it is open mid-June–September, daily 10:00–4:45, Sunday 1:00–4:45.

HOXIE HOUSE (C. 1675)

# Saugus

*Iron Works House (c. 1646)*

Saugus Iron Works National Historic Site
244 Central Street
617-233-0050

The Iron Works House is a typical seventeenth-century frame dwelling, basically medieval in character, with steep gabled roofs, ornamented overhangs, and small leaded casement windows. The interior features exposed beams, low ceilings, and authentic reproductions of seventeenth-century furnishings. It is the only surviving building of the original Iron Works complex to remain standing. The original plant, built by John Winthrop in 1650, began America's iron and steel industry and operated here for 20 years. The Iron Works House was used as living quarters and a school for iron workers. Some of the rooms are devoted to exhibits of seventeenth-century architecture, building hardware, and tools. A second-floor room is devoted to Wallace Nutting, a photographer and antiquarian who was instrumental in preserving the house. The house, now part of Saugus Iron Works National Historic Site, is open April 1–October 31, daily 9:00–5:00; winter hours, 9:00–4:00. Admission.

# Scituate

*The Cudsworth House (1797)*

First Parish Road
617-545-1083

This small, gambrel-roofed Cape, home of the Scituate Historical Society, is built around a chimney dating to 1646. The interior of the house appears as a home in the early American tradition. The furnishings have all been donated or loaned by members of the society. Of particular note is a piano brought from London in 1725, early samplers, a collection of early pewter, Staffordshire, and Chinese export porcelain. In the old kitchen, the large fireplace has a beehive oven and a huge cauldron, forged by Mordecai Lincoln, an ancestor of President Lincoln. In the shed, a loom, which is still in use, was used to weave the curtains throughout the first floor of the house. The barn houses farm tools and a coach used by Lafayette. The house is open mid-June–mid-September, Wednesday–Saturday 2:00–5:00. Admission.

## The Mann Farmhouse (late 1700s)

Greenfield Lane
617-545-1083

The construction of The Mann Farmhouse and Historical Museum spans nearly three centuries. In the cellar may be seen the original foundation of fieldstones, which dates back to the late 1600s. The main house that now stands here was built during the latter 1700s on the original foundation. It is a typical full Cape with a large central chimney. The ell was added in 1825 and served as a summer kitchen and workshop. Five generations of the Mann family lived in this house, and their artifacts, including primitive Pilgrim furniture, carpenter and shoe making tools, military items, china, toys, and early farming equipment, are on display. The grounds, restored by the Scituate Garden Club, are famous for their profusion of crocus, which bloom every spring. The house is maintained by the Scituate Historical Society and is open mid-June–mid-September, Wednesday–Saturday 2:00–5:00. Admission.

# Sheffield

## Dan Raymond House (c. 1770s)

Shefield Village Green
413-229-2694

This typical center-entrance colonial, home to the Sheffield Historical Society, is more interesting for its legend than its architecture. It was built in the 1770s by Dan Raymond, a prosperous local merchant with Tory leanings, who prompted the felling of a liberty tree set up on the village green in 1776. Charged with the offense, Raymond was forced to walk between two rows of townspeople and ask pardon of each one. The "Sheffield Tory," as he was called, later had a change of heart, for he was chosen an assessor and chairman of a committee to engage recruits for the Continental Army. He and his wife, Anne Noble, granddaughter of Sheffield's first white settler, named their ninth son George Washington Raymond. The original one-story house had been expanded several times and was restored in between 1982 and 1983. The house is open year-round every Friday, 1:30–4:00, for special events and by appointment. Donation.

# Shrewsbury

## General Artemus Ward Home (1672)

736 Main Street
508-842-8900

This was the home of General Artemus Ward, head of the Massachusetts troops during the American Revolution and chief commander at the siege of Boston (1775) until the arrival of George Washington. Partially built in 1672 and enlarged in 1785, the house has recently undergone renovations. It is an unusual pre-revolutionary house, in that the two-and-a-half-story shingled house has two front entrances and two red brick chimneys. It has been preserved as a memorial to General Ward by Harvard University and is furnished throughout with family artifacts, including the desk used by the general while in command of the Continental Army. The house is open mid-April–November, Tuesday–Saturday 10:00–12:00 and 1:00–4:00, Sunday 1:00–5:00. Free.

# Stockbridge

## Chesterwood (1901)

Williamsville Road (off Route 183 South)
413-298-3579

Daniel Chester French (1850–1931), America's foremost sculptor of public monuments, lived and worked at Chesterwood, his summer home, for 34 summers. Here he created such national treasures as the *Minute Man* (1875) in Concord, Massachusetts, and the seated *Abraham Lincoln* (1922), for the Memorial in Washington, D.C. The site features the artist's studio (1897) and the colonial Revival main house (1901) both designed by Henry Bacon, and a barn, which is now a sculpture gallery. The house, a two-and-one-half-story Georgian Revival, features French's work and his collection of furniture, paintings, and decorative arts, which span three centuries. The studio is perhaps the most interesting, with its 23-foot-high doors and a modeling table on railroad tracks that enabled French to roll his monumental sculptures outdoors to see their effect in natural light. Many of French's works, as well as his tools and equipment, can be seen in the studio and barn renovated as a gallery. Owned by the National Trust for Historic Preservation, Chesterwood is open May 1–October 31, daily 10:00–5:00. Admission.

## Merwin House (c. 1825)

39 Main Street
617-227-3956

Also called Tranquility, this late Federal-style brick house, with twelve-over-twelve windows, two chimneys, and a shingled ell added at the end of the nineteenth century, was the former home of Mrs. Vipont Merwin. It contains a collection of European and American furniture and decorative arts, mostly Victorian. It reflects the elegant lifestyle of a family who lived in Stockbridge at the turn of the century, when the Berkshires became a fashionable summer resort. It is owned by SPNEA and is open June 1–mid-October, Tuesday, Thursday, Saturday, and Sunday 12:00–5:00. Admission.

## Mission House (1739)

Main Street
413-298-3239

This plain clapboard house with a carved Connecticut Valley door (dragged by oxen 50 miles from Westfield, Connecticut) was built for the Reverend John Sargent, the first missionary to the Stockbridge Indians. In 1735, when Sargent first established his lonely outpost here, the area was a wilderness. Living in a simple cabin, he befriended the Indians and learned their language. When he later married Abigail Williams, the daughter of an English land speculator, he built a house for her on Prospect Hill. The front part of the house was Abigail's domain, while the back end had a separate entrance and long corridor, allowing the Indians access to the reverend's study. In 1927, the house was acquired by Mabel Choate, an art collector and philanthropist, who had it dismantled and moved to its present site on Main Street. It was completely restored and furnished with period pieces (some original) and is surrounded by a perennial garden with dwarf trees. There is also a small self-interpretive Indian Museum on the property. The house is maintained by the Trustees of Reservations and is open late May–mid-October, Tuesday–Saturday 10:00–5:00, Sunday, Monday, and holidays 11:00–4:00. Admission.

## Naumkeag (1885–1886)

Prospect Hill Road
413-298-3239

NAUMKEAG (1885–1886) This 26-room, shingled, gabled, and dormered Norman-style "cottage" was designed by architect Stanford White. It was built for Joseph Choate, a famous New York lawyer, who argued many important cases before the Supreme Court. He has been credited with successfully postponing the graduated income tax in America for nearly two years. Naumkeag, meaning "Haven of Peace," is surrounded by unusual landscaping and gardens, particularly the Fountain Steps, framed by birches, the brick-walled Chinese Garden, and the Rose Garden. A guided tour of the house enables visitors to see two floors furnished with the original collections of seventeenth-, eighteenth-, and nineteenth-century furnishings, porcelain, paintings, and rugs. The property is maintained by the Trustees of Reservations and is open Memorial Day–Labor Day, Tuesday–Sunday and holidays; September–mid-October, Saturday and Sunday, 10:00–4:15. Admission.

## Sturbridge
*Old Sturbridge Village*

Route 20
508-347-3362

This 200-acre living history museum is a re-creation of a typical New England farming village between 1790 and 1840. More than 40 buildings restored and relocated from throughout New England represent the range of activities and interests typical of life in the early nineteenth century. As an agricultural community, it focuses much of the attention on farm life, but there are also craftsmen, printers, tinsmiths, cobblers, blacksmiths, and village women carrying on their daily activities. Authentically costumed interpreters are on hand to talk to visitors and give demonstrations of their crafts. Several period houses, often with the housewife cooking in the kitchen or tending her herb garden, can be toured. Many seasonal activities take place here throughout the year. Gifts, food, and picnic facilities are available. It is open April–October, daily 9:00–5:00; November–May, Tuesday–Sunday 10:00–4:00. (Closed January 1 and December 25.) Admission.

# Sudbury

## Wayside Inn (c. 1700)

Old Boston Post Road
508-443-8846

One of the oldest inns in the country, this three-story, gambrel-roofed frame house was made famous by Longfellow's *Tales of a Wayside Inn*. Originally built by Samuel Howe and owned and operated by his descendants for four generations, it was called the Howe Tavern. The name was later changed to the Red Horse Tavern, and eventually, to the Wayside Inn, to capitalize on the famous poem. It was purchased by Henry Ford in the late 1920s, completely restored and furnished with authentic American period pieces. It has been ravaged by fire twice since then, but restored and refurbished each time. It remains a working inn today, offering Yankee fare and comfortable rooms at reasonable prices. There are also several museum rooms for viewing (daily 9:00–6:00). Operated by the Trustees of Wayside Inn, it is open year-round, daily, 9:00–6:00 (closed December 25). The gristmill operates April–November, and the school is open May–October. Picnic grounds. Free.

# Swampscott
## *Sir John Humphrey House (1634)*

99 Paradise Road
617-592-6258

This house was built for Sir John Humphrey, a wealthy barrister from Dorchester, England, and a member of the Massachusetts Bay Company. He was given a grant of 1500 acres in Swampscott, and when he arrived in 1634 with his wife, Lady Susan, they brought with them a supply of ammunition, heifers, and the bricks and oak beams to build this house. A two-and-a-half-story, seventeenth-century dwelling, it has a large overhang and a huge chimney. There are many interesting interior details, such as a corner staircase, carved paneling, original ceiling beams of white oak with wooden pegs, handmade bricks and mortar mixed with seaweed, and wide floorboards with handmade nails. (Such wide floorboards were often called "king's boards" because the Massachusetts Colony was required to reserve all wide timber for the king's fleet.) Four rooms are furnished with period antiques. The house, now headquarters for the Swampscott Historical Society, is open April–October by appointment. Free.

# Tisbury
## *The Jirah Luce House (1804)*

Beach Road
508-627-4441

The Jirah Luce House, a modest, two-story Cape Cod dwelling with twin chimneys, twelve-over-twelve windows, and a pedimented doorway, is named for its original owner. It has been a residence for a succession of families, including Rufus Spalding, a Tisbury physician, postmaster, and justice of the peace. It contains eight rooms of exhibits highlighting life in nineteenth-century Tisbury. The collection includes marine antiques, clothing, household goods, and toys. A strong emphasis is on marine history of the area, as Vineyard Haven Harbor was at one time an important harbor. Sometimes as many as 300 vessels would be anchored here, waiting for the turn of the tide to take them through Vineyard Sound. (Tisbury is another name for Vineyard Haven.) The Museum is maintained by the Dukes County Historical Society and is open mid-June–September. Admission.

# Topsfield
*Parson Capen House (1683)*

1 Howlett Street
508-887-8845

Considered by architectural historians an outstanding example of Elizabethan design, this weathered clapboard dwelling with a massive chimney and a high-pitched gabled roof was built by the Reverend Joseph Capen for his bride, Priscilla Appleton, daughter of an affluent Ipswich family. It was a very spacious and grand house for a minister, with its three floors and six rooms (two per floor), but the house was supposedly built with the financial help of his father-in-law. The framing beams are exposed, and the wall and ceiling areas in the parlor are plastered with seventeenth-century plaster made of cow and horse hairs mixed with lime and sand. The house is furnished with period pieces, many of them rare and unusual, such as an Essex County chest, a ventilated cupboard for storing food, and an arm chair inscribed on the back "P. Capen, 1708." Maintained by the Topsfield Historical Society, it is open mid-June–mid-September, Wednesday, Friday, and Sunday 1:00–4:40. Tea is served on Wednesday and on special occasions. Admission.

# Waltham
*Gore Place (1805–1806)*

52 Gore Street
617-894-2798

Built for Mr. and Mrs. Christopher Gore, this is one of the finest examples in New England of an estate of the Federal period. Gore was the seventh governor of Massachusetts (1809–1810) and served in the U.S. Senate from 1812 to 1816. Mrs. Gore worked closely with the architect J.G. Legrand on the plans for the house, which included a complicated floor plan of ovals, concave and convex wall surfaces of high proportions, and a graceful spiral staircase. The design of the house is a large center pavilion symmetrically connected by wings on each side, for a total length of 175 feet. The house contained many innovative features when it was built, such as a bathing tub, a Rumford kitchen, and a ventilator. It is beautifully furnished with many pieces original to the house. Gore Place is owned and maintained by the Gore Place

GORE PLACE (1805–1806)

Society and is open for guided tours mid-April–mid-November, Tuesday–Saturday 10:00–5:00, Sunday 2:00–5:00. Admission.

## The Vale/Lyman House (1793)

185 Lyman Street
617-893-7232 (house)
617-891-7095 (greenhouse)

Samuel McIntire designed The Vale, an elegant country house, for Boston merchant Theodore Lyman in 1793, and construction was completed five years later. Originally Adamesque in style with a main block with two attached wings, it was remodeled in 1882 with the addition of a third floor and interior Victorian details. Furnishings include eighteenth- and nineteenth-century decorative arts, the oval room having been restored with reproductions of the original wallpaper and furniture. The grounds of the estate were designed by an English gardener and are quite lovely. Lyman, an enthusiastic horticulturist and gentleman farmer, had greenhouses erected for the cultivation of exotic fruits and flowers. The greenhouses still display a wide variety of historic and contemporary plants and are open for tours and plant sales. The property is maintained by SPNEA and is often rented for weddings and parties. The house is open by appointment for groups of 10 or more, and the greenhouses are open year-round, Monday–Saturday 9:30–3:30. Donation.

# Wayland

*The Grout-Heard House (1740)*

12 Cochituate Road
508-358-7959

The land this house is built on was originally granted to Thomas Cakebread in 1639 as an enticement to build a gristmill to grind the corn for the first settlers of Sudbury (Wayland). Many additions and restorations have been made to this now handsome white clapboard colonial with bow windows and an ell, which was moved once from its site and then back again. It is now the home of the Wayland Historical Society, which has done a fine job of furnishing the period rooms. A children's room on the second floor with dolls and toys is particularly delightful. The house is open for many special events and on some Sunday afternoons in the spring when guided tours are given (also by appointment). Free.

# Wellesley

*Dadmun-McNamara House (1824)*

229 Washington Street
617-235-6690

DADMUN-MCNAMARA HOUSE
(1824)

At the intersection of two busy main thoroughfares (Worcester Turnpike and Washington Street) in the middle of Wellesley Hills stands this pretty, white center-entrance colonial surrounded in summertime by gardens. It originally stood about two miles up the road, at the junction of the Worcester Turnpike and Weston Road, where a tollgate was located. Daniel Dadmun, one of the early tollkeepers, built this house in 1824 on 20 acres of rolling land at that intersection. It was moved in 1975 to its present site in Wellesley Hills to become the headquarters of the Wellesley Historical Society. The house contains period rooms, special exhibits, and research archives, all relating to the history of Wellesley. It is open year-round, Monday and Saturday 2:00–4:30 and by appointment; Monday–Thursday 10:00–4:30. Donation.

# Wellfleet
## The Samuel Rider House (late 1700s)

Gull Pond Road
508-349-3785

This small clapboard house typifies an early Cape Cod dwelling of the late 1700s and early 1800s, with a central doorway and two windows on each side. The Wellfleet Historical Society, through a special-use permit from the Cape Cod National Seashore, attempts to re-create at the Rider House a Cape Cod household of many years ago. Rooms are furnished with pieces from the society's collection and with furniture placed on loan. In addition to the house, there are a woodshed, a privy, a carriage shed, and a barn where old tools are displayed. Strawberry beds, gardens, and a small orchard are carefully tended. Special exhibits are on display during July and August, Monday–Friday 2:00–5:00. Admission.

# Wenham
## The Clafin-Richards House (c. 1662–1673)

132 Main Street
508-468-2377

This mid-seventeenth-century medieval house, with gable overhangs and diamond-shaped windows, is noted for the unique ogee braces in the corner of the original dwelling room, furnished around 1600. The other three rooms of the house display architectural details and furnishings of three later periods: 1690,

1735, and 1850. On exhibit with the period furniture are outstanding examples of the museum's large collection of quilts, textiles, costumes and accessories, fans, needlework, tin, and woodenware. The museum building, a modern attachment to the house, is known for its International Doll Collection of Elizabeth Richards Horton, who was born in the Claflin-Richards House. The museum was one of the first in the country to specialize in the preservation, study, and display of old dolls, and its collection of dolls, dollhouses, and toys is excellent. Many special exhibits and activities are held here throughout the year. The house and museum are incorporated as the Wenham Historical Association and Museum, Inc., and are open year-round Monday–Friday 11:00–4:00, Saturday 1:00–4:00, Sunday 2:00–5:00. Admission.

# Westfield
## The Dewey House (c. 1735)

87 South Maple Street
413-562-3657

This museum house was originally a four-room saltbox that was renovated in the 1800s to the popular Federalist style to include a parlor, a buttery, two large bedrooms, and a child's room. Jedediah Dewey, who built this house, came to Westfield in 1667, along with his two brothers, to establish the first successful mill for sawing and grinding. The house changed hands many times but was restored to its original early farmhouse appearance in 1977 by the Western Hampden Historical Society. It is furnished throughout with period furnishings and is open for tours by appointment and at the annual Christmas Candlelight Tour in December. Admission.

# Weston
## Golden Ball Tavern (1768–1770)

662 Boston Post Road
617-894-1751

Isaac Jones, a successful merchant and local politician, built this large Georgian-style inn, which became a popular dining and dancing spot for both Tories and patriots during the pre-Revolution years. In 1775, however, the "Weston Tea Party," similar to the one in Boston, was staged here after Jones, considered "a rank Tory," continued to sell tea at the inn.

GOLDEN BALL TAVERN
(1768–1770)

It is now a unique archaeological and historic museum, with furnished period rooms showing changes made by six generations of the same family. Operated by the Golden Ball Tavern Trust, it is open April–November, Sunday and Wednesday 1:30–4:00. Admission.

## *Josiah Smith Tavern (1757)*

358 Boston Post Road
617-893-8695

This large, white, rambling building with a gambrel roof, a lean-to, and an attached barn, overlooks the town green in Weston. It was a popular stagecoach stop, often the first on the Boston to New York Post Road. During revolutionary war days, it was the scene of a spy incident, when a British officer appeared here in the guise of a countryman and, later that night, barely escaped "being tarred and feathered by thirty angry Liberty Men." The main part of the house has two rooms displaying Weston artifacts and furnishings and is the headquarters for the Weston Historical Society (open year-round, Wednesday 2:00–4:00). The restored barn is used by the Women's Community League of Weston for activities and a popular thrift shop (open September–May, Tuesdays 10:00–4:00). Free.

JOSIAH DAY HOUSE (1754)

# West Springfield

*Josiah Day House (1754)*

70 Park Street
413-734-6587

This most unique saltbox-style house is made of brick, with an unusually wide chimney and a lean-to at the rear. It is believed to be the only dated brick saltbox house of this age in the country. It was built by Josiah Day in 1754 and was lived in continuously by his descendants for well over 150 years. The Day family was prominent in local affairs. Restored and maintained by the Ramapogue Historical Society, the rooms, with huge fireplaces, are furnished largely with Day family possessions. It is open mid-June–November 1, Saturday and Sunday 1:00–5:00 and by appointment 1:00–5:00. Admission.

*Storrowtown Village (c. nineteenth century)*

Eastern States Exposition
1305 Memorial Avenue
413-787-0136

Nestled in a quiet nook of the Eastern States Exposition fairgrounds, Storrowton is the embodiment of an early New England village, with authentic, furnished period buildings surrounding a picturesque green. Philanthropist Helen O. Storrow, of Boston, founded the village in the 1920s to house home department exhibits for the Eastern States Exposition. She selected and purchased eighteenth- and nineteenth-century buildings around New England and had them taken apart and brought here, where they were carefully reconstructed. Dating from 1767 to 1834, the buildings include a steepled meetinghouse, a blacksmith shop, a tavern, a law office, and two residences—the **Phillips House** (c. 1769) and the **Potter Mansion** (c. 1776). Guided tours are given June–Labor Day, daily 11:30–4:00 and by appointment. Admission.

# Weymouth
## *Abigail Adams Birthplace (1685)*

North Street
617-878-4330

The house is a restoration of the ell section of the original dwelling where Abigail Smith Adams, daughter of a Weymouth clergyman, was born on November 11, 1744. She lived here until her marriage in 1764 to John Adams, who later became the second president of the United States. Her son, John Quincy Adams, was the sixth U. S. president. The house is furnished with early American antiques, and some of the furnishings are original to the Smith family. The house is maintained by the Abigail Adams Historical Society, and guided tours are given July 1–Labor Day, Tuesday-Sunday 1:00–4:00. Admission.

# Woburn
## *Count Rumford House (1714)*

90 Elm Street
617-933-0781

A large sign attached to the modified gambrel roof of this simple, square clapboarded country house tells you that it is the birthplace of Count Rumford. He was born here in 1753 as Benjamin Thompson, in the house his grandfather built. He became a scientific genius, best known in this country for his invention of the Rumford cooking stove, found in many of the better homes of the late eighteenth century. An

COUNT RUMFORD HOUSE (1714)

ardent Tory during the Revolution, he moved to England in 1776, and then to Germany, where he served as an administrator in Bavaria and in 1791 was named a count of the Holy Roman Empire. The house contains furnishings and artifacts pertaining to the count, particularly his inventions and an original "Rumford Roaster," one of the first fireless cookers marketed. The house is maintained by the Rumford Historical Association and is open April–October, Wednesday–Sunday 1:00–4:30; November–March, Saturday and Sunday 1:00–4:30. Free.

# Worcester
## *Salisbury Mansion (1772)*

40 Highland Street
508-753-8278

The first of the many Salisbury houses to be built in Worcester, this one was built by Stephen Salisbury, Sr., owner of the town's most successful hardware business in the late 1700s. It is a two-story clapboard and frame building of traditional colonial design. It was extensively renovated by the family in 1820 with the addition of a neoclassical portico and two elegant adjoining drawing rooms for entertaining. The

Worcester Historical Museum has restored the mansion to re-create the home life of the prominent Salisbury family during the 1830s. It is furnished with the museum's collection of period furnishings. The mansion is open year-round, Tuesday–Sunday 1:00–4:00. Admission.

# Yarmouth

## *Captain Bangs Hallet House (1740)*

Old King's Highway (Route 6A)
508-362-3021

Originally a small four-room Cape, this dwelling was enlarged in the 1840s in the Greek Revival style, with a front porch and pillars, by Captain Hallet when he retired from the China and India trade. It is now the home of the Historical Society of Old Yarmouth and is filled with period antiques and a wealth of information on the maritime history of the area. The 1740 kitchen is furnished to period with early household equipment. Next to the house are the Botanic Trails, winding for two miles through forests, fields, and pond area (maps provided at the Gate House). The house is open June–August, Monday–Friday 1:00–4:00. Admission.

CAPTAIN BANGS HALLET HOUSE (1740)

## *Winslow Crocker House (c. 1780)*

250 Old King's Highway (Rt. 6A)
617-227-3956

This Georgian-style, shingled house was originally built in West Barnstable, but in 1935 Mary Thatcher had the house dismantled and carefully reassembled in Yarmouthport. She furnished it with her own collection of seventeenth- to mid-nineteenth-century antiques, including a rare seventeenth-century wooden cradle, hooked rugs, ceramics, and pewter, which she had collected in the early part of the twentieth century. Many fine examples of furniture made by New England craftsmen in the colonial and Federal periods highlight the handsomely paneled interior of the rooms. The house is maintained by SPNEA and is open June 1–mid-October, Tuesday, Thursday, Saturday, and Sunday 12:00–5:00. Admission.

# Additional Houses

**AGAWAM**

Captain Charles Leonard House, 663 Main Street, 508-786-9421

**AMESBURY**

Mary B. Eddy House, 277 Main Street, 617-388-1361

**BARNSTABLE**

Sturgis Library, Main Street, 508-362-6636

**BEVERLY**

Long Hill, 572 Essex Street, 508-921 1944

**BOLTON**

Saywer House, 676 Main Street, 508-779-6654

**BOSTON**

W. H. Prescott House, 55 Beacon Street, 617-742-3190

**BOXFORD**

Holyoke-French House, Elm Street, 617-887-9545

**BROOKLINE**

Edward Devotion House, 347 Harvard Street, 617-566-5747

Fairsted, 99 Warren Street, 617-566-1689

**CAMBRIDGE**

Cooper-Frost-Austin House, 21 Linnaean Street, 617-227-3956

Margaret Fuller House, 71 Cherry Street, 617-547-4680

**CHARLESTOWN**

Commandant's House, Navy Yard, 617-242-5601

**CHATHAM**

Josiah Mayo House, 536 Main Street,
508-945-0342

**CHICOPEE**

Edward Bellamy House, 91 Church Street,
413-594-6496

**COHASSET**

Caleb Lothrop House, 14 Summer Street,
617-383-6930

**CONCORD**

The Wright Tavern, 2 Lexington Road,
508-369-6219

**COTUIT**

S. B. Doltridge Homestead, 1148 Main Street,
508-428-8189

**DANVERS**

Judge S. Holten House, 171 Holten Street,
508-777-1666

**DEIGHTON**

Winslow-David House, 1217 Williams Street,
508-669-5514

**DORCHESTER**

Pierce House, 24 Oakton Street, 617-227-3956

**EAST LONGMEADOW**

Historical Headquarters Museum, 25 Maple
Street, 413-527-4417

**EASTHAM**

Captain E. Penniman House, Fort Hill Road,
508-255-3421

**EDGARTOWN**

Thomas Cooke House, Cooke Street,
508-627-4441

The Vincent House, Main Street, 508-627-8017

**FALL RIVER**

E.H. Brayton House, 451 Main Street,
508-679-1071

**FALMOUTH**

Katherine Lee Bates House, 16 West Main Street,
508-548-4857

**FITCHBURG**

Vickery House, 53 Prospect Street, 508-345-1157

**GLOUCESTER**

Captain E. Davis House, 27 Pleasant Street,
508-283-0455

Stillington Hall, Quarry Road, 508-283-0332

**HAMPDEN**
   Thornton W. Burgess House, 789 Main Street,
      413-566-8034

**HANOVER**
   Stetson House, 514 Hanover Street, 617-826-6254

**HAVERHILL**
   Dustin House, 665 Hillside Avenue,
      (no telephone)

   Winnekenni Castle, 307 Kenoza Avenue,
      508-374-4626

**HOLDEN**
   The Hendricks House, Main Street, 508-852-6290

**LEXINGTON**
   Captain William Smith House, North Great Road,
      617-862-1450

**LOWELL**
   Whistler House Museum, 243 Worthen Street,
      508-452-7641

**MARLBOROUGH**
   Peter Rice Homestead, 377 Elm Street,
      (no telephone)

**MIDDLEBOROUGH**
   The Eddy Homestead, Eddyville, 508-947-3615

   Middleborough Historical Society, Jackson Street,
      508-866-4414

**MILTON**
   Suffolk Resolve House, 1370 Canton Avenue,
      617-333-0644

**NEEDHAM**
   Kingsbury-Whitaker House, 53 Glendoon Road,
      617-444-5640

**NEWBURY**
   Spencer-Pierce-Little House, Little's Lane,
      508-227-3956

**NEW SALEM**
   Whitaker-Clary House, Elm Street, 508-544-6807

**NEWTON**
   Durant-Kenrick House, 286 Waverly Avenue,
      617-235-6555

**NORTHAMPTON**
   Clapp House, 148 South Street, 413-584-0569

**NORTH ANDOVER**
   Parson Barnard House, 179 Osgood Street,
      508-686-4035

**NORTH EASTON**
   Borderland, Massapoag Avenue, 508-238-6566

## NORTH READING
Putnam House, on the green, 508-664-2156

## NORWELL
Jacob's Farm, Main Street, 617-659-1888

## OAK BLUFFS
Cottage City, Camp Ground, 508-693-0085

## ORANGE
Stephen French House, 41 North Main Street, 508-544-3755

## PLAINFIELD
Shaw-Hudson House, Main Street, 413-634-5607

## RANDOLPH
Jonathan Belcher House, 360 North Main Street 617-963-4385

## ROCKLAND
1745 House, Goddard Avenue, 617-871-1892

## ROCKPORT
Paper House, Pigeon Hill Street, 508-546-2629

## SALEM
Pioneer Village, Forest River Park, 508-744-0180

Cotting-Smith Assembly House, 138 Federal Street, 508-744-3390

Pierce-Nichols House, 80 Federal Street, 508-744-3390

## SANDWICH
Thornton W. Burgess Museum, 4 Water Street, 508-888-4668

## SCITUATE
Old Oaken Bucket Homestead, Old Oaken Bucket Road, 617-545-1083

## SOUTHAMPTON
Clark-Chapman House, Main Street, 413-527-3933

## STERLING
Sterling Historical Society House, 7 Pine Street, 508-422-6139

## STOCKBRIDGE
Old Corner House, Main Street, 413-298-3822

## STOUGHTON
M. B. Eddy House, 133 Central Street, 617-344-3904

## SUDBURY
Hosmer House, Old Sudbury Road, 508-443-8891/443-8205

Woods-Davis House, on the Town Green, 508-443-8891/443-8205

**SWAMPSCOTT**
  M. B. Eddy House, 23 Paradise Road,
    617-599-1853

**TYRINGHAM**
  Gingerbread House, Tyringham Road,
    413-243-0654

**UXBRIDGE**
  Cornet John Farnum House, Mendon Street,
    508-278-2041

**WALTHAM**
  Stonehurst, 577 Beaver Street, 617-893-0381

**WATERTOWN**
  Abraham Browne House, 562 Main Street,
    617-227-3956

  The Edmund Fowle House, 28 Marshall Street,
    617-926-9051

**WESTBOROUGH**
  Nathan Fisher House, Route 9, 508-366-7411

**WILMINGTON**
  Colonel J. Harding Tavern, 430 Salem Street,
    508-658-3311

**WORCESTER**
  The Oaks, 140 Lincoln Street, 508-829-9101

**WRENTHAM**
  Wampum House, 677 South Street
  (no telephone)

# VERMONT

## Addison

*Chimney Point Tavern (c. 1784)*

Routes 17 and 125 at Champlain Bridge
802-759-2412

Situated on the banks of the Champlain River, this is the site of one of the oldest settlements in Vermont. A small band of French colonists built a village here in the late seventeenth century. When they abandoned it at the close of the French and Indian War (1759), they burned it to the ground, and it was the grim sight of chimneys rising from blackened ruins that gave the place its name. The tavern, once known as the Barnes House, served as an inn for more than 100 years. This large, brick structure with a clapboarded ell, painted yellow with green shutters, is now in the process of restoration by the Vermont Division for Historic Preservation. It is expected to be formally opened in June 1991 with an interpretive program and people demonstrating Native American crafts and music. It will be open June 22–Columbus Day, Wednesday–Sunday 9:30–5:30. Free.

THE JOHN STRONG DAR MANSION (1795)

## The John Strong DAR Mansion (1795)

Route 17
802-759-2309

This large, square, Georgian-style house is considered one of the most elaborate brick dwellings ever erected in Vermont. It features a central gable, hip roof, Palladian window, and a pedimented porch supported by fluted columns. The interior is lavishly detailed as well, with fireplaces in each of the main rooms, their mantelpieces embellished with cornices, rope moldings, and dentils. The house was built by John Strong, an early settler, a prominent citizen, and the first judge of Addison County Court. His descendants lived here through five generations. It was purchased in 1934 by the Vermont State DAR, who restored it and furnished it in keeping with the period. Some family furniture and portraits are on display, as well as documents and interesting relics belonging to Judge Strong. It is open mid-May–mid-October, Friday–Monday 10:00–5:00. Admission.

# Brandon

## Stephen A. Douglas Birthplace (c. 1800)

2 Grove Street

A large marble monument in front of this little story-and-a-half frame cottage proclaims it to be the birthplace of Stephen A. Douglas (1813–1861). Douglas, a U.S. representative and senator and the Democratic nominee for president of the United States in 1860, was born here, and the house, with its latticed entryway, quaint double doors, low ceilings, and high mantels with huge open fireplaces, remains virtually unaltered since that time. Douglas' presidential debates with his opponent, Abraham Lincoln, became legendary and earned him the nickname, "the little giant." Stephen Arnold and his brother, relatives of Douglas, who also lived here, were sea captains who eventually settled in this area. It is believed that the house was built by ship carpenters, due to the design of the double front door, stairway, and rounded walls. The house is now owned by the Lake Dunmore Chapter DAR and contains period furnishings and Douglas memorabilia. The house is open by appointment only. (Write in care of the house, 2 Grove Street, Brandon, VT 05733.) Free.

MARVIN NEWTON HOUSE (1835)

# Brookfield
*Marvin Newton House (1835)*

Ridge Road
802-276-3325

The Brookfield Historical Society is housed in a two-and-a-half-story Federal-style house with dark stained clapboards, gable roof, and twelve-over-twelve windows. There are nine rooms in the house, many containing soapstone fireplaces, and it is furnished with period antiques, including early kitchen equipment, needlework, costumes, and old hand tools. The house is open July and August, Sunday 2:00–5:00 and by appointment. Donation.

# Brownington
*Old Stone House (1834–1836)*

Brownington Village
802-754-2022

Brownington Village has a small complex of buildings associated with the former Brownington Academy. The most important one is the four-story

granite building, built single-handedly by the then
headmaster of Brownington Academy, the Reverend
Alexander Lucius Twilight. Twilight (1795–1857) is
believed to be the first person of black ancestry to
graduate from an American college (Middlebury,
1823), as well as the first to serve in a state legislature
(Vermont, 1836–1838). Legend has it that he quarried
the stone from neighboring fields and built the house
himself with only the help of a single ox. He named
the building Athenian Hall, and it was used as a dor-
mitory for the students. The building served the
school for almost a quarter of a century and, after the
death of Twilight in 1857, it was sold to a family who
used it as a home and boarding house. The Orleans
County Historical Society acquired it in 1918 and has
used it as a museum ever since. Today it contains 25
rooms of historical exhibits from all over Orleans
County. It is open mid-May–June 30 and September
1–mid-October, Friday–Tuesday, and during July and
August, every day 11:00–5:00. Admission. The society
also owns the **Twilight Homestead** (c. 1829), which
is now undergoing renovations and, when finished,
will house much of the society's collection of early
farm tools and machinery.

OLD STONE HOUSE (1834–1836)

# Burlington

*Ethan Allen Homestead (1787)*

The Intervale
Winooski Valley Park District
802-865-4556

ETHAN ALLEN HOMESTEAD
(1787)

This reconstructed rustic, one-and-a-half-story, post and beam farmhouse is the only remaining dwelling of Vermont's founding fathers and the oldest known structure in Burlington. It was the home of one of Vermont's and America's most colorful heroes, Ethan Allen, from 1787 until his death in 1789. He lived here with his second wife, Fanny, and their children, and the homestead is a fine example of the way of life of a pioneer family living on the northern frontier at that time. The furnishings are a mixture of period

objects and accurate reproductions of decorative arts and domestic artifacts. A large new barn serves as an orientation center, with a multimedia show, gift shop, education spaces, and exhibit areas. Ongoing archaeological work can be observed as part of an open-air exhibit in progress. The property is maintained by the Ethan Allen Homestead Trust and is open May–June, Tuesday–Sunday 1:00–5:00; and July and August, Monday–Saturday 10:00–5:00, Sunday 1:00–5:00; September and October, daily 1:00–5:00. Admission.

# Calais
## Kent Museum (1837)

Kent's Corner
802-828-2291

This nineteenth-century landmark, a large brick building with four chimneys, was a favorite stagecoach stop on the Montpelier-Canada stage road. It was owned by the Kent family, who lived here for several generations and included such well-known Vermont personalities as A. Atwater Kent, a radio tycoon, and Louise Andrews Kent, long known as "Mrs. Appleyard" through her cookbooks. Now owned by the Vermont Historical Society, it houses native furnishings that portray the lifestyle of thrifty, resourceful Vermonters. The attached country store features Mrs. Kent's famous collection of miniature rooms, meticulously executed right down to tiny reproductions of Oriental rugs. It is open July 1–Labor day, Tuesday–Sunday 12:00–5:00, and weekends in fall foliage season. Admission.

# Castleton
## Higley Homestead (1811)

Main Street
802-468-5328

This brick house, with twin chimneys and twelve-over-twelve windows, is the home of the Castleton Historical Society. A marble arch and fanlight over the front door and a pedimented porch roof supporting two pillars accentuate the front entrance. Early examples of the original stenciling can be seen on some of the interior walls, while other rooms have restored stenciling. Exhibited throughout the rooms is the society's collection of nineteenth- and early twentieth-century furnishings, paintings, costumes, docu-

HIGLEY HOMESTEAD (1811)

ments, photographs, and military memorabilia pertaining to Castleton and Vermont history. The house is open on Sunday afternoons in the summer. Donation.

# Chelsea

## *Lewis House (c. 1830)*

Main Street
802-685-4860

This one-and-a-half-story country cottage, with a small Victorian "setting porch" facing the street, was built by David Hatch sometime around 1830. It was the first house in town to be wired for electric lights (in 1898). It was left to the Chelsea Historical Society by the Lewis family, who used it for 60 years as a summer place, calling it Lewis Lodge. The front parlor, with chair rails and decorated woodwork, has recently been refurbished by the society, but the old kitchen in the ell remains much as it did 100 years ago. Furnishings include costumes, manuscripts, and memorabilia relating to local history. Owned and maintained by the society, it is open during Old

Home Day, Bicentennial Day, and other local cele-  LEWIS HOUSE (C. 1830)
brations, and by request. Free.

# Fairfield

*President Chester A. Arthur Historic Site*

Off Route 36 or 108
802-828-3226

Chester A. Arthur, twenty-first president of the United
States, was born on October 5, 1829, in a small tem-
porary parsonage in Fairfield. The present structure at
this historic site, a small one-story frame house, was
constructed in 1953, from an original photograph, by
the state of Vermont as a replica of the parsonage the
Arthur family moved to in 1830. Arthur's father was a
Baptist minister, and the brick church where he
preached is located on a nearby hillside. The house is
not furnished as a historic house museum but instead
offers a pictorial exhibit of Arthur's life and career. It
is maintained by the Vermont Division for Historic

Preservation and is open June–mid-October, Wednesday–Sunday, 9:30–5:30. Free.

# Ferrisburgh

## *Rokeby (c. 1790)*

Route 7
802-877-3406

Rokeby, situated on a hill overlooking the Champlain Valley, was the home of four generations of the Robinsons, a noted Vermont family. Thomas and Jemima Fish Robinson, Quakers with a rich tradition of writing and study, settled here in 1791, and their large farm became one of the most prosperous in the valley. Throughout its history, Rokeby served as a center of family and community life in Ferrisburgh. It housed early schools, Quaker meetings, the first town library, and the town clerk's office, and was an important stop on the Underground Railway. Frugal Yankees by nature, the Robinsons saved almost every possession they ever accumulated. Today their 11-

room house is filled with two centuries of furnishings, artwork, clothing, and curios capturing the essence of decades gone by. Nearly 100 acres of the original farmlands and orchards still surround the homestead. Operated by the Rowland E. Robinson Memorial Association, it is open May–mid-October, Thursday–Sunday for guided tours at 11:00, 12:30, and 2:00. Admission.

# Grafton

In 1963, Dean Mathey, a successful New York philanthropist-financier, who had summered in Grafton for many years, established the Windham Foundation, which purchased and restored many of the businesses and several houses in this village. The foundation now owns 21 well-restored buildings, has built a cheese factory, opened a nursery and gift shop, and buried the electric, phone, and cable wires. In the **Red Barn** (behind the foundation center offices) there is a museum with old farm tools and vehicles, a replica of the original village store, a wildlife exhibit, and pictures of "before and after" restoration work.

## *The Old Tavern (c. 1801)*

Main Street
802-843-2231

Called "the most elegant little inn in all New England," this old inn has a long and proud tradition. During its first century, it was considered one of the finest stagecoach inns on the Boston–Montreal run. Some of the famous guests who stayed here during the early days included Rudyard Kipling, Teddy Roosevelt, Woodrow Wilson, Daniel Webster, Ulysses S. Grant, and Nathaniel Hawthorne. Following the Depression, a long period of decline befell the inn until it was rescued by The Windham Foundation in 1964. Modernized and winterized, this handsome white clapboard building, with a long second-story balcony, retains much of its early charm. The interior features many authentic details, such as huge hand-hewn beams, soapstone hearths, wood paneling, and old hardware on the doors. The guest rooms and the common rooms are filled with fine antiques and paintings. It is open year-round, except December 24 and 25.

THE SUMNER MEAD HOUSE
(C. 1840)

## The Sumner Mead House (c. 1840)

Main Street
802-843-2344

The Grafton Historical Society is housed in this seven-room farmhouse with attached barn that was also restored by The Windham Foundation. The house is made of solid wood, the original plank construction still intact, with clapboards on the outside and plastered walls within. On display are eighteenth- and nineteenth-century furniture, textiles, tools, paintings and prints, historical documents, artifacts from local industries, school supplies, and memorabilia relating to the history of Grafton. It is open Memorial Day–Columbus Day, Saturday 2:30–4:30, holidays, and by appointment. Admission.

## Grand Isle

### The Hyde Log Cabin (c. 1783)

U.S. Route 2
802-372-5540

Jedediah Hyde, Jr., built this one-and-one-half-story

structure, and it served as a home to members of the Hyde family for nearly 150 years. The cabin, constructed of cedar logs 14 to 18 inches in diameter, consists of one 20' x 25' room with a massive fireplace at one end and an overhead loft. It is considered one of the oldest log cabins in the United States. It contains some original furnishings, as well as furnishings from other homes in the county, agricultural and household implements, maps of the county's original grants, and other items relating to the history and settlement of Grand Isle. It is owned and maintained by the Vermont Division for Historic Preservation and is open July 4–Labor Day, Wednesday–Sunday 9:30–5:30. Donation.

THE HYDE LOG CABIN (C. 1783)

# Lyndon Center
## Shores Memorial Museum (1895–1896)

Main Street
802-626-5742/626-8547

This two-story, Queen Anne–style house was the home of an average working man and retains much of the original interior plumbing and wiring. There are eight rooms in the house, containing the original furnishings of three generations of the Shores-Gage family, which serve to illustrate the lifestyle of a typical Victorian working family of the late nineteenth and early twentieth century. Also on display are many artifacts of local historical significance. The barn behind the house has exhibits of photographs, books, and early tools. The house is maintained by the Lyndon Historical Society and is open for tours during the summer. Donation.

# Manchester

802-362-1405

The main streets of the historic area of Manchester are lined with marble sidewalks and a row of handsome old homes. Some have been converted into inns such as **The 1811 House**, once the home of Mary Lincoln Isham (Robert Todd's daughter), and **The Village Country Inn**, built in 1889 as a summer home for the Kelloggs of cereal fame. Another converted mansion, the **Yester House**, built in 1917, is now the **Southern Vermont Art Center**, with 11 galleries, a library, sculpture garden, garden cafe, and more than 400 acres with botany trails.

HILDINE (1902)

## Hildine (1902)

Route 7A
802-362-1788

Robert Todd Lincoln, the only son of President Abraham Lincoln to survive to maturity, built this Georgian Revival mansion as a summer home at the turn of the century. His decendants lived here until 1975. Tours of the 24-room mansion on the 412-acre estate begin in the restored carriage house with a slide show about Robert Todd. Proceeding into the handsome foyer, visitors are given a demonstration of the 1000-pipe organ, the same one played by the women of the family. The house is completely furnished with original pieces and memorabilia belonging to the Lincoln family, including such treasures as Abraham Lincoln's black stovepipe hat and family photos. There are more than 20 other buildings on the property, including an observatory, and the formal gardens are being restored. Many special events are held here throughout the year, and tours are given mid-May–October, daily 10:00–4:00. Christmas candlelight tours in December. Admission.

# Middlebury
## The Emma Willard House (c. 1810)

131 South Main Street
802-388-3711

Emma Willard, a pioneer in American female education, began her seminary for young women here in 1814. The large, Federal-style brick house with marble lintels over doors and windows was built for her and her husband, Dr. John Willard, around 1809–1810. It was her home for 10 years, and while living here she wrote her epoch-making *Plan for Improving Female Education*, which became the charter for the development of higher education for women in the nineteenth century. The building is now the property of Middlebury College and is used for admissions and financial aid offices. Visits can be arranged as their schedules permit, from 10:00–11:00, 12:00–1:00, 4:00–5:00. Free.

## Gamaliel Painter House (1787)

2 Court Street
802-388-7951

GAMALIEL PAINTER HOUSE (1787)

This elaborate, Federal-style house (the classically detailed doorway was a later Greek Revival addition) is situated on the most prestigious site in town. Overlooking the town green, the four first floor rooms with elegant fireplaces have recently undergone renovations. The chamber of commerce has an information center here, and one of the rooms contains an exhibit of the original drawings of the old building. **The Vermont Folklife Center**, a resource center and archive for Vermont folk art, is located on the lower level. Open year-round, Monday–Friday 9:00–5:00. Free.

## Sheldon Museum (1829)

1 Park Street
802-388-2117

Another large, Federal-style brick house that dominates the center of Middlebury is this one built by Eben Judd in 1829. Judd and his son-in-law, Lebeus Harris, operated a black marble quarry in nearby Shoreham and outfitted the house with six fireplaces of black marble. The house was purchased in 1875 by Henry Sheldon, who had a strong commitment to preserving Vermont's cultural heritage. He began collecting furniture, decorative arts, and paintings by Vermont artists, and his house soon became a repository for such things. In 1882 it was opened to the public as the Sheldon Art Museum—the first incorporated village museum in the United States. Now the Sheldon Museum, its collections have been arranged in period rooms and an old-time country store. It includes a gift shop, research center, and an award-winning garden. It is open year-round for tours June 1–October 31, daily 10:00–5:00 (except Sundays and holidays); November 1–May 31, Wednesday and Friday 1:00–4:00. Admission.

# Montpelier

In 1808, after several other cities held the distinction of being the state capital of Vermont, Montpelier was chosen as the permanent capital city. **The Vermont Museum**, operated by the Vermont Historical Society, is located in the restored nineteenth-century Pavilion Building at 109 Main Street, which was originally the site of the elegant Pavilion Hotel. The museum's vast collections and exhibits aim to interpret the history of the people of Vermont and it is open Monday–Friday 9:00–4:30; July and August, Sunday 10:00–4:00. **Redstone**, the red brick and sandstone Gothic mansion at 26 Terrace Street, once the summer home of renowned political scientist Professor John W. Burgess, is now the offices of the Vermont Secretary of State and the Vermont State Archives. It is open Monday–Friday 7:45–4:30.

# Morrisville
*Noyes House Museum (c. 1820)*

Main Street
802-888-5605

The large, red brick Federal-style house with green shutters, which sits prominently at one end of Main Street, was built by Jedediah Safford in the early nineteenth century. Now the home of the Morrisville Historical Society, it has a most attractive recessed door with handsomely detailed fanlight and sidelights, which opens into a gracious foyer. The 14-room museum contains many objects and furnishings relating to local and regional history, including the Cheney collection of more than 2000 pitchers, toys, paintings, relics from the revolutionary war period, nineteenth-century clothing, and an exhibit of early

NOYES HOUSE MUSEUM
(C. 1820)

medical instruments belonging to one of the first doctors in the region. It is open July 1–Labor Day, Friday–Wednesday 2:00–5:00, and for special events. Admission.

# North Bennington
*The Park-McCullough House (1865)*

West Street
802-442-5441

This 35-room Victorian mansion is considered an excellent example of French Second Empire style, with its elaborate gingerbread, mansard roof, cupola, and long wraparound porch. The interior is equally impressive, with 14-foot ceilings, a sweeping front hall staircase, oak and walnut paneling, parquet floors, marble fireplaces, and bronze chandeliers. It was built by Trenor Park, a young Bennington lawyer

who made a fortune in California by managing the Mariposa gold mines. He came home to build this mansion on the original farmland of his wife's family, who had settled here in 1779. The family's collection of paintings, furniture, Oriental rugs, and porcelain are well documented and on display. The spacious grounds include a Victorian garden, a grapery, a museum shop, a carriage barn that still houses the family carriages and sleighs, and a children's play-house—a tiny replica of the big house. Operated by the Park-McCullough House, it is open May 21–October 31, daily 10:00–4:00, and for special events and concerts.

THE PARK-McCULLOUGH HOUSE (1865)

# Norwich

*Hutchinson-Taylor House (1810)*

Church Street
802-649-2895

The Norwich Historical Society is housed in this small one-and-one-half-story typical Cape-style house with white clapboards and black shutters. The society's collection includes nineteenth-century furnishings, clothing, tools, maps, books, documents, and many objects relating to local history. It conducts genealogical research, guided tours, excursions, and walking tours. It is open year-round, Wednesday and Friday 2:30–4:30 and by appointment. Donation.

# Peacham

## *Peacham Historical Society*

Peacham Village
802-592-3218

Peacham is considered one of the loveliest small villages in the Northeast Kingdom. Most of the houses in the village are painted white and marked with the dates they were built. Just off the main thoroughfare, behind the country store, is a small white three-room Cape-style house with an ell that houses the Peacham Historical Society. On display in the small rooms are furniture, paintings, costumes, quilts, photographs, and documents relating to the town's history. Tours are given in summer and fall by calling the town clerk's office for an appointment.

PEACHAM HISTORICAL SOCIETY

# Plymouth Notch

802-828-3226

The Plymouth Notch Historic District contains a group of houses and buildings relating to the life of Calvin Coolidge, the thirtieth president of the United States. His birthplace, his boyhood home, his grandparents' home, the church and school he attended, the general store operated by his father, and the cheese factory (where you can purchase cheese) now operated by his son, John, can all be visited. The State Division for Historic Preservation maintains five buildings and the stone visitor's center and museum. Guided tours are available mid-May–mid-October, daily 9:30–5:00. Admission.

## *Calvin Coolidge Birthplace (c. 1840)*

This simple, almost primitive-looking building, with narrow clapboard siding and only three small windows on the front, is attached to the General Store. Calvin Coolidge was born in the downstairs bedroom on July 4, 1872. It was the first home of his parents, and when he was four years old, the family moved

CALVIN COOLIDGE BIRTHPLACE (C. 1840)

THE COOLIDGE HOMESTEAD
(C. 1850)

across the road to the larger Coolidge Homestead.
The house has been carefully restored to its appear-
ance in 1872. Most of the furnishings, donated by the
Coolidge family, are original to the house.

## The Coolidge Homestead (c. 1850)

This two-story, white clapboard farmhouse, with
large bay windows on the front and an ell with a
covered porch, is the home where Coolidge lived
most of his life. Here, in the early morning of August
3, 1923, the then vice president was awakened to the
news of Harding's death and immediately sworn in as
president of the United States by his father, Colonel
John Coolidge, a notary public. In 1956 the president's son and his wife gave the house, complete
with all the furnishings that were there on the night
of the swearing in, to the Vermont Board of Historic
Sites.

## The Wilder House (c. 1830)

This large, yellow clapboard house was the childhood home of President Coolidge's mother, Victoria

Josephine Moor. The front sitting room of the house is where she married Colonel John Coolidge. The house was originally operated as a tavern. In 1956 the state acquired the house and remodeled it to serve as a coffee shop. The Wilder Barn across the street is a large nineteenth-century structure, with hand-hewn beams pegged together and unpainted vertical pine boards with narrow battens. The gable roof is covered with cedar shingles. It contains three floors of farm tools, antiques, and machinery original to the Plymouth area.

# Proctor
*Wilson Castle (1867)*

West Proctor Road
802-773-3284

Built in the mid-nineteenth century, a quixotic blend of European styles, the castle has been the home of five generations of the Wilson family. It was originally built by Dr. Johnson, a Vermonter who married an English woman and wanted her to feel at home in the Vermont hills. Colonel Herbert L. Wilson bought the 32-room castle in the 1930s, and it remains in the

WILSON CASTLE (1867)

family. The facade of the castle is set with English brick and marble and is dominated by 19 open proscenium arches and shadowed by a towering turret, parapet, and balcony. The interiors are richly paneled, highlighted by 84 stained-glass windows and 13 fireplaces finished with imported tiles and bronze. The furnishings are elaborate museum pieces from the Far East and Europe. The 15-acre estate is complete with cattle barns, stables, carriage house, gas house, and aviary. It is now maintained by the Wilson Foundation, Inc., and is open mid-May–October, daily 9:00–6:00. Admission.

# Reading
## Reading Historical Society House (c. 1830)

Main Street, Felchville Village
802-484-7250

The Reading Historical Society is located in a small, two-story, nineteenth-century house in the little village of Felchville. Once a parsonage and private home, it now contains an extensive collection of memorabilia relating to town history. Working life of past generations of townspeople is documented through exhibits of early agricultural and commercial tools. Family life is presented through photographs, portraits, clothing, household articles, musical instruments, and furniture. The society is also a repository for early town records and church documents. The museum house is open July and August, Monday, Wednesday, and Friday, and by appointment 2:00–4:00. Donation.

# Ripton
## Homer Noble Farm (Robert Frost Cabin)

Route 125
802-388-6451

The cabin where Robert Frost wrote some of America's favorite poetry is situated on the grounds of the Homer Noble Farm, now owned by Middlebury College (Breadloaf Campus). This small, rustic cabin in the woods (behind the white Noble farmhouse) was Frost's summer home for the last 23 years of his life. During this time he was closely associated with the famous Breadloaf Writer's Conference, in which he was an active and important participant. An annual event, "A Day with Robert Frost in Frost

Country," is held here in August. At that time the cabin is open to visitors (transportation from the Wayside Area is provided), films on Frost are shown, and walks along the Robert Frost Trail can be taken.

# Shaftsbury
## *The Peter Matteson Tavern (c. 1780)*

East Road
802-447-1571

The earliest town records of this tavern show that Peter Matteson, who came here from Rhode Island in 1762 with his parents and eight brothers, was among eight residents of the town licensed to keep "houses of Public Entertainment." Little else, however, is known of the early history of this typical eighteenth-century, restored Georgian-style farmhouse with a long ell. It remained in the family until it was sold to Beatrice Breese in 1926, who remodeled parts of the house, filled it with her collections of eighteenth- and nineteenth-century antiques, and named it Topping Tavern. Upon her death the property was given to The Bennington Museum, which operated it as a public museum. Ravaged by fire in 1976, it has undergone extensive research and restoration and was renamed for the original owner. It is the site of museum-sponsored craft demonstrations, open houses, overnights, and the annual Apple and Harvest Festival. Admission. Call for information and open house dates.

# Shelburne
## *Shelburne Farms (c. 1899)*

Harbor Road
802-985-8686

Approximately 1000 acres remain today of a magnificent 4000-acre estate amassed by Dr. and Mrs. William Seward Webb (Lila Vanderbilt) in the late nineteenth century. Considered one of the grandest estates in New England when it was built, it overlooks Lake Champlain, one of the most beautiful waterfront settings in Vermont. The 110-room summer "cottage" was built in the grand style of many of the Newport, Rhode Island, mansions, with multigables and irregular eaves, tall chimneys, enclosed porches, and sweeping, landscaped grounds (created by Frederick Law Olmsted). The main house is now an inn and restaurant (open mid-May–mid-October), while the rest of the estate, including an immense five-story, 416-foot barn and an elaborate coach barn, is now used for educational and cultural purposes. It is operated by a nonprofit corporation, Shelburne Farms Resources, Inc., and daily tours of the grounds are given June 1–October 15, 9:30–3:30. Throughout the year, cultural events, craft fairs, a Harvest Festival, and a Winterfest are held. Admission.

## Shelburne Museum

U.S. Route 7
802-985-3346

Considered one of the finest outdoor museums in the country—often compared to Sturbridge Village (Massachusetts) and Ford's Deerborn Village (Michigan)—this vast collection of Americana was started in 1947 by Electra Havemeyer Webb. Situated on 45 acres of well-maintained grounds are 37 period homes and historic structures housing a collection of more than 200,000 pieces of American antiquity. Most of the houses and buildings were dismantled, moved here from various parts of New England, reconstructed, and restored to pristine condition. The houses, filled with excellent period antiques and representing a variety of early New England modes of living, are the **Dutton House** (1782), **Prentis House** (1733), **Vermont House** (1790), **Stencil House** (c. 1790), **The Stagecoach Inn** (c. 1783), **Stone Cottage** (c. 1840), **Dorset House** (c. 1840), and **Sawyer's Cabin** (c. 1800). **The Electra Havemeyer Webb Memorial Building**, a beautiful Greek Revival–type home, constructed in 1967, houses six rooms that were removed from the Webbs' Park Avenue apartment in New York City. The rooms were reconstructed in exacting detail and contain their original furnishings and exquisite artworks by Degas, Rembrandt, Monet, Manet, and others. Many other buildings and unique treasures, such as the S.S. *Ticonderoga*, a round barn, and a covered bridge, are included in this "collection of collections." Shops, picnic and food facilities, and a free jitney that circles the grounds are available. It is open mid-May–mid-October, daily 9:00–5:00. Admission.

# Springfield

*The Springfield Art and Historical Society (c. 1861)*

9 Elm Street
802-885-2415

This stately brick house, high on a hill in downtown Springfield, was originally a Victorian mansion but underwent considerable alterations in the early 1900s. The addition of a third floor with dormers, balustrade, and four tall pillars gave it the nickname, "The Pillars." The house was donated to the town by its last owners, Mr. and Mrs. Edward Miller, to be used as a center for the arts. In addition to serving as an art museum, with galleries displaying paintings, drawings, and primitive portraits, as well as works by local artists, several rooms are used by the historical society for displaying items relating to the history of Springfield. The museum, which offers tours, lectures, and art classes, is open May–October, Tuesday–Friday 12:00–4:30, Thursday evening 6:00–8:00. Donation.

THE JUSTIN SMITH MORRILL
HOMESTEAD (1848)

# Stratford
*The Justin Smith Morrill Homestead (1848)*

Stratford Village
802-828-3226

Justin Smith Morrill (1810–1898), former member of
the U.S. Senate and the Congress, built this fanciful
17-room Gothic Revival "cottage," adapting forms and
details of the period to suit his own needs and vision.
Elaborate exterior details, such as a steeply pitched
gable roof with finials and bargeboards, Tudor moldings, bracketed canopies, windows of varying sizes,
and the rosy pink paint on the flush board siding of
the house, make the house look like something out
of a fairy tale. The interior details are equally as fascinating, with ornate Gothic woodwork and Victorian
furnishings, all original to the house. Several outbuildings, gardens, and landscaped grounds complete
the estate. It is owned and maintained by the
Vermont Division for Historic Preservation and is
open mid-May–mid-October, Wednesday–Sunday
9:30–5:30. Free.

# Vernon

*The Governor Hunt House (1789)*
Governor Hunt Road
802-257-1416

Elegant in its simple lines, this solid colonial house is highlighted by its front entrance, with pilastered columns supporting a triangular pediment, and double doors topped with a rectangular transom. It was recently restored to its original beauty by the Vermont Yankee Nuclear Power Corporation, which now owns the property. The house was built by Jonathan Hunt (1738–1823), a leading member of society who held numerous public office's and whose home was the center of much activity. The house is still unfurnished, but an informative tour, complete with a descriptive booklet with floorplan and pictures showing the restoration of the house, is given on weekdays, year-round 10:00–2:00. Free.

# Weston

*Farrar-Mansur House (1797)*
On the Common
802-824-6781

FARRAR-MANSUR HOUSE (1797)

Captain Oliver Farrar built this Federal-style house to serve as a home for his growing family, as well as an inn. The inn soon became the center of community life. The first town meeting was held here in 1800, and town meetings continued to be held here until the 1830s. The ballroom served for local courts, dances, and as early as 1820, plays were held here. (The popular Weston Playhouse, next door, is the oldest professional summer theater in Vermont.) The house was acquired by the Mansur family in 1857 and served them as a home for four generations. In 1932 the house was given to the town and is now operated by the Weston Historical Society as a house museum with collections of furniture and many items relating to local history. It is open June–October, Tuesday–Sunday 2:00–5:00. Free.

# Wethersfield
## *Reverend Dan Foster House (c. 1776)*

Wethersfield Center Road
802-263-5230/263-5333

REVEREND DAN FOSTER HOUSE (C. 1776)     The oldest section of this house—the rear ell—

includes a huge revolutionary war period fireplace. The 1785 addition, a Federal-style farmhouse, was built for the first settled minister to Wethersfield, the Reverend Dan Foster. It later served as as inn, the post office, and the home of the local blacksmith. A replica of a blacksmith's shop with a working forge is on the grounds. The house is maintained by the Wethersfield Historical Society, which holds special exhibits every summer displaying items pertaining to local history. It is open late June–early October, Thursday–Monday 2:00–5:00 and for special events. Donation.

# Windsor
## The Old Constitution House (1777)

16 North Main Street
802-828-3226

Often called the "birthplace of Vermont," the Old Constitution House is one of Vermont's most important historic sites. It was here that the state's first constitution was adopted on July 8, 1777. Vermont's constitution was the first in the country to prohibit slavery and to establish universal manhood suffrage. The two-story frame building, with a long open porch across the front supported by six Doric columns, was a tavern during its early days, owned by Elija West. The general assembly often met here. The building was originally located in the center of town, but it was moved to its present location in 1914 for preservation purposes. Fully restored, it is furnished with eighteenth- and nineteenth-century furniture, paintings, and historic Vermont memorabilia. Maintained by the Vermont Division for Historic Preservation, it is open May–mid-October, daily 10:00–5:00. Free.

# Woodstock
## Billings Farm and Museum (1871)

Route 12
802-457-2355

Billings Farm was established in 1871 by Vermont native Frederick Billings, a lawyer, businessman, and philanthropist. He imported dairy cattle directly from the Isle of Jersey, kept careful records of milk production, and bred selectively to improve the herd. He planted more than 10,000 trees in the Woodstock area, becoming one of the early conservationists in the state. Today the farm is a living museum of nineteenth-century Vermont family farming, featuring extensive exhibits, a restored and furnished 1890 farmhouse, and a working dairy farm. **The Farm House**, a large rambling Queen Anne structure with steep gabled roofs and high chimneys, was built in 1890 for George Aitken, the farm manager, and his family. The interior is typical of the Victorian period, with the addition of the latest household inventions and gadgetry available at that time. Four original barns have been remodeled to house exhibits on rural life in late nineteenth-century Vermont. The farm is open to the public May–October, daily 10:00–5:00, and for special occasions in the winter (Thanksgiving and Christmas tours). Admission.

## The Dana House (1807)

26 Elm Street
802-457-1822

Another handsome Federal mansion with a classic pilastered and pedimented doorway is the Charles Dana House, now home to the Woodstock Historical Society. Completed in 1807 and occupied for the next 140 years by the notable Dana family, it has nine period and theme rooms. Extensive exhibits and collections focus on the decorative arts from the early nineteenth century and include silver, glass, ceramics, and textiles. The adjoining Canady Gallery features etchings by John Taylor Arms, who had a studio in nearby Pomfret. The library contains more than 800 volumes of local history, reference material, early photographs, and genealogical material. Behind the house and the barn (with its exhibits of early farm implements) is a lovely garden and landscaped grounds reaching down to the Ottauquechee River. The house is open May–October, Monday–Saturday 10:00–5:00, Sunday 2:00–5:00. Admission.

## Ottauquechee DAR House (1807)

On the Green
No telephone

Tillie Parker came to Woodstock from Bethel in 1806 and opened a tavern in his home. The following year he built, on the adjoining land, this large, two-story frame house with a Palladian window above the doorway. The structure was erected purposely to

accommodate the members of the Vermont legislature, which met in Woodstock that year. In 1922, the Ottauquechee Chapter, Daughters of the American Revolution, purchased the building and have since maintained it as a historic house museum and as a chapter house for their meetings. The seven rooms are furnished in early Americana and exhibit collections of revolutionary war memorabilia, doll furniture and toys, decorative arts of the period, and items relating to local history, especially of the Woodstock Railroad. The house is open June–August, Monday–Saturday 2:00–4:00. Free.

OTTAUQUECHEE DAR HOUSE
(1807)

# Additional Houses
*(Area code 802)*

**ALBANY**
Hayden Mansion, Route 14 (P.O. Box 1, 05820)

**BARNET CENTER**
Goodwillie House, Barnet Center, 633-2611

**BRIDPORT**
Bridport Historical Society Museum House, Route 22A, 758-2654

**CANAAN**
 "Jacob's Stand" (Ward Library), Town Green, 266-3088

**EAST POULTNEY**
 Eagle Tavern, On the Green, 287-9498

**ESSEX JUNCTION**
 Anna Early House, 51 Park Street, 878-8687

**FRANKLIN**
 Log Cabin, Route 120, 285-6505

**MARLBORO**
 Ephraim H. Newton House, Village (Box 276, 05344)

**MIDDLEBURY**
 Seymour House, 3 Main Street, 388-2260

 John Warren House, 88 Main Street, 05753

**MIDDLETOWN SPRINGS**
 The Community House, Town Green, 05757

**SPRINGFIELD**
 Hartness House, 30 Orchard Street, 885-2115

**WINDSOR**
 Windsor House, Main Street, 674-5910

# NEW HAMPSHIRE

## Ashland

*Whipple House Museum (1837)*

Pleasant Street
603-968-7716

This 12-room farmhouse with attached barn was originally built as a two-family dwelling by Obadiah Smith in 1837. He lived on one side and his married daughter, Frances Hoyt, lived on the other. It has been owned and passed down through five generations of the same family for 133 years. The last descendant, Dr. George Hoyt Whipple, a distinguished pathologist and Nobel Prize winner, gave the house to the Ashland Historical Society in 1970. It is furnished with many original family pieces, as well as artifacts pertaining to the history of Ashland, and particularly, Dr. Whipple. The house is open July and August, Wednesday and Saturday 1:00–4:00. Free.

WHIPPLE HOUSE MUSEUM (1837)

# Canterbury Center
*Canterbury Shaker Village (1780s)*

Shaker Road
603-783-9511

Canterbury Shaker Village was founded in the 1780s, the sixth of 19 Shaker communities that flourished from Maine to Kentucky during this period. Within this communal village, as in the others, the Shakers practiced equality of the sexes and races, common ownership of goods, celibacy, and pacifism. At its peak in 1860, Canterbury had grown to accommodate some 300 people who lived, worked, and worshipped within a complex of 100 buildings on 4000 acres of land. They made their living from farming, selling seeds and herbs, manufacturing medicines, and making crafts. Today, consisting of 22 buildings, it is one of only two remaining communities with living Shakers. Tours conducted by interpretive guides and demonstrations by skilled craftsmen help to explain the Shaker traditions. Lunch, snacks, and four-course candlelit dinners are served in the Creamery Restaurant (open year-round). The village is open early May–mid-October, Monday–Saturday 10:00–5:00. Admission.

# Center Sandwich

*Elisha Marston House (c. 1848)*

North Sandwich Road
603-284-6269

This Cape Cod–style house, with an ell and an attached barn, and surrounded by a low, white picket fence, represents the predominant architectural type found in Center Sandwich. This one is enhanced by corner pilasters and a central doorway surrounded with small window panes. It was built by Elisha Marston, a skilled shoemaker, who lived here until his death at the age of 101. It was then occupied by his son, Dr. Enoch Marston, who had his medical office here. It is now headquarters for the Sandwich Historical Society and contains furnishings and artifacts relating to the history of Center Sandwich. It is open June–September, Tuesday–Saturday 11:00–5:00. Free.

# Concord

*Pierce Manse (1838–1840)*

14 Penacook Street
603-224-9620

PIERCE MANSE (1838–1840)

Franklin Pierce, fourteenth president of the United States (1853–1857), lived in this attractive modified Greek Revival house from 1842 to 1848, when he moved to Concord with his wife and two sons to establish a law firm. The house was saved from demolition in 1966 by The Pierce Brigade, who moved it to its present location (Concord Historic Park, near the state house). It has been restored to the mid-nineteenth-century style, retaining the gun-stock corner posts, gun cabinet in the front hall, and original floors. Many of the furnishings belonged to Pierce or other members of his family; some pieces are known as "White House Pieces." Pierce's oldest son, Franky, died here of typhus in 1843, and his younger son, Benny, was later killed in a train accident in 1853, just two months before Pierce was inaugurated as president. Pierce left from here in 1846 to go off to the Mexican War, and it is speculated that he did not wish to return to the house because "the rooms would have been haunted by the memory of Franky's death." The house is open mid-June–mid-September, Monday–Friday 11:00–3:00, and by appointment. Admission.

## The Upham-Walker House (1831)

THE UPHAM-WALKER HOUSE
(1831)

18 Park Street
603-224-2508

The Upham-Walker House, a two-and-one-half-story brick Federal-style mansion with an attached wooden wing and stable, has changed little since it was built in 1831. It was built by Nathanial Upham two years before he was appointed to Superior Court at the age of 32. "Judge Upham," as he was always called, resigned from the bench in 1842 to become the principal figure in the development of the Concord Railroad and in the growth of the capital city. He was also influential in helping Franklin Pierce attain the presidency in 1853. The house remained in the family for four generations (Judge Upham's daughter married Joseph B. Walker) and reflects the changing tastes of its prominent, civic-minded owners for more than 150 years. The house was purchased by the state of New Hampshire in 1978, and although most of the furnishings were auctioned off, some were acquired by the state and are on display in the restored house. Call for visitors' information.

# Conway

*Eastman-Lord House (1818)*

EASTMAN-LORD HOUSE (1818)

100 Main Street
603-447-5551

William Kimball Eastman came to Conway in 1818 to begin a thriving mill business. During that same year, he began construction of his two-and-a-half-story colonial home. The house, extensively renovated in 1845, has undergone many changes. It is now maintained by the Conway Historical Society as a 17-room museum. Interesting features are the two borning rooms, an authentic Victorian parlor, and a reconstructed sleeping loft. Complementing the eclectic furnishings of the other rooms, the society displays a constantly changing array of vintage clothing from their enormous costume collection. The house is open Memorial Day–Labor Day, Wednesday 2:00–4:00 and 6:00–8:00, Tuesday 5:00–7:00, and by appointment. Donation.

# Cornish

ASPET, SAINT-GAUDENS
NATIONAL HISTORIC
SITE (C. 1800)

## Aspet, Saint-Gaudens National Historic Site (c. 1800)

Route 12A
603-675-2175

Augustus Saint-Gaudens, one of America's greatest
sculptors, made his summer residence and later, his
permanent home, in Cornish. The house was originally an old tavern known as "Huggins Folly," a
large, brick, Federal structure that he painted white,
and to which he added roof dormers and a long
columned porch along the west side, where guests
could watch the sunset over Mount Ascutney. He
thoroughly remodeled the interior and landscaped
the grounds extensively. Today the original furnishings are retained in both the house and studio, and
copies of some of his most important works are displayed throughout the grounds. During the season,
contemporary art exhibitions are held in the Picture
Gallery and concerts are held on the grounds. Both
are open to the public. The estate is administered by
the National Park Service, U.S. Department of the
Interior, and is open May–October, daily 8:30–4:30.
(The grounds are open 8:00–dusk.) Admission.

# Derry

*Robert Frost Farm (c. 1880)*

Route 28
603-432-3091

This typical New England two-story, white clapboard
farmhouse, with the front door to one side and a
large bow window next to it, was the home of Robert
Frost and his family from 1901 to 1909. Two of his
most famous poems, "Home Burial" and "The Death
of the Hired Man," were written here, and many of
his later works drew from his experiences on the
Derry farm. The house was restored and furnished to
its turn-of-the-century period by his daughter Leslie,
who was born here. The large barn, where an intro-
ductory video is shown, contains Frost exhibits.
There is a half-mile nature trail, that takes you past
the "Mending Wall" and other scenes filled with
Frost's poetic images. Operated by the State Division
of Parks, the Frost Farm is open Memorial

ROBERT FROST FARM (C. 1880)

Day–September 1, Wednesday–Sunday 10:00–6:00. Admission.

## Dover

### *Woodman Institute (1675, 1813, 1818)*

182–192 Central Avenue
603-742-1038

The Woodman Institute is a complex of three buildings spanning three centuries of New Hampshire history. **The Woodman House** (1818) was the residence of Mrs. Annie E. Woodman, who left her house and a sum of money for the creation of an institution for the study of local history and art and for free lecture courses. The house has been converted into a history museum and contains extensive exhibits on natural history and science relating to New Hampshire's environment. **The Hale House** (1813), next door to the Woodman House, was the home of John P. Hale, the famous abolitionist U.S. senator from 1840 to 1872. It is now used to house the institute's vast historical collection, and one alcove is devoted to a display of Senator Hale's furniture and memorabilia. The **Damm Garrison House**

(c. 1675) is a colonial garrison house, moved from its original site, three miles away, to the grounds of the institute. It contains more than 800 period items, including furniture, cooking utensils, clothing, farm tools, and cradles (particularly, a rare one for twins). The houses are open April 1–January 31, Tuesday–Saturday 2:00–5:00. Lectures and special exhibits are held throughout the year. Donation.

WOODMAN INSTITUTE (1675, 1813, 1818)

# Exeter
## Gilman Garrison House (c. 1690)

12 Water Street
603-436-3205

This remodeled Georgian-style clapboard house masks the original dwelling that stood here—a fortified garrison house built by John Gilman to protect his sawmill. Some of the original features, such as massive, heavy dovetail timbers, "loop-hole windows," a puncheon floor, and scratch-molded beams, can still be seen within. A model of the original portcullis doorway, which could be opened and lowered during an Indian raid, is on exhibit. Much of the furniture in the house was locally made, and some of

LADD-GILMAN HOUSE
(C. 1721)

the pieces are original to the house. One such piece is a crude desk used by Daniel Webster when he was a student boarder here. The house is maintained by SPNEA and is open June 1–October 15, Tuesday, Thursday, Saturday, and Sunday 12:00–5:00. Admission.

## Ladd-Gilman House (c. 1721)

(Cincinnati Hall)
1 Governor's Lane
603-772-2622/778-1805

This large, rambling, yellow clapboard house is the headquarters for the Society of the Cincinnati in the State of New Hampshire. Members of the society, which was formed in 1783 with George Washington as the first president general, are all direct descendants of the officers of the Continental Line. The house, originally a two-story brick dwelling built by Nathaniel Ladd, was sold to his cousin, Colonel Daniel Gilman, in 1747 and enlarged considerably. It remained in the Gilman family and underwent more remodeling, until it was purchased by the society in 1920. The house served as the State Treasury from 1775 to 1789, when Nicholas Gilman was acting as first treasurer of New Hampshire, and as the governor's mansion during the 14-year term of John Taylor Gilman. The house is handsomely furnished with furniture, portraits, prints, documents, and memorabilia of the revolutionary war period. It is open to the public year-round, on Tuesdays and Sundays 12:00–5:00 and by appointment. Donation.

## The Moses-Kent House (1868)

One Pine Street
603-778-1803

This multiform Victorian mansion includes several different styles of architecture, including a mansard roof with an off-center tower, bracketed cornices, rusticated wall surfaces, windows of varying proportions, and double porches. It was built by Henry C. Moses, a successful wood dealer, and later was home to George E. Kent and then his son Richard. The Kent family owned and operated the Exeter Manufacturing Company, which strongly influenced the economy of the town of Exeter from the last half of the nineteenth century through the first half of the twentieth century. Today the museum rooms may be seen with the original furnishings of 1903, when the Kents first lived in the house. The landscaped grounds were designed by the firm of Frederick Law Olmsted. The house is open year-round, Tuesday 1:00–4:00. Admission.

# Fitzwilliam
## Amos J. Blake House (1837)

On the Common

This modified Greek Revival–style house with two front doors was built by Levi Haskell in 1837 and in 1865 became the home and law office of Amos Blake, community leader, town official, and state legislator. The house is now owned by the Fitzwilliam Historical Society and, through their efforts, has been completely restored and refurnished to its mid-nineteenth-century appearance. There are 13 rooms on view, including Mr. Blake's law office with most of its original furnishings, the consulting room of Dr. George Emerson, a longtime Fitzwilliam physician, and an old-time schoolroom. The museum is open late May–mid-October, Saturday 10:00–4:00, Sunday 1:00–4:00, and by appointment. Donation. Write the society at P.O. Box 87, Fitzwilliam, NH 03447.

# Franconia
*The Frost Place (c. 1830)*

Ridge Road
603-823-5510

This simple farmhouse, with a front porch looking out over the White Mountains, was purchased by Robert Frost upon his return from England in 1915. He lived here until 1920 and then used it as a summer residence until 1938. Several rooms of the house contain some original furnishings, signed first editions of his works, a rare collection of his Christmas card poems, and other memorabilia. Located behind the house is a half-mile-long poetry trail, dotted with plaques inscribed with well-known Frost poems that were written while Frost lived here. Each summer a poet in residence lives here and gives readings in the old barn. Maintained by the Town of Franconia, the house is open Memorial Day–June 30, Saturday and Sunday 1:00–5:00; July and August, daily except Tuesday, 1:00–5:00; Labor Day–Columbus Day, Saturday and Sunday 1:00–5:00. Admission.

THE FROST PLACE (C. 1830)

# Franklin

*Daniel Webster Birthplace (1773)*

105 Loudon Road
603-271-3556/934-5057

DANIEL WEBSTER BIRTHPLACE
(1773)

Ebenezer Webster built this two-room frame house for his wife and two children, and it was here that their third child, Daniel, was born on a snowy January day. The famous orator, congressman, and two-time secretary of state lived here for only three years, but in 1913 the Webster Birthplace Association restored it as a memorial. Much of the house is believed to be original, and the fireplace was rebuilt using the original handmade bricks and hearthstone. Furnishings are typical of the period, and some items on display belonged to Daniel Webster in the latter period of his life. It is now maintained by the New Hampshire Division of Parks and Recreation and is open late-May–June 30, Saturday and Sunday 10:00–6:00; late June–Labor Day, daily 10:00–6:00. Admission.

# Hancock

## Charles Symonds House (1809)

Main Street and Bennington Road
603-525-4106

This beautifully restored, two-story brick Federal building was built by Jacob Ames, an accomplished local builder. It is a fine example of the period, with a shallow hipped roof and corner chimneys. It has few adornments except for the unusual semi-elliptical doorway set between widely spaced sidelights. It is now owned by the Hancock Historical Society and houses a collection of furniture, china, books, old New Hampshire tools, and local historical data and heirlooms. It is open June and September, Saturday 2:00–4:00; July and August, Saturday and Wednesday 2:00–4:00. Admission.

# Hanover

## Webster Cottage (1780)

32 North Main Street
603-646-1110

The Webster Cottage, a small, typical, one-story farmhouse, with two bedrooms built under the eaves, is owned by Dartmouth College and is maintained and operated by the Hanover Historical Society. It was built in 1780 as a residence for Abigail Wheelock, daughter of Dartmouth's founder. In 1801 Daniel Webster, then an undergraduate at the college, lived here and climbed the narrow staircase to his room in the garret on the second floor. The house is furnished in the period of Webster's time and contains his desk, chair, books, and "spirits box." The house was also the birthplace of Henry Fowle Durant, founder of Wellesley College. It is open Memorial Day–Columbus Day, Wednesday, Saturday, and Sunday 2:30–4:30. Donation.

# Hillsboro

## Pierce Homestead (1804)

Route 31
603-464-5858

The Pierce Homestead was built in 1804 by Benjamin Pierce, two-time governor of New Hampshire, the year his son Franklin was born. The two-story Federal house was a reflection of Benjamin's prominent standing in the community and became a gathering place for many great men of the state and nation. In the ballroom on the second floor, local militia groups were drilled by Pierce, who had served under Washington in the revolutionary war and later formed the first brigade of militia in Hillsborough County. His son Franklin, who was to become the fourteenth president of the United States, lived here from his birth until his marriage in 1834. Period furnishings and Pierce memorabilia are on display. It is operated by the New Hampshire Division of Parks and is open late May–mid-October, Saturday and holidays 10:00–4:00, Sunday 1:00–4:00; also July and August, Friday 10:00–4:00. Admission.

# Keene

## Colony House Museum (c. 1817)

104 West Street
603-357-0889

This handsome, brick Federal house with a shallow hipped roof has a columned entryway with a fanlight and arched window above. It was the home of Horatio Colony, the first mayor of Keene. It now serves as a museum for the Historical Society of Cheshire County, Inc., and contains an outstanding collection of glass from the early glass factories once located here, and Hampshire Pottery, which was produced in Keene between 1871 and 1923. Other displays include collections of locally produced toys, silver, furniture, musical instruments, and archival material for researchers. The society offers many educational programs throughout the year, and the museum is open June 1–Labor Day, Tuesday–Saturday 11:00–4:00; Labor Day–Columbus Day, Saturday 11:00–4:00, and by appointment. Admission.

## Wyman Tavern (1762)

339 Main Street
603-357-3855

The Wyman Tavern was built by Captain Isaac Wyman in 1762 and operated as a tavern by the Wyman family for 40 years. From this two-and-one-half-story frame dwelling, 29 minutemen started their march to Lexington and Concord in April of 1775,

WYMAN TAVERN (1762)

under the command of Captain Wyman. The Reverend Zedekiah S. Barstown made his home in the tavern for 55 years and conducted a private school here. The tavern is maintained by the Historical Society of Cheshire County, Inc., as a period house museum representing the period from 1770 to 1820 with fine antiques, books, and paintings. It is open June 1–Labor Day, Thursday–Saturday 11:00–4:00.

## Lancaster

*John Wingate Weeks Historic Site (1910–1913)*

Mount Prospect
603-788-4004/271-3556

The estate of John Wingate Weeks, an early conservationist, U.S. congressman, U.S. senator, and secretary of war under Presidents Harding and Coolidge, is located on a most impressive site affording a 360-degree panoramic view of mountain splendor. The main house, called the "lodge," is built of fieldstone and stucco, with a gable roof covered with red terra cotta tiles. The most outstanding feature of the house is the 30 x 70-foot living room, which makes up the entire second floor. Huge windows and balconies take full advantage of the lodge's mountaintop setting. Most of the woodwork and trim in the lodge is dark oak, as is the furniture in both the living room and dining room. Signed photographs of many of the dignitaries who visited here are displayed on the walls. The space that originally contained six bedrooms has been converted to a display area for exhibits tracing the history of forestry and conservation in New Hampshire. The property is maintained by the New Hampshire Division of Parks and Recreation and is open late June–Labor Day, Wednesday–Sunday 10:00–5:00; September–mid-October, Saturday and Sunday 10:00–5:00. Admission.

# Littleton

*Charles F. Eastman Mansion (1884)*

(Community House)
141 Main Street
603-444-5711

Built by Charles F. Eastman, one of Littleton's "lumber barons" during the late nineteenth century, this

CHARLES F. EASTMAN MANSION (1884)

Queen Anne Victorian treasure is now the town's Community House. The exterior is a profusion of jutting features and angular projections incorporating bay windows, porches, dormers, and chimneys. Seven types of wood were used throughout the interior of the house, and particularly notable is the handsomely carved cherry woodwork in the wainscoting throughout the first floor and the front hall staircase. Most of the period furnishings were contributed by local citizens who are justly proud of their Community House. Call for a free tour (weekdays year-round).

# Manchester
*General John Stark House (1736)*

2000 Elm Street

GENERAL JOHN STARK HOUSE (1736)

The boyhood home of General John Stark, national hero, Indian fighter, and a brigadier general of the Continental Army during the revolutionary war, is a small, one-story frame structure with a gable roof, center chimney, and clapboard walls. Many of the original features of the house are still visible, includ-

ing hand-stenciled walls, old wood flooring, some original window panes, three fireplaces with wide-wood paneling, and a beehive oven. The furnishings are all authentic eighteenth-century pieces, many from members of the Stark family. The house, owned and operated by the Molly Stark Chapter of the DAR, is open September–May by appointment only, and for small groups, docents in costume are sometimes provided. Donation. Write to General John Stark House, 2000 Elm Street, Manchester, NH 03104.

## Isadore J. and Lucille Zimmerman House (1952)

223 Heather Street
603-669-6144

Frank Lloyd Wright, one of America's most influential modern architects, designed this brick and wooden structure for the Zimmermans in 1952. The house is designed with the landscape and natural surroundings in mind, and large plate glass windows along the back of the house seem to bring the outdoors inside. Most of the furniture in the house was also designed by Wright. Long shelves were designed for the dining area to showcase the Zimmermans' twenti-

ISADORE J. AND LUCILLE ZIMMERMAN HOUSE (1952)

eth-century sculpture and pottery collection. Mr. Zimmerman, a successful urologist, and Lucille, a psychiatric nurse, left the house to the Currier Gallery of Art in 1988. Guided tours are given year-round, Thursday–Sunday 10:30–2:30 (reservations required). Visitors should purchase their tickets at the Currier Gallery, where they will then be bused to the house.

# Milton
## *Jones Farm (c. 1780)*

(New Hampshire Farm Museum, Inc.)
Route 16, Plummer's Ridge
603-652-7840

The Jones Farm, approximately halfway between Boston and the White Mountains, has long been known to travelers as the Halfway House. It is a long, rambling collection of buildings, running 277 feet in length, including the original Cape-style farmhouse built in the 1780s and furnished with period antiques. The collection is one of the longest sets of New England connected farm buildings in existence. It shows 200 years of the evolution of architecture and was owned continuously by the same family for five

JONES FARM (C. 1780)

generations. It is now home to the New Hampshire Farm Museum, an organization dedicated to collecting and preserving tools and artifacts of New Hampshire's agricultural heritage. Tours, exhibits, demonstrations, craft workshops, and many educational programs are conducted throughout the summer months and on some weekends in the winter. It is open late June–Labor Day, Tuesday–Sunday 10:00–4:00. Admission.

# Moultonborough
## Lucknow (1913)

(Castle in the Clouds)
Route 171
603-476-2352

Lucknow, the former country estate of eccentric multimillionaire Thomas Gustave Plant, took many years, thousands of workmen, and millions of dollars to build. Situated on a promontory in the heart of the Ossipee Mountain Range, it consists of thousands of acres of woodlands with ponds, trout streams, waterfalls, thick forests, all interlaced with 85 miles of carriage roads and horse trails. Plant was an inventor, and the stone castle, made from granite blasted out of the surrounding hillside, contains numerous modern conveniences practically unheard of at the time of its construction. The roof is made of Spanish slate, and all of the exterior and interior woodwork is hand hewn. The windows, many of them handpainted and depicting scenes from the estate, are of brass and leaded glass. Many of the original furnishings remain, and in addition to tours of the estate and grounds, horseback riding and hay rides are available. Privately owned, the estate is open mid-June–mid-October, daily 9:00–6:00.

# Nashua
## Abbot-Spalding House (1804)

5 Abbot Street
603-883-0015

This large, square, Federal-style house with a low hipped roof and balustrade was the home of a succession of prominent Nashua citizens, particularly Daniel Abbot, who formed the Nashua Manufacturing Company, the first cotton mills in Nashua. The house was a common meeting ground of the famous and the influential of New Hampshire. The furnishings are fine pieces collected by the Spalding family, the last residents, including glass, china, and paintings. Owned by the Nashua Historical Society, the house is located next to their museum, the Florence H. Speare Memorial Building, which contains exhibits of local history. Admission to both buildings is free and they are open February–November, Saturday 1:00–4:00, and by appointment.

# New Ipswich
## *Barrett House (1800)*

(Forest Hall)
Main Street
617-227-3956

Forest Hall, an elegant, three-story, Federal-style country residence with a long attached carriage shed, is located in the center of a picturesque village. It was built by Charles Barrett, Sr., an entrepreneur and industrialist, for his son, and descended in the family until 1948, when it was given to SPNEA. The 12 museum rooms, including a music room/ballroom on the third floor, contain some of the society's most

BARRETT HOUSE (1800)

important examples of eighteenth- and nineteenth-century furniture and antique musical instruments, passed down through the Barrett family. The extensive grounds include a Gothic Revival summer house on a terraced hill behind the main house. The house is open June 1–October 15, Thursday–Sunday 12:00–5:00. Admission.

# New London
## *The Scytheville House (1820)*

Little Sunapee Road
603-526-6564

The New London Historical Society maintains a collection of early 1800s buildings in an outdoor museum setting. This complex includes the Scytheville House, the Pleasant Street School, the Griffin Barn, the Colby-Greenwood-Seamans Store, a blacksmith shop, and several smaller structures. The buildings were donated to the society over a period of years by local residents, dismantled, and moved to this site. Members worked together to restore each building and to furnish them with period antiques. The Scytheville House is furnished as a workingman's home during the period just prior to the Civil War. Many special events, such as exhibits, demonstrations, art festivals, and Halloween and Christmas open house, are held here throughout the year. Admission for some programs.

# Passaconaway
## *The Russell-Colbath House (1832)*

Kancamagus Highway
603-447-5448

This one-and-a-half-story, wood-frame Cape with a center chimney was built by Thomas Russell and his son Amzi between 1831 and 1832 and was the home of their descendants until 1930. Russell and his four sons operated a sawmill in the area, and for a time, his son Amzi ran a store from the house. It is one of the few houses, and the oldest, built along New Hampshire's most scenic highway, the Kancamagus. Now owned by the U.S. Forest Service, it has been restored and furnished with period antiques. It also serves as an information center, providing visitors with information about the Kancamagus Highway

THE RUSSELL-COLBATH HOUSE (1832)

and related facilities. It is open late June–Labor Day, daily 10:00–4:00. Free.

# Peterborough
*The Peterborough Historical Society*

19 Grove Street
603-924-3235

A large, neo-Federal, U-shaped brick building in the center of Peterborough houses the many and varied collections of the Peterborough Historical Society. More than 250 years of the town's history is on display here, from the tools of the earliest settlers to a properly dressed seamstress seated in the Victorian parlor. Of particular interest are the two little restored **Mill Houses** (1840s) behind the museum, where the mill girls lived when the town was a thriving textile center. The museum complex is open September–June, Monday–Friday 1:00–4:00; July and August, daily 1:00–4:00. Admission.

# Portsmouth

In 1630 the early settlers who came to this seacoast area named it Strawbery Banke for the abundance of wild strawberries found along the shores. But as the tiny village grew into a major shipbuilding port, rivaling Boston and other Massachusetts ports, the name Portsmouth seemed more appropriate. The days of the swift clipper ships are long past, but left behind is a legacy of some of the finest nineteenth-century sea captains' houses to be found anywhere along the coast of New England.

## Governor John Langdon Mansion (1784)

143 Pleasant Street
603-436-3205

Of the 43 properties owned by SPNEA, this house is considered their finest and most historic. It was built by John Langdon, a wealthy merchant and ardent supporter of the Revolution, who later became governor of New Hampshire. Inside and out, this house emphasizes the best of Georgian features—fluted corner pilasters, a hipped roof with balustrades and dormer windows, and a central portico topped with a circular porch pavilion. When George Washington

GOVERNOR JOHN LANGDON MANSION (1784)

visited here in 1789, he described it as "the finest house in Portsmouth." The interior woodwork is embellished with elaborate wood carving, and the rooms are furnished with family antiques—also considered some of the finest in SPNEA's collection. The house is open June 1–mid-October, Wednesday–Sunday 12:00–5:00. Admission.

## Jackson House (c. 1664)

Northwest Street
617-227-3956

Believed to be the oldest house surviving in New Hampshire, this medieval-looking wood-frame house, with long sweeping rooflines and leaded glass windows, typifies the early colonial dwellings of New England. Built by Richard Jackson, a cooper and shipwright, and occupied by his descendants for more than 250 years, it is now one of the eleven study houses maintained by SPNEA for architectural preservation research. It is simply furnished in keeping with its era and is open by appointment only. Admission.

## John Paul Jones House (1758)

Middle and State streets
603-436-8420

Captain Gregory Purcell, a master mariner, built this handsome two-story frame house with a gambrel roof for his bride, Sarah Wentworth, niece of Governor Benning Wentworth. After the captain's death, however, his wife had to take in boarders to support herself. Her most famous boarder was the dashing young Captain John Paul Jones, who came to Portsmouth in 1777 to command the frigate *Ranger*, which was in the process of being built on nearby Badger's Island. The house is now owned by the Portsmouth Historical Society and contains a wide and varied collection of Americana, particularly pertaining to Portsmouth's maritime history. A model of Jones' famed frigate is also on display. The museum house is open for guided tours mid-May–mid-October, weekdays 10:00–4:00; July–October, Sunday 12:00–4:00. Admission.

## Moffatt-Ladd House (1763)

154 Market Street
603-436-8221/742-7745

This beautiful, three-story, late Georgian mansion
with dentils around the shallow hipped roof, a
balustraded captain's walk, and stone quoins accentu-
ating the corners of the building, was built by another wealthy sea captain, John Moffatt. The front hallway, with its elaborate paneling and wood carving,
"Bay of Naples" wallpaper, and grand staircase, is
considered one of the most gracious in New England.
It is furnished with exceptionally fine antiques, and
the grounds are terraced with formal gardens.
Adjoining it is the shipping office and counting-
house. Owned by the Society of Colonial Dames in
New Hampshire, the house is open mid-June–mid-
October, Monday–Saturday 10:00–4:00, Sunday
2:00–5:00. Admission.

## Rundlet-May House (1807)

364 Middle Street
603-436-3205

RUNDLET-MAY HOUSE (1807)

This impressive, large, wooden three-story Federal house has changed little since it was built by merchant James Rundlet in 1807. Situated on a terrace raised above the street, it is surrounded by its original outbuildings, including a coach house, stables, barn, and privy. The estate was occupied continuously by descendants of James Rundlet until it was given to SPNEA. It is furnished with fine furniture made by Portsmouth craftsmen and wallpapers imported from England. The grounds include flower gardens, orchards, and a cemetery for family pets. It is open June 1–mid-October, Wednesday–Sunday 12:00–5:00. Admission.

## Strawbery Banke

603-433-1100

The settlement of Strawbery Banke, an outdoor museum of 10 acres with more than 40 buildings dating from the seventeenth to nineteenth century in various stages of restoration, is a unique attraction. Seven furnished houses of different eras show the changes in lifestyle and architectural fashion over a period of 350 years. These houses include the

STRAWBERY BANKE

**Thomas Bailey Aldrich House** (1790), **Chase House** (1762), **Drisco House** (1790), **Governor Goodwin Mansion** (1811), **Captain Keyran Walsh House** (1876), **Captain John Wheelwright House**, and the **Pitt Tavern** (1766). Several more restored houses are used for specific exhibits or to illustrate early house construction. Visitors can tour the neighborhood on their own or take a guided tour. Staff members are stationed in each house to answer questions. Strawbery Banke is open May 1–October 31, daily 10:00–5:00. Candlelight strolls are held weekend evenings in early December. Admission.

## Warner House (1716)

150 Daniel Street
603-436-5909

Built by Captain Archibald Macpheadris, a wealthy and prominent member of the King's Council, this house is regarded as among the finest urban brick residences of the early eighteenth century in the country. Many distinguished descendants have lived in the house, including Governor Benning Wentworth and the Honorable Jonathan Warner. Among the many interesting features of the house are six mural paintings on the staircase wall, an early example of marbleizing in the dining room, beautiful paneling in several rooms, and a lightning rod on the west wall, said to have been installed under the personal supervision of Benjamin Franklin, who was a frequent visitor here. The house is furnished with excellent antiques of the period, including some Portsmouth pieces, and several family portraits by the English artist Joseph Blackburn. The house is owned by the Warner House Association and is open mid-May–mid-October, Tuesday–Saturday 10:00-4:30. Admission.

## Wentworth-Coolidge Mansion (1750)

Little Harbor Road
603-436-6607

This rambling, 42-room, wooden structure has a very irregular roof line, which is the result of several buildings being attached at various times. The main portion of the house was built by Benning Wentworth, the first royal governor of New Hampshire (1741–1767), who made his home here until his death in 1770. It was also the seat of government and the center of social life in Portsmouth dur-

WENTWORTH-COOLIDGE
MANSION (1750)

ing his term, and one wing of the house was built for a council chamber. The house, partially furnished and with ongoing restoration, is maintained by the New Hampshire Division of Parks and Recreation and is open May–June 30, Saturday and Sunday 10:00–5:00; July 1–Labor Day, daily 10:00–5:00. Admission.

## *Wentworth-Gardner House (c. 1760)*

140 Mechanic Street
603-436-4406

The Metropolitan Museum of Art purchased this handsome Georgian house in 1918 and planned to move it to Central Park. Fortunately, they did not, and it remains on its original site. It was built by ship's carpenters commissioned by Madam Mark Wentworth as a wedding gift for her son Thomas, the younger brother of Governor John Wentworth. The exterior wide clapboarding, rusticated to imitate cut stone, is enhanced by quoining, pedimented windows, and a "swan's neck" pediment on the attractive front door. The interior woodwork is most outstanding, said to have taken three master carpenters 14 months to execute. Handpainted wallpapers, Dutch-

tiled fireplaces, and ornate mantels are enhanced by fine period antiques. It is operated by the Wentworth-Gardner and Tobias Lear Houses Association and is open mid-June–mid-October, Tuesday–Sunday 1:00–4:00. Admission.

THE CLARK HOUSE (1778)

# Wolfeboro
## *The Clark House (1778)*

South Main Street

The Clark House, a white clapboard revolutionary war era farmhouse with a large central chimney, was built by Joseph Clark in 1778, and is part of a small complex of buildings on Main Street that is owned and maintained by the Wolfeboro Historical Society. It is fully furnished with period antiques, including the first piano in Wolfeboro. There is also a large collection of pewter and china on display, and one room is devoted to textiles with exhibits of quilts, bed linens, and samplers. It is open July–Labor Day, daily (except Sunday) 10:00–4:30, and by appointment. Write to Wolfeboro Historical Society, Wolfeboro, NH 03894.

# Additional Houses
*(Area code 603)*

**ATKINSON**
Stephen Peabody House, Academy Road,
362-4760

**BETHLEHEM**
Rocks Estate, Glessner Road (Route 302),
444-6228

**CENTER OSSIPEE**
Squire Lord's House, Lord's Hill, 539-4803

**CHARLESTOWN**
The Fort at No. 4, Route 11, 826-5700

**DERRY**
Pinkerton House, 12 North Main Street, 432-2528

**CORNISH**
The Chase House, Route 12A, 675-5391

**HUDSON**
Alvirne Hills House, 211 Derry Road
(no telephone)

**LANCASTER**
Wilder-Holton House, Main Street, 788-2328

**NORTH GROTON**
Mary Baker Eddy House, Hall's Brook Road,
786-9943

**RUMNEY**
Mary Baker Eddy House, Stenson Lake Road,
786-9943

**SANBORTON**
The Lane Tavern, Sanborton Square, 286-3564

# MAINE

## Auburn
### *Knight House Museum (1796)*

Great Falls Plaza
207-784-0586

This little one-and-a-half-story Cape Cod–style house
with a large central chimney and small-paned windows is the oldest frame house in Auburn. It was
moved to its present site where it overlooks the
Androscoggin Waterfalls and is surrounded by herb
and flower gardens. It has been painstakingly restored with funds raised by Auburn citizens. Named
for the last family that lived in the house, it has been
furnished with period antiques contributed by local
residents. Adjacent to the house is a one-room shoe
shop with tools and equipment used during the mid-
nineteenth century. It is open during July and August,
holidays, and by appointment. Donations.

## Augusta
### *Blaine House (1833)*

162 State Street
207-289-2121

Just across the street from the Bulfinch-designed State
House is the official residence of the governor of
Maine, Blaine House. Originally a Federal mansion,
this long, two-story frame residence has undergone
many changes and additions over the years. Its
gleaming white clapboards and black shutters, colon-
naded porch, hipped roof with twin cupolas, and
beautifully landscaped grounds all add to its impressive appearance. It was built by Captain James Hall
of Bath, a master mariner, during the same year the
State House was being built. In 1862 it was purchased by Congressman James G. Blaine, considered
the most prominent Maine political figure of the nineteenth century. It is furnished with many of the original Blaine family furnishings. Steeped in Maine history, the house is open to the public year-round,
Monday–Friday 2:00–4:00, excluding holidays, with
tours on the half hour. Free.

# Bangor

## Isaac Farrar Mansion (1845)

17 Second Street
207-941-2808

Isaac Farrar, a wealthy lumberman, merchant, and president of the Maritime Bank of Bangor, commissioned architect Richard Upjohn to design this two-and-one-half-story, brick Greek Revival mansion in 1833. Today, it retains many of its original features, such as carved mahogany paneling, curved and slotted bookcase doors, marble fireplaces, and stained-glass windows. For many years it was the home of the Bangor Symphony's Northern Conservatory of Music, and thus was given the name "Symphony House," which many still know it by. It is now owned by the Bangor-Brewer YWCA. Four rooms on the first floor have been restored and furnished with American Empire pieces. It is open year-round, Monday–Friday 9:00–4:00, with tours available. Donation.

## Thomas A. Hill House (1834–1836)

159 Union Street
207-942-5766

Another example of noted architect Richard Upjohn's early work, this two-story, brick Greek Revival mansion, with its columned, three-sided portico, is now the home of the Bangor Historical Society. It was built for Thomas Hill, a prominent local businessman and attorney, and later occupied by Mayor Samuel Dale. The elegant double parlor boasts an unusual handcarved room divider with Corinthian columns and an arabesque frieze. Tall, gilded mirrors, ornate chandeliers, and Victorian furnishings throughout are reminders of the days when Mayor Dale entertained many distinguished visitors, such as President Ulysses S. Grant. The upstairs now hosts changing exhibits relating to local history. Open for guided tours February–mid-December, Tuesday–Friday and Sunday 12:00–4:00.

# Bethel

## Dr. Moses Mason House (1813)

15 Broad Street
207-824-2908

This classic Federal house is a two-and-one-half-story frame structure with a center-entrance doorway framed with sidelights and a graceful fanlight. It was the home of Dr. Moses Mason (1789–1866), one of Bethel's most prominent citizens and U. S. congressman (1833–1837). His wife, Agnes Straw Mason, was a leader in the temperance movement in Oxford County. The house contains eight period rooms appropriately furnished to reflect the life and times of Dr. and Mrs. Mason. Of particular note are the murals on the front hall stairway by Rufus Porter, an important early American painter. The house is now the headquarters of the Bethel Historical Society and is open July 1–Labor Day, daily except Monday, 1:00–4:00, and by appointment. Admission.

# Blue Hill

## Holt House (1815)

Water Street
No telephone

The Holt House, one of the early homes at the head of the bay in this scenic little seaside village, was built by Jeremiah Thorndike Holt, the grandson of Nicholas Holt, one of the earliest settlers of Blue Hill. Skillfully restored by craftsmen and members of the Blue Hill Historical Society, it remains virtually in its original form. The stately entrance hall provides access to six of the nine rooms, eight of which have a fireplace. The rooms feature recessed shutters and fine woodwork, and old stencil decorations whose patterns have been reproduced and replaced on the restored walls. The house is furnished with period pieces donated or on loan—some made by local craftsmen. It is operated by the Blue Hill Historical Society and is open July and August, Tuesday–Friday 1:00–4:00. Donation.

## Jonathan Fisher Memorial (1814)

Main Street
207-374-2780

Jonathan Fisher, a most unusual, talented, and educated man, came to the pioneer village of Blue Hill in 1796 as the first "settled" pastor of the Congregational Church. Not only did he design and build his own two-story, four-room frame house by himself, he made most of his own furniture, farmed his land, concocted medicinal remedies, wove hats, made buttons from animal bones, and still found time to paint portraits and landscapes and write poetry and books. The house is furnished with many original paintings, furniture, manuscripts, and other items belonging to the parson and his family. The house is maintained by the Jonathan Fisher Memorial, Inc., and is open July 1–mid-September, Monday–Saturday 2:00–5:00. Admission.

# Boothbay Harbor
## *Elizabeth Reed House (1874)*

70 Oak Street
207-633-3666

Home of the Boothbay Region Historical Society, this interesting Italianate sea captain's house was built for Captain Freeman Reed and left as a gift to the town by Elizabeth Reed. The house itself, as well as the exhibits inside, featured prominently in the history of this area. Along with period furnishings and nineteenth-century household appliances, it contains an outstanding collection of photographs pertaining to

ELIZABETH REED HOUSE (1874)

local maritime affairs, and artifacts and memorabilia. It is open July and August, Monday, Wednesday, Friday, and Saturday 10:00–4:00, and by appointment. Admission.

# Brunswick

## *The Harriet Beecher Stowe House (1804)*

63 Federal Street
207-725-5543

This white frame house, with a high-pitched roof and twin chimneys, was the home of Harriet Beecher Stowe from 1850 until 1870. It was here, while her husband, Calvin Stowe, was a professor of religion at nearby Bowdoin College, that Stowe wrote her famous indictment of slavery, *Uncle Tom's Cabin.* Henry Wadsworth Longfellow lived in the house when he was a student at Bowdoin, and was often visited by his good friends Nathaniel Hawthorne and Franklin Pierce. The house is now an inn, with a motel and a restaurant, but the rooms associated with Mrs. Stowe and her work have been preserved and are intact. The inn is open year-round and visitors may browse in the Stowe rooms and the gift shop.

THE HARRIET BEECHER STOWE HOUSE (1804)

## Joshua L. Chamberlain House (c. 1825)

226 Main Street
207-729-6606

This Federal-style home, with Victorian Gothic additions, is the partially restored home of Joshua L. Chamberlain and pays tribute to his roles in the Civil War, as president of Bowdoin College, and as state governor. He is noted for his heroic defense at Gettysburg and for being the only Union officer to receive a battlefield promotion from General U.S. Grant. The restored rooms are filled with period furnishings, many original to the house, and exhibits of Civil War memorabilia, providing a look at the life and career of this Civil War general. The house is now owned by the Pejepscot Historical Society and is open Memorial Day–Labor Day, Thursday and Friday 10:00–3:00, and by appointment. Admission.

## Skolfield-Whittier House (1857)

SKOLFIELD-WHITTIER HOUSE
(1857)

Pejepscot Historical Museum
159–161 Park Row
207-729-6606

This large, brick Greek Revival-Italianate "double house," with an ornate cupola and tall chimneys, was built for two sea captains, Alfred and Samuel Skolfield. Alfred's side of the house was home to three generations of Skolfields. The 17 rooms are furnished with fine examples of Eastlake, Rococo, and Elizabethan Revival styles, as well as paintings and several pantries filled with china and glass. The other side of the house is now occupied by the Pejepscot Historical Society, one of Maine's oldest historical organizations, and features a special centennial exhibit and a look at changing visions of history over the past 100 years. The Pejepscot Museum is open year-round, Monday–Friday 10:00–3:00, (free), and the Skolfield-Whittier House is open Memorial Day–Labor Day, Thursday and Friday 10:00–3:00 (admission).

# Calais
*Holmes Cottage (c. 1804)*

241 Main Street
207-454-3100

This little, one-story frame house is the oldest house in Calais and is now a museum run by the St. Croix Historical Society. Calais, Maine's only international city, is situated on the west bank of Passamaquoddy Bay at the mouth of the St. Croix River, a U.S. and Canadian boundary. The house is filled with collections of early furniture, Indian relics, and maps and photographs pertaining to local history. The cottage was home over the early years to the first three doctors who came to practice in this busy border-crossing town. It was deeded to the historical society by Josephine Moore, a direct descendant of Dr. Job Holmes. It is open July and August, daily 1:00–5:00 and by appointment. Donation.

# Camden
*The Conway House (c. 1770)*

Conway Road
207-236-2257

One of the earliest houses in the region, this small Cape Cod–style farmhouse was built by Robert Thorndike, one of the first white settlers in the area. The property was acquired by Mary Meeker Cramer,

THE CONWAY HOUSE (C. 1770)

president of the Camden-Rockport Society in 1961, and restoration work by the society began. Many of the original features can still be seen. Members of the society furnished the house with authentic pieces of household items in use in the eighteenth and early nineteenth centuries. The nearby Mary Meeker Cramer Museum, built in 1969, is furnished with period costumes, early glass, paintings, documents, and regional memorabilia. There is also a barn filled with a collection of carriages, sleighs, farm implements, and early tools, and a restored blacksmith shop. The Camden Garden Club has landscaped the grounds with native plants common in New England before 1860. The buildings are open July and August, Tuesday–Friday 10:00–4:00. Admission.

## Norumbega (1886)

61 High Street
207-236-4646

Norumbega, designed in the popular Queen Anne style of the late 1800s and built of fieldstone and wood with a three-story turret, porte-cochere, balconies, terraces, and leaded-glass windows, is one of the few remaining baronial mansions that once dot-

NORUMBEGA (1886)

ted the coast of Maine. It was built by Joseph B. Stearns, the inventor of duplex telegraphy, which revolutionized the telegraph industry and made him a millionaire. Decorated throughout with period furnishings, Norumbega is now a sumptuous bed and breakfast but can be visited from 11:00–1:00 any day year-round. (Guest rooms may not be available for viewing.)

# Campobello Island

*Franklin D. Roosevelt Home (1897)*

Route 774
506-752-2997

The former summer home of President Franklin D. Roosevelt is the centerpiece of the 2600-acre Roosevelt-Campobello Park, administered jointly by the United States and Canada. The 34-room, shingled, Dutch colonial "cottage," occupied by Roosevelt from 1905 to 1921, is typical of the summer homes built during this period. The first floor rooms are large and airy, while the second floor has a long center hallway with many small dormitory-type bedrooms lining each side (17 bedrooms in all). The house has been meticulously preserved with all the original furnishings intact, right down to FDR's famous felt hat and the huge megaphone used by Eleanor to call the children to dinner. At the reception center, an introduction to the island and the Roosevelt family is provided by way of several films shown alternately every hour on the hour. Visitors can stroll leisurely through the rooms of the house (where guides are posted to answer questions) and around the landscaped grounds and gardens. It is open from Memorial Day–mid-October, daily 9:00–5:00. Free.

FRANKLIN D. ROOSEVELT HOME (1897)

# Columbia Falls

## Ruggles House (1818)

Main Street
207-483-4637

This modest-sized but elegant Federal-style house, with a handsome doorway with an arched window above, was built by Judge Thomas Ruggles, a wealthy lumber dealer, merchant, postmaster, and militia captain. Its most remarkable feature is the interior wood carving, done by an English woodcarver with his pen knife, and taking more than three years to complete. Another special attraction of the house is the impressive flying staircase, rising from the center hall, without lateral support, to the landing and then dividing into two half-flights. The house is furnished with period antiques, many original to the house. It is maintained by the Ruggles House Society and is open June 1–mid-October, weekdays 9:30–4:30, Sunday 11:00–4:30. Donation.

# Damariscotta

## Chapman-Hall House (1754)

Main Street
No telephone

CHAPMAN-HALL HOUSE (1754)

This small, Cape Cod–style house, with a large central chimney, an ell, and nine-over-six windows, is the oldest surviving building in Damariscotta. Its survival is credited in large part to Nathaniel Chapman, the skilled housewright who built it. His craftsmanship is seen in the old kitchen, with its deep beams that run the entire width of the house, the planked ceiling, paneling, and original floors. Other rooms reflect changes made in later periods of ownership of the house. The house is furnished with period antiques and an herb garden and eighteenth-century rose bushes are on the grounds. It is owned and maintained by the Chapman-Hall House Preservation Society, Inc., and is open mid-June–mid-September, Tuesday–Sunday 1:00–5:00. Admission.

# Ellsworth
## Colonel Black Mansion (1824-1828)

West Main Street
207-667-8671

Also called Woodlawn, this three-story, brick Federal country house, with a columned portico and balustrades, was built as a combination home and office by John Black, a young land agent from England. It took three years to build, as the bricks came by sea from Philadelphia and the skilled workmen from Boston. Three generations of the Black family lived in this house, and it remained virtually unchanged throughout their ownership. The estate, with all the original rich furnishings, decorative objects, and historical artifacts, was bequeathed to the public by the grandson of John Black in 1928 and has since been administered by the Hancock County Trustees of Public Reservations. Located at the rear of the house are a restored country garden and a carriage house filled with interesting old carriages and sleighs. It is open June 1–October 15, Monday–Saturday 10:00–5:00. Admission.

# Farmington
*Nordica Homestead (c. 1840)*

Holly Road
207-778-2042/778-2855

This simple, Cape Cod–style farmhouse has been pre
served as a memorial to Lillian Nordica, born here as
Lillian Norton, America's first internationally
acclaimed soprano (1857–1914). She was particularly
noted for her Wagnerian roles, having studied under
Wagner's widow, and sang in all the great opera
houses in the world and before all the crowned
heads of Europe. Three rooms of the house are
devoted to her memorabilia, particularly a large collection of her operatic and concert costumes, made
by Worth of Paris, and stage jewelry (although the
stones are not genuine, they were cut by Tiffany).
The house is owned and maintained by the Nordica
Memorial Association and is open June 1–Labor Day,
daily except Monday, 10:00–12:00 and 1:00–5:00, and
by appointment. Admission.

# Gorham

*Baxter House (1797)*

South Street
207-839-5031

This large, Federal-style house, with an attractive doorway and many fine details throughout, is the birthplace of the Honorable James Phinney Baxter, former mayor of Portland, and was the home of his son, Percival P. Baxter, governor of Maine from 1921–1924. It was donated to the town by the Baxter family as a museum and contains many original pieces of furniture. Other early American furnishings are contributions from local families and pertain to the history of Gorham. It is owned by the town of Gorham and is open July and August, Wednesday 2:00–5:00. Donation.

# Hampden

*Kinsley House (1794)*

83 Main Road
207-862-3003

During the War of 1812 the British set up an encampment on the grounds surrounding this two-and-a-half-story, Federal-style farmhouse. It is now the home of the Hampden Historical Society, and was the location of Hannibal Hamlin's law office. Hamlin, a prominent lawyer, senator, and governor of Maine, became vice president of the United States under Abraham Lincoln. The restored office contains many of Hamlin's personal belongings. The house features rooms of different periods, with many fine pieces of Federal and Victorian furniture. Also on the grounds are a blacksmith shop and a carriage house. The house is open April 1–October 1, Tuesday 10:00–4:00 and by appointment. Free.

# Harpswell

*Eagle Island*

Casco Bay
207-774-6498/846-9592 (for transportation)

Sitting high above the rocky shores of this small island, the former home of Admiral Robert E. Peary, North Pole explorer, looks out across the waters of

Casco Bay. Two huge, fortress-like structures form the base of the house. One of them was a cistern built to store up to 40,000 gallons of rain water; the other, facing north, was Peary's library and workshop, and its porthole windows were salvaged from old ships. The house, the only one on this 17-acre island, is made with the island's native rock and wood. Many stuffed and mounted arctic birds, most of which were prepared by Peary himself, are displayed throughout the house. Now owned by the state of Maine, the home is preserved as it was when Peary lived here, filled with memorabilia from his life on the island and his explorations. It is open mid-June–Labor Day, daily 10:00–6:00. Free. Call *Kristy K.* for transportation (boat fee).

# Houlton
## *Marion Woodbury MacIntyre Home (c. 1905)*

Aroostook Historical and Art Museum
109 Main Street
207-532-4216

This attractive, two-story Greek Revival building, with a columned portico and hipped roof, is the fourth house to be built on the same spot by the prominent Woodbury family. When it was built it was considered the finest house in Houlton. It is now the home of The Aroostook Historical and Art Museum, and most of the original features of the house—woodwork, fireplaces, stairway, marble sinks—have been kept intact. Houlton is the oldest community in Aroostook County, and the museum's collections reflect this. Among the costume collection in the parlor are several wedding gowns dating from 1840 to 1920. The house is open June–September, Monday–Friday 10:00-12:00 and 1:00–4:00. Donation.

# Jay
## *Holmes-Craft Homestead (c. 1820)*

Jay Hill (Route 4)
207-645-2653/645-2723

This classic, two-story Federal-style house, with a shallow hipped roof and tall chimneys, is thought to have been built as early as 1803. Many of its early architectural details, such as feathered clapboards and twelve-over-twelve windows on the exterior, and hand-hewn timbers, wide pine floorboards, and original hardware on the interior, have been well preserved. It is furnished with early nineteenth-century period antiques, including a chair made prior to the Civil War by Arana Holmes. Maintained by the Jay Historical Society, it is open June–September by appointment and on special occasions, including an annual open house on the second Saturday in August. Donation.

# Kennebunk

## Taylor-Barry House (1803)

24 Summer Street
207-967-2751/985-3608

Designed and built by architect Thomas Eaton for a prominent local family of shipmasters and shipowners, this Federal-style house is particularly known for its interior appointments. Elaborately carved moldings, doorways, corner cupboards, and paneling are highlighted by colorful stenciling attributed to the itinerant stenciler Moses Eaton. Four rooms are decorated with the original Federal and Victorian furnishings of the prominent Lord and Barry families that occupied the house. The studio of the last owner, Edith Barry, a twentieth-century painter, is at the rear of the house. Exhibits on local artists and authors are occasionally held in the house. It is operated by the Brick Store Museum, a local history museum and center for crafts and the arts in southern Maine. The museum, which also sponsors architectural walking tours of Kennebunk's historical district, has a craft and gift shop. The museum is open Tuesday– Saturday 10:00–4:30, and the house is open June– September, Tuesday–Friday 10:00-4:30. Admission.

# Kennebunkport

## The Nott House (1851–1853)

Main Street
207-967-2751

Also known as White Columns, this outstanding Greek Revival matchboarded and clapboarded house, with its Doric colonnade and bold triangular pediment, has been a town landmark since 1853. It was built by Eliphalet Perkins III, a descendant of one of Kennebunkport's founding families, and remained in the family until it was given to the Kennebunkport

Historical society in 1981. Eliphalet's son, Charles Perkins, who became a wealthy merchant in his own right, spared no expense in his purchase of art and decorative appointments for his home. The house retains all the original French wallpapers, carpets, paintings, and furniture reflecting the taste of affluent Victorians. It is open mid-June–mid-October, Wednesday–Friday 1:00–4:00. Admission.

THE NOTT HOUSE (1851–1853)

# Livermore
*Norlands (1868)*

Route 4
207-897-2236

Five nineteenth-century buildings, consisting of the rambling, white clapboarded Washburn farmhouse, attached farmer's cottage, a library, church, and schoolhouse, situated on 450 acres of farmland and woodland comprise a unique living history museum. Norlands was once the home of the extraordinary Washburn family, among whose ancestors were the seven sons of Israel and Patty Washburn. In a single generation they served as two governors, four congressmen, a U. S. senator, a Navy captain, an Army general, a secretary of state, and two foreign ministers. Today, participants come to the restored Nor-lands farm for an adult live-in program that offers an in-depth, total involvement experience of rural life as it was lived in northern New England a century ago. Special programs for school children are also conducted here. Guided tours are given July and August, Wednesday–Sunday 10:00–4:00. Admission.

# Machias

## Burnham Tavern Museum (1770)

Main Street
207-255-4432

This two-story, clapboard structure, with a gambrel roof and central chimney, was built just seven years after the settlement of Machias. Job Burnham built it not only as a tavern for the early settlers to gather and drink but as a home for his wife and 11 children. It is the oldest building in the area and the only building in eastern Maine that boasts of revolutionary war history. In 1775 the British escort ship *Margaretta* was captured by a group of local citizens "armed with guns, swords, axes and pick *[sic]* forks" aboard the tiny sloop *Unity*. Following the battle, which was considered the first naval engagement of the Revolution, the tavern was used as a hospital. It has been restored and maintained as a museum by the Hannah Weston Chapter, DAR, who have owned it since 1910, and it is furnished in the period of the revolutionary war. It is open late June–Labor Day, Monday–Friday 9:00–5:00 and by appointment. Admission.

# Machiasport

## Gates House (c. 1800)

Route 92
207-255-8461

Considered the first Federal-style residence to be built in the area, this house was purchased at auction by Nathan Gates, a trader, in 1813 and remained in the Gates family about 120 years. The two-story, L-shaped, frame structure features twelve-over-twelve windows, a shallow hipped roof, and a fanlight over the front door. The rooms are furnished with early American antiques; one room is devoted to a maritime exhibit and another, to a genealogical library. It is headquarters of the Machiasport Historical Society and is open June–mid-September, Monday–Friday 12:30-4:30. Donation.

# Newfield
*Willowbrook at Newfield (nineteenth century)*

Route 11
207-793-2784/793-2210

Willowbrook at Newfield is a restored nineteenth-century village depicting trades and crafts of the period and featuring two early homes, **The William Durgin Homestead** (1813) and **The Dr. Isaac Trafton Homestead** (1856). This extensive restoration is the work of Donald F. King, who began buying buildings in the 1960s after a devastating 1947 fire left the village a virtual ghost town. The restored village now totals 27 buildings, including a country store, bank, schoolhouse, fire house, barber shop, farm buildings and numerous trade shops, displaying more than 10,000 items relating to the history of Newfield. Both of the homesteads, typical nineteenth-century New England farmhouses, are furnished with Victorian antiques. The museum, privately owned, is open mid-May–September 30, daily 10:00–5:00. Admission.

# New Gloucester
*The Shaker Museum (1783)*

Sabbathday Lake, Route 26
207-926-4597

The United Society of Believers, better known as the Shakers, founded one of their largest communities in America here in the little village of New Gloucester in 1783. One of the nation's oldest communal religious organizations, the Shakers established more than 25 buildings on this site, of which more than half remain today. Nine of the plain, unadorned frame buildings—classic examples of Shaker architecture—predate 1850. Housed in various structures are numerous collections of furniture, textiles, folk art, song books, early American tools, and farm implements, demonstrating the simple, yet inventive and productive lifestyle of the Shaker community. The museum is open Memorial Day–mid-October, Monday–Saturday 10:00–4:30. Admission.

# New Sweden
*Lindsten Stuga (1894)*

Route 161
207-896-3018

In the summer of 1870 a band of 51 hardy Swedes left their homeland bound for new homes in northern Maine. The 22 men, 11 women, and 18 children traveled by ship, rail, barge, and wagon train, arriving at this site, which they quickly christened "New Sweden." Today, New Sweden and the neighboring towns of Stockholm and Westmanland form a colony where Swedish culture and tradition are still kept very much alive. Their early immigrant houses were made of logs, and several have been preserved. Lindsten Stuga, behind the New Sweden Historical Museum, is one such log cabin, and is furnished with the belongings of its original owners, the Lindsten family. Both the museum, containing furnishings, handcrafted items, tools, equipment, sleighs, pictures, and historical documents of the early settlers, and Lindsten Stuga are open mid-June–Labor Day, Tuesday–Saturday 12:00–4:30, Sunday 2:00–5:00, and by appointment. Donation.

# Phillips
*Phillips Historical Society (c. 1825)*

Pleasant Street
207-639-2011/639-2088

This large, Federal-style house, built by Joel Whitney around 1825, is now considered one of the best small-town rural museums in the state. Rooms are arranged with furnishings of local first families, mostly of the nineteenth century, but there are some eighteenth-century pieces as well. Also featured is an extensive display of narrow-gauge Sandy River and Rangeley Lakes Railroad material. Phillips was headquarters for this railroad, which ran from 1899 to the 1950s. (A restored train operates on a one-mile track about a mile away.) The museum house is open in August, Friday and Saturday 2:00–4:00, and by appointment June–October. Donation.

# Pittston
*Major Reuben Colburn House (1765)*

125 Arnold Road
207-582-7080

This sturdy, two-story, clapboard country colonial house, with a large central chimney, is one of the few remaining houses along the famous route taken by Benedict Arnold on his ill-planned march to Quebec in September of 1775. Major Colburn, who built this house, was instrumental in helping to build the small boats for Arnold's troops. The house is now headquarters of the Arnold Expedition Historical Society and is in an excellent state of preservation. Each room reflects one of the classic architectural periods in which the family furnished the house during their 188 years of occupancy. It is furnished throughout with original period pieces on loan from a private collection. The house is open July and August, weekends 10:00–5:00, and by appointment. Admission.

# Portland
*Neal Dow Memorial (1829)*

714 Congress Street
207-773-7773

This late Federal-style brick mansion was the lifelong home of Neal Dow, one of the prominent men of the reform movement in the nineteenth century. Twice mayor of Portland, member of the state legislature, lobbyist, and candidate for the presidency of the United States on the Prohibition Party ticket (1880), he was a force in the politics of the day. He was responsible for drafting the famous "Maine Law," making Maine the first state to prohibit alcohol. His home is now the state headquarters of the Maine Woman's Christian Temperance Union. Features of the memorial rooms are furnishings of the varied periods original to the house, portraits and other fine paintings, silver and china, and memorabilia of Dow's military and political career. Guided tours are given year-round, Monday–Friday 11:00–4:00. Free.

*McLellan-Sweat Mansion (c. 1800)*

111 High Street
207-775-6148

McLELLAN-SWEAT
MANSION (C. 1800)

This magnificent, three-story, Federal-style brick town house has a semicircular entrance portico with fluted Doric columns, graduated window openings, and a full balustrade. It was originally built by Hugh McLellan, a wealthy Portland merchant. The fourth owner, Lorenzo de Medici Sweat, left it to his widow, who in turn willed it to the Portland Society of Art (now the Portland Museum of Art, a complex of three buildings). Featured within is an unusual flying staircase, fine detail in the paneling and woodwork, and three neoclassical chimney pieces with both carved woodwork and molded plaster ornamentation. (At this writing the house is temporarily closed for restoration. Call for information.)

## Tate House (1755)

TATE HOUSE (1755)

1270 Westbrook Street
207-774-9781

Built by George Tate, mast agent for the British Royal
Navy, this large, Georgian-style house has several dis-
tinguishing features. Its clapboards are still unpainted,
and the house is one of two residences in Maine with
an unusual clerestory in the high gambrel roof. The
interior boasts fine paneling, raised moldings, a wide
stairway, and a cove ceiling in the front hall. Each of
the eight rooms has a fireplace opening into one
enormous chimney. The rooms, filled with fine examples of period furniture, textiles, and tablewares,
reflect the lives of the prominent and well-to-do Tate
family. The house is owned by the National Society
of Colonial Dames of America in the State of Maine
and is open mid-June–mid-September, Tuesday–
Saturday 11:00–5:00, Sunday 1:30–5:00. Admission.

## Victoria Mansion (1858)

109 Danforth Street
207-772-4841

Also known as the Morse-Libby House, this large
ornate brownstone, with a central square tower rising
above two stories, is designed in the Italian villa
style. It is considered to be one of the finest examples of nineteenth-century architecture to survive in
the United States. The interior is extravagantly
designed with carved mahogany, rosewood, and
chestnut paneling, marble fireplaces, ceiling murals,
etched and stained glass, and elaborate light fixtures.
It features an ornate drawing room, Gothic library,
chestnut-paneled dining room, and Turkish smoking
room. It was built for Ruggles Sylvestor Morse, a
Maine native, who made his fortune in the hotel business, and most of the furnishings reflect the wealth
and taste of this Victorian entrepreneur. It is owned
by the Victoria Society of Maine and is open
June–August, Tuesday–Saturday 10:00–4:00, Sunday

1:00–4:00; September, Tuesday–Saturday 10:00–1:00, Sunday 1:00–4:00, and by appointment. Admission.

## Wadsworth-Longfellow House (1785)

485 Congress Street
207-772-1807/774-1822

This late Georgian-style brick house, set behind a tall wrought-iron gate and surrounded by old-fashioned gardens, was the boyhood home of the poet Henry Wadsworth Longfellow. It was built by his maternal grandfather, General Peleg Wadsworth, and was the first house in Portland to be built of brick. The house, occupied by three generations of Longfellows, is furnished with their original possessions, and the "Rainy Day Room" (named for Longfellow's first poem, *The Rainy Day*, which was written in this room) is filled with Longfellow memorabilia. He returned here many times in his later life, visiting his sister, who left the house to the Maine Historical Society to serve as a memorial to her famous brother. The Society's headquarters and library are adjacent to the house. The house is open June–early October, Tuesday–Saturday 10:00–4:00. Garden open year-round. Admission.

# Rockland

## Farnsworth Homestead (1854)

21 Elm Street
207-596-6457

The Farnsworth Homestead is a stately, mid-nineteenth-century, Greek Revival town house with a classic pilastered front entrance. It was the home of the prominent Farnsworth family, who lived here from 1854 to 1935. It was inherited by Lucy Farnsworth, the last surviving child, who, upon the death of her mother in 1910, pulled down the shades and lived as a recluse the rest of her life. When Lucy's death was discovered in 1935 investigators found a stash of money and her will in a cupboard. Her will stated that the homestead be maintained as it was in her lifetime and that an art museum be built on the property. Accordingly, the house is preserved as an outstanding example of a fine Victorian home, with all its original furnishings intact. The adjoining art museum, subsequently built and now ranking as one of the finest regional art museums in the nation, features American, European, and Oriental art, with

FARNSWORTH HOMESTEAD (1854)

emphasis on the artists of Maine. The homestead is open June 1–September 30, Monday–Saturday 10:00–5:00, Sunday 1:00–5:00, and the museum is open year-round. Admission.

# Searsport

*Penobscot Marine Museum*

Historic District
Main Street
207-548-2529

Searsport has a long history as a shipbuilding center and a port for foreign trade vessels, but during its heyday in the 1870s, it was particularly known as the home of more than 285 sea captains. The Penobscot Marine Museum Historic District is a cluster of seven buildings, including a church, library, town hall, gallery, and three former sea captains' houses. The **Fowler-True-Ross House**, built by William Fowler, is of Federal design and was the residence of three generations of ship captains. It is completely furnished with an original nineteenth-century collection of furniture. The **Jeremiah Merithew House** (c.

1860) serves as an exhibit area displaying some of the museum's outstanding maritime collections. The **Nickels-Colcord-Duncan House** (c. 1880), now used as offices for the museum, is decorated with tables, paintings, and other artifacts from the the mid-nineteenth-century trading days with China and Japan. The museum buildings are open Memorial Day–mid-October, Monday–Saturday 9:30–5:00, Sunday 1:00–5:00, and for lecture, film, and concert series throughout the year. Admission.

# Sedgwick
## *Reverend Daniel Merrill House (1795)*

Route 172
207-359-2547

This simple, two-and-a-half-story house, with symmetrically placed unadorned windows and a classic early Georgian front entrance, was built for the first minister of Sedgwick, the Reverend Daniel Merrill. The Reverend Merrill, who was later one of the principal founders of Colby College, was apparently a very persuasive minister, for his church became the largest Congregational gathering in the District of Maine. It is now home to the Sedgwick-Brooklin Historical Society and contains many interesting artifacts of local history, as well as a historical library. Throughout the summer the society holds special exhibits and outdoor events such as flea markets, craft shows, and antique auto meets. The house is open July and August, Sunday 2:00–4:00. Free.

# South Berwick
## *Hamilton House (c. 1785)*

Vaughan's Lane
603-436-3205

This distinguished, white clapboarded, foursquare Georgian house stands high on a hill overlooking a tributary of the Piscataqua River. It was built on a grand scale for Colonel Jonathan Hamilton, who had risen from humble beginnings to become the most prominent merchant in the region. In later years the house was the setting for Sarah Orne Jewett's romantic historical novel, *The Tory Lover*. The house has recently been refurbished to reflect its early twentieth-century appearance. The furnishings, original to the house, are mostly Federal, with some country and painted pieces. Of particular note is the extensive landscaping, which includes an elaborate formal perennial garden, flowering trees and shrubs, and a charming garden house. The house is now the property of SPNEA and is open June 1–mid October, Tuesday, Thursday, Saturday, and Sunday 12:00–5:00. Admission.

## Sarah Orne Jewett House (1774)

5 Portland Street
207-384-5269

The home of Sarah Orne Jewett, one of New England's most celebrated writers, is enclosed behind a white picket fence on a busy corner in the center of town. It was considered quite elegant in its day with its hipped roof, flared eaves, and three large dormers across the front. Jewett, who wrote such classics as *Country of the Pointed Firs* and *Country Doctor*—describing small-town activities in a nineteenth-century town—lived most of her life and did most of her writing in this house. The interior has been refurbished, re-creating the appearance of the house dur-

SARAH ORNE JEWETT HOUSE
(1774)

ing her lifetime. Her own room has been preserved intact, and other rooms contain fine paneling and original eighteenth- and nineteenth-century wallpapers. The house is owned and maintained by SPNEA and is open June 1–mid-October, Tuesday, Thursday, Saturday, and Sunday 12:00–5:00. Admission.

# South Bridgton

*Peabody-Fitch House Museum (1797)*

Ingalls Road
207-647-2765

This simplified, Georgian, center-chimney farmhouse was once the home of the prominent Peabody family, early settlers of Bridgton. It is now part of the Bridgton Historical Society complex, located in an unspoiled rural setting, and includes a firehouse, blacksmith shop, and "temperance barn." The 10-room house is furnished with locally made artifacts and presents a picture of rural farm life at the time of the Civil War. The society also maintains and old fire station on the property, which houses the library and archives. The museum is open mid-June–Labor Day, Tuesday–Saturday 1:00–3:00 and by appointment. Admission.

# South Windham

*Parson Smith House (1764)*

93 River Road
617-227-3956

Parson Peter Thatcher Smith built this substantial Georgian-style house himself and lived here until his death in 1826. The region was sparsely settled in the mid-eighteenth century, and it was considered quite unusual for a house of such fine design and furnished in such high style to be found in this location. The house remained in the family until it was bequeathed to SPNEA in 1952, and, consequently, remains in excellent and nearly original condition. The interior features fine Georgian paneling and several folding partitions, a handsome staircase, and a remarkable eighteenth-century kitchen. It is furnished throughout with original family pieces. It is open mid-June–September 1, Tuesday, Thursday, Saturday, and Sunday 12:00–5:00. Admission.

# Standish

*Marrett House (1789)*

Route 25
617-227-3956

Originally built as a typical Maine farmhouse in the mid-eighteenth century, this house acquired its Federal and Greek Revival additions in later years. It became the home of the Reverend Daniel Marrett on his appointment to the local parish in 1796 and remained in the family for over 150 years. During the War of 1812, gold and silver coins from the Portland treasury were stored in the "best" parlor of the house for safekeeping. Iron locks on the parlor door and floor supports testify to this fact. Original period furnishings, reflecting the evolution of taste and patterns over 150 years, are on display, and the large flower and herb gardens have been restored. The property is owned and maintained by SPNEA and is open mid-June–September 1, Tuesday, Thursday, Saturday, and Sunday 12:00–5:00. Admission.

# Thomaston

*Montpelier (1929–1931)*

High Street
207-354-8062

MONTPELIER (1929–1931)    This is a replica of the home of Major General Henry

Knox, a revolutionary war hero, which once stood on the banks of the St. George River. The original house, a magnificent, Federal-style, two-story building, with an elliptical central facade and a balustrade topping the clerestory, has been faithfully reproduced as a tribute to one of Maine's most famous residents. General and Mrs. Knox lavishly entertained distinguished American and foreign visitors in their elegant home, which features high ceilings, long windows, an oval dining room, and a semiflying staircase. The 18 rooms are furnished with colonial and Federal period antiques, many of them belonging to the Knox family, as well as some personal possessions of the general. It is operated by the Bureau of Parks and Recreation, Maine Department of Conservation and is open Memorial Day–Labor Day, Wednesday–Sunday 9:00–5:30. Admission.

# Van Buren
*Acadian Village*

Route 1
207-868-2691/868-5405

The village consists of a collection of more than 16 reconstructed and relocated buildings dating from 1785 to the early 1900s, which exemplify the lifestyle of the hardy Acadians who settled in this area after being driven out of Nova Scotia in 1855. All of the buildings, including houses, school, church, railroad station, general store, barber shop, and blacksmith shop, are furnished with period pieces and open to the public. A newly built art museum features rotating art shows. The village is operated by the Living Heritage Society and is open mid-June–Labor Day, daily 12:00–5:00 and by appointment. Admission.

# Washburn
*Benjamin C. Wilder Farmstead (1852)*

Main Street

This typical, white frame farmhouse, with a pitched roof and gables, is distinguished by its 71-foot-long wraparound porch. It was built by Benjamin Wilder, a descendant of the original settlers, who became postmaster of Washburn and proprietor of the general store. It was acquired by the Salmon Brook Historical Society in 1985, and extensive repairs and remodeling restored it to its original status. The rooms are furnished with period antiques. A large red barn, replacing the original one, which burned down in 1938, has recently been built and is now the Aroostook County Agricultural Museum, containing an extensive collection of farm tools and both hand- and horsepowered farm machinery. It is open mid-June–mid-September, Saturday and Sunday 1:00–4:00 and by appointment. Write P.O. Box 71, Washburn, ME 04786.

# Waterville
## Redington Museum (1852)

64 Silver Street
207-872-9439

This white clapboard Federal-style farmhouse is enhanced by Doric columns supporting a second story porch with a decorative balustrade. It was built by a pioneer settler, Asa Redington, who fought in the Revolution and was one of the members of Washington's elite honor guard. The house, occupied by Redington descendants for more than 100 years, was presented to the Waterville Historical Society in 1924 and has been open to the public as a museum since 1927. The rooms are furnished with late eighteenth- and nineteenth-century furnishings from the Redington family, as well as many other pieces belonging to early local families. Attached to the house is the LaVerdiere Apothecary Museum, a replica of an early apothecary building, which houses an extensive collection of pharmaceutical antiques. The house is open from mid-May–September, Tuesday–Saturday 2:00–6:00. Admission.

# Weld
## Weld Historical Society (c. 1841)

Weld Village
207-585-2586

In the center of the town of Weld are several vintage buildings restored and maintained by the Weld Historical Society. The Museum House (c. 1842) is a high-posted, clapboard Cape-style house, with paired chimneys and five bays. It is furnished with period pieces donated by townspeople. The Document Room contains photographs, genealogical records, diaries, and many artifacts reflecting eighteenth- to early twentieth-century life in this small, rural, mountain village. Other buildings include the original Town House (c. 1845) and a doctor's office (c. 1880). The buildings are open July and August, Wednesday and Saturday 1:00–3:00 and by appointment May–September. A Heritage Day Fair is held the last Saturday in July, 10:00–3:00. Donation.

# Wiscasset

## *Castle Tucker (1807)*

Lee Street
207-882-7364

Built by Judge Silas Lee, this large, Georgian-style house, with huge windows overlooking Wiscasset harbor, was thought to resemble a castle in Dunbar, Scotland. It was later purchased, complete with all its furnishings, by Captain Richard H. Tucker, Jr., third generation of ship captains and owners. He and his wife made several changes, including the addition of a large glass and brick piazza. The house remains in the hands of Captain Tucker's descendants and is

MUSICAL WONDER HOUSE (1852)

open to the public July and August, Tuesday–Saturday 11:00–4:00, and by appointment during June and September. Admission.

## Musical Wonder House (1852)

18 High Street
207-882-7163/882-6373

This handsome, Greek Revival house, with pilastered double doors and double framed dormers, was built by two ship captains, Scott and Clark. The interior features an impressive flying staircase, classical moldings, period wallpapers, and Victorian furnishings, providing a unique setting for what is considered one of the most extensive music box collections in the world. Each room displays a variety of restored antique musical boxes, from an early talking machine to a giant, full orchestral musical box with matching table. Several different tours of varying lengths and prices are conducted at the house. The museum is privately owned and open Memorial Day–mid-October, daily 10:00–5:00. Admission. The gift shop is open until Thanksgiving (no admission fee).

## Nickels-Sortwell House (1807)

Main Street
617-227-3956

Considered one of New England's most elegant Federal mansions, this three-story, frame town house was the residence of a prominent Maine shipmaster, Captain William Nickels. Its richly decorated facade of a story-high entrance portico with Corinthian pilasters and fanlight is topped by a second-story Palladian window and a crescent-shaped third-story window. An impressive interior feature of the house is the elliptical staircase, which is illuminated by a third-floor skylight. In the early 1900s the property was acquired by Alvin Sortwell, a mayor of Cambridge, Massachusetts, who restored it. It was deeded to SPNEA in 1958, along with the colonial revival furnishings belonging to the Sortwell family. It is open June 1–September 30, Wednesday–Sunday 12:00–5:00. Admission.

# York
*The Emerson-Wilcox House (1742)*

Lindsey Road
207-363-4974

This trim, colonial frame house served as a general store, tailor shop, tavern, and home for Edward Emerson's large family in the eighteenth century. Emerson, one of the village's leading citizens, provided the military broadcloth that clothed the local patriots during the Revolution. Later, the Emerson Tavern hosted such notables as General Henry Knox, the Marquis de Lafayette, and Presidents John Quincy Adams and James Monroe. Today it offers a series of period room settings covering the years 1740 to 1840 and displays many fine pieces from the Old York Historical Society's collection of American decorative arts. It is maintained by the Old York Historical Society and is open mid-June–September 30, daily, and on Columbus Day weekend, 10:00–5:00. Admission.

*The Elizabeth Perkins House (c. 1730)*

THE ELIZABETH PERKINS
HOUSE (C. 1730)

South Side Road
207-363-4974

This lovely, old frame colonial house, surrounded by well-landscaped lawns and gardens, is situated on the banks of the York River. It was lived in as a summer home by the Perkins family for several generations. Both Mrs. Newton Perkins and her daughter Elizabeth, early collectors and historians, were leaders in the local preservation movement and left the house, complete with the furnishings, and grounds to be preserved as a museum. The central part of the house, now the dining room, was probably all there was to the original small cottage built by Joseph Holt in 1732. It is maintained by the Old York Historical Society and is open mid-June–September 30, daily, and on Columbus Day weekend, 10:00–5:00. Admission.

# York Harbor
*Sayward-Wheeler House (1718)*

79 Barrell Lane
603-436-3205

Like many other merchants' houses along the coast of Maine, the principal entrance to this large frame Georgian colonial is on the water side. Originally built in 1718 and enlarged in the 1760s, it was the residence of Jonathan Sayward, a merchant and civic leader who retained the respect of the community despite his Tory sympathies. Sayward lived in this house until he died in 1797, making few changes in it throughout his lifetime. Similarly, his grandson and great-grandchildren, out of respect, kept the house and its furnishings virtually intact. Most objects in the house were never rearranged, and some of the wall hangings have their original hardware. Important collections of Queen Anne and Chippendale furniture, family portraits, and china brought back as booty from the expedition against the French at Louisburg in 1745, are in excellent condition. The house and its contents were bequeathed to SPNEA by the heirs in 1977. The house is open mid-June–mid-October, Wednesday–Sunday 12:00–5:00. Admission.

# Additional Houses
*(Area code 207)*

**CAMDEN**
  Whitehall Inn, (Edna St. Vincent Millay room), 52 High Street, 236-3391

**CASTINE**
  The John Perkins House, Court Street, 326-8753

**DENNYSVILLE**
  Lincoln House, Route 1, 726-3953

**ELLSWORTH**
  Stanwood Homestead Museum, Bar Harbor Road, 667-8460

  Sheriff's Home (Hancock County Jail), State Street (no telephone)

**FAIRFIELD**
  History House, 42 High Street, 453-2998/ 453-6867

**FREEPORT**
  Enoch Harrington House, 45 Main Street, 865-0477

  Pettingill Farm, Pettengill Farm Road, 865-0477

**KENNEBUNKPORT**
  The Wedding Cake House, Summer Street, 985-6866

**KEZAR FALLS**
  History House, Main Street, 625-4667

**KINGFIELD**
  Amos G. Winter House, Winter Hill, 265-5421

**MONMOUTH**
  Blossom House (Monmouth Museum), Route 132, 933-2287

**SCARBOROUGH**
  Hunnewell House, Black Point Road (no telephone)

**SKOWHEGAN**
  Skowhegan History House, Norridgewock Avenue, 474-3140

**SOUTH CASCO**
  Hawthorne's Boyhood Home, Hawthorne Road, 655-3349

**STRONG**
  Vance and Dorothy Hammond Memorial, Main Street, 684-4483

**SUNSET**
Salome Sellers House, Route 15A (Deer Isle), 348-2886

**THOMASTON**
Knox Farmhouse, Knox Street, 354-2295

**WILTON**
Wilton Farm and Home Museum, Canal Street, 645-2091

**WISCASSET**
Jailer's Home (Lincoln County Museum), Village, 882-6817

**WOOLWICH**
Woolwich Historical Museum, Route 1, 443-4833

# ALPHABETICAL LISTING BY HOUSE

### NEW HAMPSHIRE

### MAINE